THE
TURNING
TIDE

PAT ROBERTSON

THE TURNING TIDE

WORD PUBLISHING
Dallas • London • Vancouver • Melbourne

Unless otherwise indicated, all Scripture references are from The New King James Version (NKJV), Copyright © 1979, 1980, 1982, Thomas Nelson, Inc., Publisher. Other Scripture quotations are from:

The King James Version (KJV).

The Holy Bible, New International Version (NIV), Copyright © 1973, 1978, 1984 International Bible Society, and are used by permission of Zondervan Bible Publishers.

The Living Bible (TLB), Copyright © 1971, Tyndale House Publishers, Wheaton, Illinois. Used by permission.

Library of Congress Cataloging-in-Publication Data

Robertson, Pat.
    The turning tide : the fall of liberalism and the rise of common sense / Pat Robertson
    p.   cm.
Includes bibliographical references.
ISBN 0–8499–0972–4
ISBN 0-8499-3694-2 (mass paper)
    1. United States—Politics and government—1993– .   2. United States—Politics and government—1989–1993.   3. Liberalism—United States—History—20th century.   4. Conservatism—United States—History—20th century.   I. Title.
E885.R63–1993
320.973—dc20   93–5935
                                                                        CIP

569   OPM   9 8 7 6 5 4 3 2 1

Printed in the United States of America

Contents

Acknowledgments

This is a book about common sense and hope. While it addresses social, political, and ethical issues, it is first and foremost a book about the practical matters we all deal with every day. It is a book about the dramatic changes taking place in our culture and the signs of a visible shift in private thinking about public matters. Most essentially, it is about the importance of your home, your family, your individual choices, and your values.

Any work that examines a broad range of public and private concerns must deal with both risks and opportunities, and this book offers both good news and bad. But my perspective has been that we have come to an unprecedented moment in our history—a time when the potential for positive change has never been greater. In the midst of political turmoil and discontent, we are seeing a renewal—a reawakening —of the personal values and beliefs that have sustained this nation throughout its history. This is the true source of America's hope. We have grown through our struggles, and there is a new sense of maturity abroad—a new commitment to the things that really matter.

For their assistance in preparing this work, I would like to thank the following: Dr. Jim Nelson Black for his assistance in the development and preparation of the manuscript; CBN News Director Drew Parkhill for his research and fact checking; Steve Fitschen of the American Center for Law and Justice for his legal research; and Beverly Milner of my staff for typing the frequent additions and revisions to the manuscript. For their support and encouragement during the writing of this work, I would also like to thank my colleagues and staff at the

Christian Broadcasting Network and Regent University. My special thanks to Kip Jordon, Joey Paul, David Moberg, and Byron Williamson of Word Publishing for their dedication and professionalism. I hope this book is further encouragement to Keith Fournier and Jay Sekulow of the American Center for Law and Justice and to Ralph Reed of the Christian Coalition. My heartfelt appreciation to my wife, Dede, for reading and commenting on the work as it developed. Finally, I want to thank you, the reader, for your willingness to weigh and consider these pressing concerns, and to experience the turning tide.

Pat Robertson
Virginia Beach, Virginia

Preface

The morning after the 1992 general election, Americans woke up to the news that a sixties liberal had won the White House and that both houses of Congress were suddenly in the hands of a Democrat majority. Political analysts credited the Democrats' victory to a combination of voter anger and the third-party challenge of Ross Perot that had shifted the political balance, creating an odd set of reactions. Bill Clinton became President of the United States with a mere 43 percent plurality.

As the average American considered this new circumstance and thought about what might come from the new liberal alliance, millions tuned to "The 700 Club" to see what Pat Robertson would make of the situation. A former presidential candidate and an outspoken advocate of conservative political action, Robertson had stumped for George Bush and was clearly in a position to offer a reasoned assessment. But what he actually said came as a shock to many: "This election," he said, "may be the best thing that has ever happened to America."

No one was prepared for that statement. Visibly surprised by the remark, even Pat's co-hosts seemed speechless. *The best thing that has ever happened to America?* How could that be? "Because," Pat continued, "four years of Bill Clinton will bring this entire nation to its knees." And *that's* the best thing that could happen to America, he maintained.

As hard as it was to foresee at that time, that is precisely what did happen. By the 1994 mid-term elections, it seemed apparent that the electorate had seen enough of Mr. Clinton's clearly liberal agenda—government support for abortion-on-demand, gays in the military, approval of fetal tissue research, appointment of two dozen self-proclaimed homosexuals to high government office, and a health care plan guaranteed to bankrupt the nation. Savvy political watchdogs called the 1994 election not only a vote against dangerous policies but also a clear repudiation of liberalism in general and a return to common sense values. Around the world the election of 1994 was being hailed as a new day for America.

U.S. News & World Report called the election "a Republican tide that swept Democrats out of Congress and statehouses." Reporters summarized the election, saying, "The storm was driven by a chorus of complaints about Americans' lives and leaders: jobs too insecure, wages too sluggish, families too fragmented, streets too dangerous, government too big, taxes too high, lobbyists too powerful, welfare too cushy, illegal aliens too costly, campaigns too nasty, politicians too arrogant." Every network and virtually every news commentary on the elections proclaimed that a "tidal wave" had struck the country, changing the political landscape of the nation. Yet in the summer of 1993—over a year before—as he was writing *The Turning Tide*, Pat Robertson set forth the reasons why the downfall of liberalism in America was inevitable.

By the time the dust settled the morning after the election, Republicans had gained fifty-one seats in the House of Representatives and eight in the Senate, giving them a clear majority in both houses. Suddenly the GOP held thirty state governorships, including the state of Alabama, whose former Democrat governor switched parties. For the first time in forty years, conservatives would control the halls of government, and it was also clear that Pat Robertson's amazing prophecy contained in the pages of *The Turning Tide* had come to pass.

In *The Turning Tide*, Pat Robertson peered into the general discontent of mainstream America. He saw the unhappiness over the failure of public education, the anger with the bias of the news media, and the outrage over the collapse of law and order. He could see Americans were angry with the assault on religious values and the demoralization of their children. Pat also recognized that the men and women who took office in 1992 had failed to keep faith with the people who elected them, and he believed the voters would have the final word. The proven aftermath of 1994's tidal wave at the polls revealed just how serious "We the People" were about turning things around.

Pat Robertson encouraged Americans to rally for such a turning point in 1988 when, as a presidential candidate, he called for a "restoration of the greatness of America through moral strength, faith in God, and a resurgence of individual self-reliance." As he stumped across the nation, he reminded Americans that throughout history, cultures came crashing down through deterioration from within when moral values began to unravel. He called for a national renewal of the faith of America's founding fathers.

As you read this book, you may feel the winds of national renewal blowing, but be aware that Pat Robertson will be the first one to tell you that we're not there yet. "The liberal agenda has been at large in this land for more than forty years," he observes, "and it may well take that long to reverse it. Faith, commitment, and fierce determination will be needed, if we are to point the way to real renewal."

Pat Robertson's prophetic voice was right. Liberal rule helped drive Americans to their knees and into the voting booths. Only it didn't take four years. It took two.

The Publisher
January, 1995

1

The Wave
of the Future

I WAS SITTING IN MY STUDY working over the draft of this book when the phone rang. It was Jay Sekulow, chief counsel of the American Center for Law and Justice, calling to tell me that the first 1993 case concerning student-initiated graduation prayer had been litigated and that we had won a resounding victory. This was one tangible bit of good news that the excesses of liberalism in America may be coming to an end.

Sometimes little things can have enormous significance: a tiny hole in a dike, a slight fissure in a dam, a bit of metal fatigue in an airplane wing, or one wrong harmonic on an old bridge that sets the whole structure swaying until it suddenly collapses. Such mysteries are common in nature, but they happen just as often in human nature.

For more than thirty years, liberals have forbidden little children to pray in schools. One liberal teacher even forced a sixth grader to stand in punishment because he mentioned God during recess. Another teacher broke a child's pencil because it said "Jesus Is Lord." Such callous behavior has been common in classrooms.

But now, despite the anguished cries of liberals, once again youngsters in America will be able to pray to God at school graduations. A court has ruled that Christian students in America are protected by the First Amendment to the United States Constitution and can no longer be persecuted by the American Civil Liberties Union (ACLU), People for the American Way, the National Organization for Women (NOW), the National Education Association (NEA), or any of the other forces of the Radical Left.

Like a starburst on the Fourth of July, a movement began, and we could witness the explosions on campuses all across the land. First one child, then a hundred, then a thousand, then seven thousand children chose to pray publicly at their graduation ceremonies. It was their right and their privilege as free citizens, and no alien power could scold them into silence.

Can this be what America has been waiting for? Are we finally witnessing a return to common sense in this nation? That is what this book is all about. It is this important question: As we see liberalism, excessive government, planned central economies, and attacks on religious freedom collapsing in country after country, is there hope that the tide is turning in America as well? Will the dramatic events signaling the fall of liberalism and the rise of common sense all around the globe wash over the shores of the United States? In the pages that follow I will attempt to answer that question by examining both the positive trends that are emerging today as well as the dangers that must be overcome.

The Vision Thing

Jay's call was not the only evidence of the change coming. Just one week earlier, I learned that pro-family candidates supported by the Christian Coalition had won 57 percent of the school board races they entered in New York City. These conservative candidates were up against a militant homosexual and lesbian coalition championed by David Dinkins, the liberal mayor of the New York, who had previously said that the views of Pat Robertson were "repugnant to the people of New York City." The results of this election were an indication that Mayor Dinkins was, once again, incorrect in his assessments.

Earlier still, I had received news from a city in Idaho where an attempt had been made to force the teaching of homosexuality in the schools. In the school board elections, Christian Coalition-backed candidates won four out of five seats in a hotly contested local election. This and other important victories in recent months, coupled with the unprecedented surge of political action and grass-roots citizen involvement all across this nation, offer resounding proof that the mood of the public is changing. But is this apparent return to sane and responsible policies the beginning of a rebirth or perhaps only a brief and meaningless phase?

In these pages I will examine these questions in considerable detail, not only to illustrate how the changes we are seeing today have come about, but what this historic moment may mean to the future well-being of our nation. I will address the situation in government, the law, the educational establishment, the media, and in many other areas of American life. In addition, I will look closely at the rise of common sense in politics, in business and the private sector, as well as in the home, the family, and the church.

As we look at what appears to be a sudden shift of public opinion back toward practical, common-sense solutions to our problems, I believe we have every right to be optimistic. Yes, we need to be cautious. We are not home free just yet. But this trend to the Right has actually been building for a long time. Many conservatives were caught off guard by the results of the November 1992 elections when liberals took control of the Senate, the House of Representatives, and the White House. But rather than halting the momentum of the swing toward common sense, it is clear now that the liberal victories of 1992 actually helped give momentous strength and vitality to the movement—more than anything else could have done. Now we can see the enemy more clearly than ever before, and the inevitable social, political, and economic disasters to come from Clintonomics—and government's social engineering—will show once and for all what liberalism hath wrought.

It should also be said that the odd circumstances which led to the liberal victory in 1992—particularly the role played by Ross Perot—actually helped to consolidate the groundswell of clear-eyed conservative sentiment in this country and to bring forth a mood of public outrage against liberalism. So the kinds of grass-roots political engagement we are seeing today are clearly a phenomenon that has not been seen in this country for more than 220 years—since the Boston Tea Party of 1773 and the climactic events it precipitated. And what is happening today is nothing short of a revolution.

Beyond all the rhetoric and ballyhoo of the Clinton administration, the American people recognize the characteristic signature of the liberal agenda, including its fascination with bloated bureaucracy, exploitation of the taxpayer for the sake of bigger and bigger government, and all the other socialized programs connected with issues such as health care and the environment. Thanks to prime-time news coverage by CBN, CNN, C-Span, and to a lesser degree the major networks, very little of the good or the bad news is hidden anymore. And combined with an unprecedented public fascination with politics and government—incited, in fact, by dramatically higher taxes, collapsing public education, and the high visibility of the AIDS epidemic, homosexuality, abortion, and condoms and sex education in the public schools—tens of thousands of deeply concerned voters are watching these events with rapt attention.

In the Public Eye

The emergence of popular new voices, such as radio-television talk-show host Rush Limbaugh, is another sign that America is listening. A significant minority cares passionately, and others are being persuaded. They are informed, they know what is wrong, and they just don't buy the Left's tired solutions to our problems. Limbaugh along with such prominent voices as former Education Secretary William Bennett, Representative Robert Dornan, Senator Bob Dole, and others are being listened to as never before. Every sleight of hand by government and every public act is being witnessed by the nation and the entire world. And the most surprising part of all is that this public awareness and involvement, arising largely because of the Clinton election, has empowered common-sense democracy and traditional American conservatism in ways unimaginable just a short time ago—particularly during the twelve years of Reagan-Bush leadership.

As I focus on each of these areas in the pages that follow, we have to ask, "How did these things come to be?" As Clinton's public ratings continue to plummet, we see more and more examples of the wounds the administration's radical social agenda is inflicting on the Democratic party. But people are asking, "Where on earth did these radical ideas come from?" Were they something the Democrats just stumbled into—some new visitation of Enlightenment ideology—or are they a reflection of something deeper and more worrisome? Were they part of some deliberate plan, or a mere accident of history?

I recently read an essay that reported on the deliberate attempt by socialists in Europe—primarily in France and Spain—to undermine the traditional structures of society in order to bring those nations down to a level that would approximate the Third World. The objective, according to this writer, was to amalgamate the entire world into a socialist model based on current Third-World practices.

Even if such theories may sound a bit extreme, the evidence is overwhelming that the Left—guided by some kind of Orwellian vision of "social equality"—is striving toward a leveling of our culture and the replacement of traditional democratic freedoms with a one-world government in the hands of the "politically correct" elites. But more on that later.

Perhaps the most damning comment on the perspectives of the liberals in government was delivered by Irving Kristol in his provocative article, "The Coming Conservative Century," which appeared in the *Wall Street Journal* on February 1, 1993. Here, less than two weeks after the star-studded Clinton inauguration, was as brilliant and prophetic a statement of political vision as I have read in many years. In the piece, Kristol, a fellow of the American Enterprise Institute in Washington, D.C., and publisher of *The National Interest*, made the statement, "liberalism is at the end of its intellectual tether."

While the Democratic party may have won the election, he said, its liberal agenda is contrary to the tide of public opinion and counter to the tide of history as well. But once in office, the liberal Democrats will display, first, their political impotence and then their penchant for divisive social programs and government meddling in the private affairs of the American people.

One example of meddling, Kristol goes on to say, is the area of secular humanism and the attempt to obscure the natural connections between culture and conscience under the rubric of the separation of church and state. But he offers a stern warning, saying:

> For the past century the rise of liberalism has been wedded to the rise of secularism in all areas of American life. In the decades ahead, the decline of secularism will signify the decline of liberalism as well. Already on the far-left fringes of liberalism itself, artists and philosophers are welcoming the collapse of a "secular humanism" that they find sterile and oppressive. They can offer nothing with which to replace this liberal-secular humanism. But others can, and will. Today, it is the religious who have a sense that the tide has turned and that the wave of the future is moving in their direction.[1]

Then he says, "In the meantime, we are enduring a 'prolonged spasm of liberal fanaticism,' paid for by a doctrine of 'sacrifices'—which means higher taxes. And they promote the doctrine of victimization, by which government becomes the benefactor of every special interest group, without any reference to the more necessary and natural principles of 'self-control' or 'self-reliance.'"

But finally, Kristol offers the proposition that in order to defend itself against the crisis of liberalism run amok, America must come back to three pillars of conservative wisdom:

1. A renewed faith in economic growth
2. Renewed pride in our country
3. Inclusion of men and women who hold strong religious convictions.

Concerning the economy, he writes that the government must return to the view that national prosperity can grow only when business and industry are healthy. Disincentives to growth and to wealth building will inevitably damage not only individuals, but American business and our prospects for trade and political influence abroad. It was Calvin Coolidge who made the comment, "The chief business of the American people is business." But Kristol would add that America's business is also the world's business, and, by extension, what is good for American business is good for the world.

Rethinking Our Priorities

To regain our position of respect in the world, America must first gain a new respect for its own role in international affairs. As the only remaining superpower, we need to recognize that we are not only a military power to be reckoned with but also the world's moral leader and the best example of how democratic capitalism is supposed to work. The disastrous trends toward multiculturalism, anti-Americanism, anti-capitalism, and historical revisionism being pushed by liberals and other leftists in the universities only serve to further degrade America's image at home and abroad. But there is change on the horizon, and the coming conservative century will see a renewed respect for a strong, resilient, and self-confident America with a revitalized sense of national destiny.

But Kristol's final remarks must not be missed; he writes that, while religious people can seem troublesome at times, with an allegiance to God rather than the state, they have become a mighty force and an important ally in the struggle for republican democracy. Truly, America desperately needs a restoration of civic virtue and self-restraint in all areas of public and private life. We need to rediscover the lessons of responsible behavior and self-reliance, and religion helps us to see those ideals in concrete terms.

The Democrats will never welcome the religious, writes Irving Kristol, but if the Republican party should fail to embrace those who are motivated by religious convictions, it will be at the party's own peril. He concludes: "One way or another, in the decades ahead they will not be denied." How very right he is!

But something else is perfectly clear as well. Bill Clinton's popularity has fallen week by week since his January 20 inauguration. Just five months into the new regime, a *Times-Mirror* survey showed a continuing steady decline in the Democratic leader's popularity in every category.

The *New York Times* concluded that the root of Clinton's problem was his poor performance as a manager. And CEOs of leading U.S. corporations contacted by the editors said that on top of all these apparent political weaknesses, there is a serious management gap in the Clinton administration. Seventy-one percent of the Fortune 500 CEOs polled in a May 1993 survey disapproved of the president's job performance. The cover story of the July 19, 1993, issue of *Forbes* magazine reported that Barton Biggs, the chief investment adviser of Morgan Stanley, is moving the bulk of its $40 billion in pension funds to Europe and Asia because of what he fears Bill Clinton's policies will do to the United States stock market. "We want our clients' money as far away from Bill and Hillary as we can," Biggs said. "The President is a negative for the U.S. market. I'm embarrassed that I voted for him and contributed money to his campaign."

What happened to change the public's perception of their "candidate of change"? The new administration's agenda was bold and called for top-level management, but the Clinton White House staff is surprisingly young, inexperienced, idealistic, and apparently incompetent. Even with the rescue attempt being launched by former Reagan staffer David Gergen, it has become increasingly clear that there is a gulf of immense proportions between this president's pre-election promises and his actual capacity for deficit reduction.

The most recent Cahners Index of Business Confidence, cited in the *New York Times*, showed the new administration's approval rating sagging badly after a brief period of post-election euphoria. Why this doubt and pessimism? The writer offered three suggestions. First, Clinton's promise of a new Democratic agenda turns out to be just one more visitation of the all-too-familiar liberal tax-and-spend theory. Washington consultant Ted Van Dyck said that the new president "misread his mandate and essentially overweighted the taxes and spending side in his basic package. It's already the largest tax increase in history. Combining it with healthcare reform could cripple the economy."[2]

Second, senior executives feel Clinton's plans are anti-business and anti-growth. And third, virtually all of those consulted believe that the president is neither qualified nor capable enough to be the leader of the nation. The White House is full of overexalted neophytes with no experience in government; yet most have shown that, by instinct and by education, they are essentially anti-government and anti-capitalist in their thinking. Irving Shapiro, former chairman of the DuPont Corporation, told the *New York Times*, "There's a great question of credibility on whether they are really cutting spending. The public can't put its finger on anything."[3]

Maybe this is because the administration is still trying to have it both ways. As one example, Democratic Senator Daniel Patrick Moynihan, chairman of the Senate Finance Committee, said on "This Week with David Brinkley" on June 6, 1993, that his party was not as interested in making any actual tax cuts as they were in *appearing* to make them. In fact, the only way they can erect all their planned new spending programs is to raise vast new sources of money. No wonder some have labeled the Democrats' economic initiatives "smoke and mirrors."

Salvation by Society

In the November 16, 1992, issue of *Newsweek*, columnist George F. Will wrote that Bill Clinton, as the sixth Democratic president since Woodrow Wilson, will be leading a party "still awash with Wilsonian liberalism's desire to conscript the individual into collective undertakings." Underlying liberal idealism is a notion once described by Peter Drucker as "salvation by society." This is the belief that society—not personal faith, nor industry, nor even individual initiative—will lead individuals to transcendence and spiritual perfection, and this through the ministrations of more and bigger government.

This is the view that gave us FDR's New Deal, JFK's New Frontier, LBJ's Great Society, and Jimmy Carter's Shared Sacrifices. All these programs proved to be, not only draining on the public purse, but unrealistic and idealistic solutions to very real problems. Such liberal remedies have consistently failed to achieve either transcendence or economic balance, yet they come back to haunt us every few years.

A year ago Mrs. Louise Smith from Boone, Iowa, sent me a yellowed copy of the *Saturday Evening Post* dated December 15, 1934. Its feature story was by former President Herbert Hoover, written one year after the start of Roosevelt's New Deal. Hoover's account of the rhetoric of 1933 sounds exactly like an account of the liberal rhetoric of today. It said:

> We are told by men high in our government, both legislative and administrative, that the social organization which we have developed over our whole history is "outworn" and "must be abandoned." We have been told that it has failed. We are told of "outworn traditions," that we have come to the 'end of an era,' that we are passing through a 'bloodless revolution.' We are also told that the American system "is in ruins," that we must "build on the ruins of the past a new structure."

Writing with extraordinary insight, the former president continued:

> No one with a day's experience in government fails to realize that in all bureaucracies there are three implacable spirits— self-perpetuation, expansion, and the incessant demand for more power. . . . These spirits are potent and they possess a dictatorial complex. They lead first to subversive influence in elections. They drive always to extension of powers by interpretation of authority, and by more and more legislation. . . . In their mass action they become the veritable exponents of political tyranny.

I have frankly never seen a more insightful or prescient exposition of the dangers our nation faces from the incessant demands of a permanent bureaucracy that has grown exponentially since the 1933–34 era to what it is under Clinton today.

So we ask again: Is the disenchantment with Bill Clinton an indication that the American people have finally seen through the liberal rhetoric? When will the nation be ready to cast aside the rotting carcass of the New Deal, the Fair Deal, and the Great Society and return government back to the people?

Economist Milton Friedman, winner of the 1976 Nobel Prize for economics, calls a spade a spade. In his response to a *Wall Street Journal* poll of the nation's top economists, Friedman leveled stern criticism at the Clinton agenda, saying:

> President Clinton calls for widespread sacrifice by the many through higher taxes, and concentrated benefits to the few through additional government spending—"contributions" and "investment," in Clinton doublespeak. The country needs precisely the reverse: widespread benefits to the many through lower taxes and lower spending, and concentrated sacrifice by the few through abolishing numerous government programs that, if they were ever justified, no longer are: agricultural subsidies and price supports, Rural Electrification Administration, Amtrak, subsidies to the humanities, arts, broadcasting, to mention only a few.

Then the economist goes on to say:

> These programs cost taxpayers a multiple of any gains to the intended beneficiaries. In agriculture, for example, most of the money pays for the growing, storing and disposing of food rendered "surplus" by high government fixed support prices, and for administering the program. Little of the money trickles down to the individual farmer. Would consumers regard the lower prices for food that would follow the ending of these subsidies and price supports as a sacrifice?[4]

Feeding the Monster

Other economists cited in the *Journal* article agree with Friedman's conclusion that "Government is already too big, too intrusive, too destructive of our civil liberty." Yet it is increasingly apparent that Bill Clinton intends to walk America farther down the same old garden path. Friedman counsels that increasing the size of government at the expense of the individual or of private business will mean slower economic recovery, contrary to the administration's claims. It will bring with it intolerable levels of government spending and a federal deficit of truly crisis proportions.

More government, higher taxes, and increased government interference in our lives, he says, will only make the nation's problems worse—most of which, as Friedman says, were created by "excessive and inefficient government." Our primary and secondary education are an international disgrace. Despite massive social programs, crime is exploding in all sectors of society and the inner city has become unmanageable.

In addition, the rising costs of health care are a direct result of government regulation; yet the administration wants to emasculate the industry by nationalizing medical care, enacting more regulations, and disastrously dabbling in an industry that could be better served by a common-sense policy that once again gives the recipient of healthcare a voice in the relationship between the insurer and the healthcare provider. Today, more and more people are coming to see the federal government as the monster that devoured not only New York City but the entire nation. And most Americans believe it is time for a change. A radical change.

When I addressed the conferees at the Twentieth Annual Conservative Political Action Conference in Washington, D.C., in February 1993, I warned that the solution to the enormous fiscal problems of big government are not merely to be found in so-called secular solutions. I spoke of the dangers and the enormous cost brought about by the moral conflict throughout our society. Just as the floods, hurricanes, tornadoes, and other storms of the past three years are without precedent, so the storm of immorality has never been so rampant. Never in history has there been such an all-out assault on Christian faith and the family values that guided this nation from its foundation.

The twin thrusts of the statist society—assault on religious faith and huge centralized government—have done a deadly work in our land. Here's a sample: The homicide rate in the United States today is greater than that of every other industrialized nation. The cost of crime in America exceeds $100 billion each year. We have more than 1.1 million inmates behind bars, which gives us the highest percentage incarceration rate in the world—ten times that of Japan, Sweden, Ireland, and the Netherlands. Every day sixteen thousand crimes occur on or near our school campuses. That means that each year there are more than three million crimes involving schoolchildren in this country. National education standards are among the lowest in the entire world while juvenile crime is the highest. Apparently crime is the only thing our young people are learning well.

On "The 700 Club" we have reported the shocking difference in our public schools before and after prayer was removed. In the 1940s, teachers considered talking out of turn, chewing gum, and running in the halls to be the greatest problems in the schools. Today, teachers are confronted with drug and alcohol abuse, teen pregnancies, and teen suicide.

But there are other areas where America leads the world, and the connection is not incidental. We are number one in the world in divorce. We are number one in the West in teenage pregnancies. We are number one in voluntary abortions. We are also number one in illegal drug use, and number one in illiteracy. According to a report in *U.S. News & World Report*, 22.2 percent of all white children born in 1980 and 82.9 percent of all black children born the same year will be dependent on welfare before they reach age eighteen. Among whites, 19 percent of all births today are to unwed mothers. Among blacks the rate is 65 percent, compared to just 19 percent in the 1940s.

The crisis facing America today is not a financial crisis. Despite what government is telling us, we do not have a financial crisis; we have a moral crisis. Everything else, whether it is the litigation explosion, the rising bankruptcy rate, the rising divorce rate, raging illiteracy, or the rising crime rate, grows out of that one problem. And we can never solve the other issues until we come to the heart of the problem, which is the problem in the human heart. But the tide is turning.

A No-Win Situation

Today the federal government throws more than $226 billion a year at the poverty problem with no solution in sight. We have already spent more than $3.5 trillion in the so-called War on Poverty since 1965, and the commercial streets in many of our city centers today are more dangerous and blighted than even the worst ghettos were in 1965.

But there is an even worse plague upon the land, with more than fifty-six million Americans suffering from some type of sexually transmitted disease—which we refer to now by the euphemism STD. Many of these diseases are disfiguring and potentially life threatening, and we know that the AIDS epidemic is sweeping the land with, by some projections, as many as 1.4 million cases nationwide. And even while the government is going through violent contortions over the healthcare "crisis," expressing alarm over the rising cost of medical treatment, we are spending as high as $140,000 per person for each individual suffering with AIDS and related diseases. That means the cost to treat one hundred thousand AIDS sufferers could exceed $14 billion; the cost to be paid by taxpayers for treating a projected one million AIDS cases could top $1.4 trillion, which would be twice the amount we currently spend on all healthcare nationwide.

Of course, an epidemic this size will bankrupt the insurance companies and shatter all known healthcare systems. The White House has called for higher taxes to meet our exploding deficit. In fact, President Clinton's plan, pushed through Congress by the Democratic party, promises to become the largest tax increase levied on any nation in human history. But now we see that the potential cost of healthcare for people suffering from self-inflicted sexual diseases will, in all likelihood, exceed all categories in that budget. Yet in the face of irrefutable logic, the president is legitimizing sodomy by insisting that homosexuals serve in his government and in the military.

This country was founded on common sense. Our founding fathers came here to escape the unreasonable demands of bureaucrats and tyrants; they came here for free speech and free exercise of their religious beliefs. Yet just 386 years after the first boatload of dissenters landed at Jamestown, Virginia, and planted here the Christian cross, we seem to have lost our way. Common sense and plain truth have been lost in the halls of government, and violence and immorality stalk the land.

Instead of compelling the armed forces to admit homosexuals, the American people are saying, Let the president take a stand against this immoral lifestyle. Instead of seeking appropriations for billions of dollars more for AIDS research, let him declare that we will treat AIDS as any other communicable disease—as a virus, not as a protected civil right. Instead of issuing executive orders facilitating abortions, abortion counseling, federal funding of abortions, or licensing the use of the RU-486 abortion pill, let him call for moral restraint and a renewed emphasis on the virtues of the home, the family, and the church. Let him call for an end to no-fault divorces, and let him challenge Americans to renew their vows of allegiance to God and country. Let him call for a bold new commitment to sound public school policy based on historical authority and strong families that love and support their children. These are the keys to America's future. And these are the "changes" Americans really want from their president and their national leaders.

A Winning Coalition

A few years ago I had a chance to speak privately with President Ronald Reagan about the prospects for positive changes in America. I said that I hoped he could somehow get Congress to see the light. From his point of view, he said, it doesn't matter if they see the light as long as they feel the heat. I thought that was an excellent perspective because, when it comes down to it, Congress and our national leaders will only change when they see that the people will no longer settle for business as usual. The real power of government in democratic nations belongs to "We, the people." We are the ones who can turn up the heat.

Marlin Maddoux recently wrote, "I firmly believe, if we respond correctly, the Clinton election could become our spiritual Pearl Harbor, a wake-up call that did its job." And I believe he is right. A resurgence of moral vitality and personal resolve will be needed to turn the tide to our advantage. But the alarm has been sounded, and if common-sense conservatives move boldly, the entire fortress of liberalism will fall.[5]

From this vantage point, we can see that the Clinton years are the last gasp of the liberal social agenda. The Democrat-controlled government must now live or die by its own medicine, and now that they have won control of the executive and legislative branches of government, they will have no one to blame for their failures but themselves. And who can doubt what must follow?

At the same time, voices of common sense are rising from the people in the streets, from men and women in the local precincts, and from the platforms and pulpits of our noble institutions. Today, as never before in history, men and women who agree on certain key principles of democracy have agreed to overlook the things that keep them apart in order to concentrate on the things that bring them together. It is one of the most exciting movements in the history of this nation. Fiscal and economic conservatives, political realists, Protestants, pro-family Roman Catholics, conservative and orthodox Jews, and many others who agree on essential values are coming together to bring about meaningful change.

Great movements often have small beginnings. The collapse of Eastern European communism began with the cry of one old woman who dared call Nicolae Ceausescu a liar. And even though conservatives often seem outgunned in the media and in the public square, we have a great weapon—we have truth on our side. As we examine the evidence of a resurgence of common-sense values in our society, I believe we will also come to see the Clinton victory of 1992 as the stroke that felled the liberal colossus in America. As long as the liberals were on the outside looking in, they could exalt their vision of "change." But now that they have their moment in the sun, it is clear that they are out of their depth, with neither a vision, nor a platform, nor a track record acceptable to the American people.

I firmly believe that the conservatives of America have the winning message if we are willing to enunciate it boldly, to stand by our principles, and to make a coalition together against those who would seek to break our resolve.

William Shakespeare wrote, "There's a tide in the affairs of men which, when taken at its flood, leads on to victory." That tide is rising now. It is abroad in the land. With the sudden collapse of Soviet communism and the imminent death of European socialism, the fatally flawed principles of American-style liberalism are suddenly visible to the entire world. Yes, liberals hold the reins of power for a time. But that is precisely what is needed to waken the nation. For like the storms and the other "acts of God" pummeling our land, we have this brief moment to recognize where we have failed, to turn from our wicked ways, and to recommit ourselves to changes that will make a lasting difference.

Everything we treasure depends on how we respond to this challenge.

2

The Tide of Freedom

IT WAS A SUNDAY NIGHT IN February 1993. The streets
of Paris glistened with rain as the black Citroen sped along the Quai
D'Orsay toward my hotel next to the American embassy at the Place de
la Concorde. My host was a prominent French attorney who, along with
his wife, raised thoroughbred racehorses at their farm in Normandy. My
traveling companions and I had been their guests for an unbelievably
delicious dinner at a lovely restaurant called *l'Orangerie* located not too
far from the Cathedral of Notre Dame in the oldest part of Paris, the
Ile de la Cité.

I had come to Paris to examine a product line produced by a French
firm. Yet fifteen minutes into my first meeting, the owner of the company
began trying to sell me, not just his products, but his entire company.

This was such a surprising overture, I asked myself why the owner
of a successful business would want to sell it to a stranger he had known
for only fifteen minutes. In a country with all the evidences of prosperity—elegant shops, luxury hotels, incredible cuisine, highways jammed
with cars—was there something terribly wrong?

Later, over dinner at *l'Orangerie* on Sunday night, I began to get the
answer. My dinner host, a devout Roman Catholic, shocked me when he
asked, "In America do the liberals attack religion?" I was surprised at his
question but quickly sketched out the vendetta against religious values

that had been waged for the past thirty years in the United States by liberal courts, liberal educators, and the liberal media.

I then replied, "Why do you ask? Have you had the same problem in France?"

His answer was very direct. "From the moment Mitterrand and the socialists took power in France they began an attack on religion by the government, by the press, and by the schools. Under French socialism, children are educated to believe in humanism and atheism."

He then began to question me about the reason for my trip to his country. I told him about the company I had come to visit and explained that within minutes of our meeting the owner of the business had offered to sell me his company.

"Watch out," he warned, as if I needed a warning. "The socialists have made it so difficult to do business that no one is hiring."

"What do you mean, no one is hiring?" I asked.

"Here is our dilemma," he went on. "The socialists have mandated so many benefits for workers that a businessman must add 50 percent, in some cases 100 percent, to his total payroll costs. But that's not all. It is very hard to lay off workers when business is slow. A businessman who terminates a worker must pay an amount equal to one year's pay. We have high unemployment in France now because businessmen simply cannot assume the high costs and future liability that comes along with every new worker." I later learned that a record three million Frenchmen, or 10.5 percent of the work force, were unemployed.

Then he concluded, "If you buy a business here, all those problems will be yours."

I laughed and then in deference to the others at our table we changed the subject. But in the quiet of his car on the ride back to the hotel I got the real answers. "Tell me," I asked, "how heavily are you taxed personally?"

"There are several taxes," he replied. "My personal income tax rate is 57 percent. Then there is a wealth tax on all my property. Then a capital gains tax."

I interrupted, "Do you mean that you pay a tax each year on the value of your securities?"

"Yes," he continued, "a tax on everything we own. And the tax collectors are very thorough."

"But what about the French value added tax?" I asked.

"The VAT is 18.9 percent and is added to the price of everything we buy," he replied.

"I don't see how you can endure a system like this," I blurted out. "Why don't you go to Switzerland or Monte Carlo to escape?"

"I am a Frenchman," he replied. "I come from an old French family and I will not be forced out of my country. But of course you are right. Life under socialism is intolerable. Unless the politics of our country are changed, I am certain that France will be destroyed!"

As I left Paris the next day, I thought about the likely political consequences of such intense feelings. I could not believe that the passion to overthrow the tyranny of the French liberal humanists was held exclusively by my host. I knew that the burden of crushing taxes, wasteful and inefficient government, government meddling in business, schools dedicated to atheism, and the other pressures on French families would inevitably lead to some sort of a revolution at the polls.

Indeed, within a month of my visit, the French socialists were not merely defeated in parliamentary elections, they were annihilated, losing all but 70 of their 277 seats. When the smoke cleared, 207 socialists had been defeated and the new parliament held 484 members of the center right alliance—an unprecedented 84 percent majority of the 577-seat National Assembly.

The new conservative prime minister, Edouard Balladur, outlined his two concerns in a 110-minute speech to the French parliament. He said that France, because of socialism, now faces the gravest economic situation since World War II, along with a pernicious "moral crisis" in the cities—especially among young people.

As to the socialists, one wire service described them as "traumatized, crushed, and humiliated," having suffered a political blow that "French commentators compared to Napoleon's defeat at Waterloo."

"P.S.," according to a longtime Socialist party supporter, Marc Chemalli, "no longer stands for Parti Socialiste but post-scription, not so much a party as an afterthought." In France, too, the tide is turning. Liberalism is in retreat; common sense is rising.

What Happened in Eastern Europe

My mind goes back to a little church in Timisoara, Rumania, in the spring of 1990—three years before my visit to France.

I stood looking out the window of the study of Pastor Laszlo Tokes onto the narrow street outside. Here, in December 1989, a small crowd had gathered in support of their beloved pastor. It seemed that his views were considered by his bishop to be contrary to the official government line, and therefore Tokes was to be transferred to a parish in a remote mountain village.

But why would that draw a crowd? Only five years before, the government of Nicolae Ceausescu had been imprisoning and brutally torturing dissident Roman Catholic and Orthodox priests. I had learned of one brave priest who was tortured and mutilated and then forced to serve mock communion with the elements comprised of his own feces and urine.

This was the same country where a brave Lutheran pastor, Richard Wurmbrand, was not only chained, imprisoned, and starved but tortured by sadistic guards who took delight in searing deep wounds in his chest and back with red-hot pokers.

This was a country where, by order of the dictator, no birth control was permitted and defective babies were taken from their parents and forced to grow up deformed and without love in virtual isolation. Where the government decreed that each normal baby would be given an injection of blood even if the needle employed had been used many times before and might be infected with the deadly virus that causes AIDS.

This was Rumania, the land of police spies, officially sanctioned kidnapping and murder, suppression of religion, and a reign of terror. What, then, could church members be thinking of to gather in protest of nothing more serious than an ecclesiastical transfer? But Rumania in 1989, like France in 1993, had come to that moment in time when people would no longer endure the tyranny of the Left. In the small street outside Pastor Tokes's study, the tide in Rumania began to turn. Here is how it happened.

At first only a few dozen people gathered in support of their pastor. Then the crowd grew to a thousand. Tokes opened the big double windows of his study and begged the crowd to disperse. He knew the sadistic wrath of Ceausescu's dreaded Securitate, and he did not wish their retaliation on these innocent church members. "Go home. Obey the law," he pleaded. "God will take care of me."

But his entreaties were in vain. As news of the protest spread, the crowd grew so large that it filled the small side street next to the church and spilled over into the main thoroughfare. Then, as their numbers swelled, the crowd surged into the central plaza of the city. Soon there were a hundred thousand people shouting over and over again to their atheistic masters, "God is alive! God is alive! God is alive!" Then they began singing a song familiar to many American churchgoers that speaks of the second coming of Christ. "He's coming soon! He's coming soon! Jesus is coming soon!"

By this time the Securitate had positioned men with high-powered rifles on the rooftops of the buildings that surrounded the central plaza. On command they opened fire on the unarmed civilians gathered below. As many as two thousand men, women, and children fell on the blood-soaked pavement. The rest of the crowd scattered, running for their lives.

This massacre was not done in secret. As the news spread like wildfire throughout Rumania, a wave of revulsion began building among the people.

Then on December 17, 1989, a huge crowd assembled in the city square in the capital city of Bucharest. Large loudspeakers were set so that Ceausescu could be heard as he came out on the balcony of the Communist party headquarters facing the square. Supposing that this was one more staged event for public relations purposes, Ceausescu began his usual sugarcoated version of spin control.

Midway through his speech, from deep in the huge crowd came the voice of one old woman. "You're a liar!" Then those around her picked it up. "You're a liar!" Then more and more until a huge roar filled the streets crying in unison. *"You're a liar!"*

Those who may have seen news footage of the event saw Ceausescu waving both hands in front of his face in a gesture that seemed to say, "Stop it. No. This isn't in the script." But the crowds didn't stop, because the tide had turned.

Ceausescu, the all-powerful dictator, fled the platform and went into hiding. He and his family flew to a retreat outside Bucharest in their white helicopter, but to no avail. By December 23 the popular resistance had captured the despot and hauled him back to the capital for a speedy hearing and judgment. Ceausescu and his wife were executed by a firing squad on Christmas Day, and the news pictures of these events were flashed to a stunned world.

Future Shocks of Freedom

Nowhere was this news received with more chagrin that in Moscow. The Soviets could only stare in disbelief as their entire Communist apparatus in Rumania collapsed. The prisons were closed, the executions stopped, the Securitate forces seemed to evaporate, a democratic constitution was adopted, elections were held, and suddenly the people had freedom. Obviously freedom does not guarantee economic prosperity, just the right of the people to seek a better life for themselves and their families. But that first step to a new life had been taken boldly.

The turning tide in Rumania did not merely signify a political change; it signified a profound moral change as well.

Modern liberalism is not merely economic and political control of people's lives by repressive government. Under communism it meant an open embrace of atheism, and in countries like France and the United States it has meant a vitriolic repression of historic Judeo-Christian religious values.

But just as people cannot long endure economic and political oppression, neither can their spirits and souls endure an existence without hope and without ultimate meaning. Like a black-and-white photograph of a scene from 1890, their lives lack spark, excitement, and vitality. Everything is drab and colorless. Because the authorities in the liberal paradigm have rejected the wisdom that flows from the time-honored biblical concepts of law, family, sexual morality, individual freedom, and ultimate accountability to God, their actions become more and more capricious, unreasonable, and lacking in common sense. Then because the innate common sense of people refuses to reso-nate with the arbitrary foolishness emanating from their ruling elites, the people in power find it necessary either to face a breakdown of au-thority or step up the use of force.

But once the tide turns and liberalism collapses, the new regime instinctively reaches out to religious values to provide a foundation for its policies. In Rumania, after the fall of communism, the new govern-ment sent an urgent message to the churches. "Please supply us with teachers of religion," the officials pleaded, "so that they may go into our schools and teach our children Christian principles."

On my visit to Rumania, I was honored not only with the oppor-tunity to meet with the new president, Ion Iliescu, but with the televi-sion authorities as well. They eagerly accepted our offer to supply them with programs.

Our series of 104 animated cartoons of Bible stories, *Superbook* and *Flying House*, are in beautiful color and were dubbed into flawless Ruma-nian. The government broadcasting authority aired them at 7:30 each weeknight throughout the whole country. The response of the people was electrifying. The CBN office in Bucharest has to date received 1.2 million letters requesting further information about the Bible.

CBN Group Vice-President Michael Little met with the chief of staff to President Iliescu in Bucharest about a year ago to discuss the airing of the Bible-based programs. Imagine Michael's surprise to hear the following from one of the highest officials of the new Rumanian government. "I am an atheist. I do not believe in God. I do not believe in Jesus Christ. *But we know that in order to build a just society we must build it on the principles of the Bible. We want your Bible stories*" (empha-sis added).

Stingers Wound the Bear

Yet Rumania is not an isolated example. Close your eyes and think back to 1986. America stared across a chasm of nuclear terror to what seemed to be an implacable foe in the Soviet Union. The arms race was in full tilt. Our leaders talked of throw weight of ICBMs, megatons of thermonuclear bombs, Pershing missiles v. SS20 missiles, sea-based intercontinental ballistic missiles, nuclear carriers, and constant satellite alertness. In short, the Evil Empire versus The Land of the Free and the Home of the Brave.

Then the tide began to turn. Despite the outcry of doctrinaire liberals, Congress approved a small supply of arms, most notably the shoulder-launched "Stinger" ground-to-air missile, to the Afghan resistance fighting the Soviet troops that had invaded their nation. Up to this time the Soviets had brutalized Afghan civilians and demoralized the guerrilla forces. Their principal weapon was the seemingly invincible MiL-24 Hind helicopter gunship. But with Stinger missiles now in the possession of the Afghan Mujahadeen freedom fighters, Soviet helicopter gunships were regularly blown out of the sky. Then Afghan troops enlisted by the Soviets began to desert and bring Soviet-supplied tanks, weapons, and ammunition with them. It was clear that the Soviets could never win militarily in Afghanistan.

In a short time the hundred-thousand-man Soviet army turned tail and went home. They had lost men, heavy armor, and vast sums of money, but most of all they had lost face.

The myth of Soviet military invincibility was shattered once and for all. In truth, behind the mighty colossus was a third-rate economy that was on the verge of collapse. In the final analysis, Soviet liberalism was based on hot air, bluster, massive propaganda, and *the lack of moral resolve on the part of its opponents. All it took was a few modern weapons in the hands of a determined band of resolute and deeply religious mountain fighters to turn the tide.*

The rest is history. The collapse of communism in the Soviet Union, Poland, East Germany, Hungary, Bulgaria, Rumania, and Albania took place so fast that now communism seems like a largely forgotten relic of some far-distant bad dream.

Just think, virtually overnight the terrible demons that tormented hundreds of millions have vanished. The Berlin Wall has been demolished, the prisons are closed, secret files are opened, military hardware is either rusting or being sold on the streets, dictators have been replaced by elected parliaments, state-owned enterprises are being rapidly privatized, and central-command economies have given way to free enterprise and the free market.

Lest we get too giddy at all this, we must remember that restoring, repairing, and retraining the institutions, customs, and thought patterns of people who have known nothing but regimentation for most of their lives is not going to happen overnight.

But what we must understand is that the collapse of the Soviet Union, as the most visible expression of a modern government based on the twin pillars of secularism and Marxist-Leninist communism, proved the moral and economic bankruptcy of state socialism. The death knell has been sounded worldwide for any other attempt to create a system of bureaucratic organizations based on those failed principles.

And I might add emphatically that the tide flowing against liberalism and against the sterile secularized society is so strong worldwide that it will clearly engulf the dominant liberalism and secularism of the governing elites in the United States. More about that later.

Fire of Faith

One aspect of the collapse of communism in the Soviet Union that has received scant attention in the predominantly liberal media of America is the engulfing fire of religious faith in that formerly atheistic country.

Anecdotal evidence is legion, but consider these reports from the heady days when freedom was restored. Muscovites were seen kneeling outside of Lenin's tomb while turning to faith in Jesus Christ. Gifts of Bibles were greeted with tears, and the Holy Book was reverently kissed. One story has it that when an announcement was made to the Russian parliament that free Bibles were being given away in the lobby of their building, the entire body rose from their seats and went to the lobby to receive this treasured gift.

CBN—with the full cooperation, first, of Soviet television and, later, Russian and Ukrainian television—began broadcasting spiritual programs from the European border of Russia as far away as Vladivostok. Scientific audience surveys indicated that our programs had an astounding one hundred million viewers. The numbers of those projected to have made a spiritual commitment to Christ as a result numbered in the tens of millions.

CBN opened offices in Moscow (in one of Lenin's former headquarters) and in Kiev in the Ukraine. To date our Russian and Ukrainian staff have responded to more than seven million letters from the wonderful people who pour out their hearts to us as they seek a personal experience with Jesus Christ. The mail coming to our offices as a result of our continuing television programs averages twenty-two thousand pieces a day, more than a hundred thousand pieces per week. We offer Bible correspondence courses, and now our enrollment has exceeded five hundred thousand students throughout what is now called the Commonwealth of Independent States.

But that's not all. Boris Yeltsin, whose mother was a Christian believer, has requested that teachers of the Christian religion be encouraged to teach biblical principles in the Russian schools. Not only are the Russian churches participating, but many U.S. churches and parachurch organizations such as Campus Crusade for Christ and Walk Through the Bible have been welcomed.

I am a student of secular and ecclesiastical history, and, to the best of my knowledge, never in the history of the Christian church has there been a heartfelt spiritual revival with the magnitude and fervor of what is now taking place in a land that only two years ago was our sworn enemy.

We are seeing nations in Eastern Europe claw their way back from the abyss where their leadership abandoned religious faith, broke up stable families, removed the discipline of the free market, and tried to substitute the decisions of a few bureaucrats for the millions of economic decisions that make up a free market.

They also are discovering the same common-sense truths that were held so firmly by the founders of the United States. They realize that they cannot bring up a generation of law-abiding, honest citizens capable of freedom without the self-restraint that only religious faith can bring. They realize instinctively that law and order can only be brought about in an atheistic dictatorship at the point of a gun aided by a network of spies and informants. They realize that freedom without religious belief will lead inevitably and suddenly to anarchy and lawlessness.

Their thinking immediately calls to mind the words of the first and second presidents of the United States:

> Reason and experience forbid us to expect public morality in the absence of religious principle.
>
> George Washington

> We have not a government strong enough to restrain the unbridled passions of men. This constitution was made only for a moral and a religious people. It is wholly inadequate for any other.
>
> John Adams

How exciting that the post-communist leaders are eagerly embracing the common-sense truth that the liberal elites in America have been so eager to destroy. But in America, too, the tide is beginning to turn.

The Rise and Fall of Japan

The events in Europe, startling as they are, may one day pale into insignificance in light of what is taking place in Asia.

My first visit to Asia was in 1951, courtesy of the United States government. In those days Douglas MacArthur, the supreme allied commander, functioned as the "American Caesar." From his office in the Dai Ichi building close by the Imperial Palace of the Japanese emperor and the famed Frank Lloyd Wright Imperial Hotel, MacArthur not only commanded the allied forces resisting the combined communist forces of mainland China and North Korea, he was also the military governor of occupied Japan as well. The United States had crushed the Japanese in World War II. MacArthur and Admiral Chester Nimitz had received the unconditional surrender of the Japanese high command at a historic ceremony on the deck of the battleship *Missouri* anchored in Tokyo Bay, September 2, 1945.

MacArthur had pulled off one of the extraordinary acts of bravery for which he was famous. He flew in an unarmed C-47 transport plane without fighter escort directly into the Tokyo airport. He could have been mobbed, torn limb from limb. Instead he was greeted with courtesy—later adulation. MacArthur relied on one thing. The Japanese believed that their emperor was a god, and the message was passed to the Japanese people that their emperor "willed" a safe arrival for MacArthur.

When I reached Japan as a twenty-year-old Marine lieutenant, the Japanese economy was flat on its back. When I sit in the cockpit of a sleek, turbo-charged, three-hundred-horsepower Nissan ZX sports coupe, I can't help remembering the short taxi rides from Kyoto to Camp Otsu, where I was stationed, in a Japanese taxi powered by a rear-mounted charcoal burner that not only toasted the backs of the passengers but could scarcely power the vehicle over the small hills in the area.

After the war, Japan was a bombed-out, primitive ruin that had just lost its god. MacArthur saw the spiritual vacuum developing in the collective soul of the Japanese people and implored the churches of America to send Bibles and ten thousand missionaries. But the churches of America were too preoccupied with filling the needs of the new families moving into newly built, sprawling suburbia.

The spiritual tide did not begin to turn for Japan, but the economic tide did. MacArthur gave them the framework to move from feudalism into an ordered democracy based on American constitutional law. And one lone American management consultant, W. Edwards Deming, gave their leaders a very simple formula, most of it based on biblical values, for business management and business success.

Living by the System

Armed with American-style constitutional freedoms and a basic American code of management principles, the Japanese set out to build from the ashes a new society. They put into practice the very principles of conduct that the post-war American elites were debunking. And as the folly of liberalism began the long, slow weakening of the time-honored traditions of America, application of traditional American management principles enabled the Japanese during the eighties to sprint ahead of us in virtually every area of industrial competition.

According to Karel van Wolferen in his book, *The Enigma of Japanese Power*, the Japanese "employ neither law, nor religion, nor systematic articulate, intellectual inquiry as a means of evaluating their socio-political arrangements . . . there being thus nothing outside the System to overrule or judge it, the System can only judge itself."[1] Therefore what van Wolferen calls "Japaneseness" or "the System" has actually become the new religion of Japan. Robert C. Christopher also pointed out, "In a poll taken in 1979, only 19 percent of all Japanese between the ages of sixteen and nineteen professed any religion at all. That was the lowest percentage reported for any major nation in the non-Communist world."[2]

This lack of any moral and ethical framework other than their own "Japaneseness" leaves Japan either sociologically very vulnerable or, alternatively, a very dangerous economic competitor to the rest of the world.

Now in the 1990s it appears that the tide for the Japanese is starting to turn against them. We gave them representative government and the techniques of industrial wealth, but we left them impoverished in spirit. And it is the spiritual deficit that is beginning to exact a bitter toll. A recent report coming out of Japan indicates that the Japanese economy is beginning to get bogged down with the same type of procedural red tape American businessmen complain about in the

United States. However, even in a recession, Japanese unemployment is 2.2 percent and the government has a large savings pool available to stimulate the economy.

Time magazine reported in its April 19, 1993, issue that nobody yet knows how the shakiness of Japanese banks will affect the economy, but estimates of bad debts run to a huge $300 billion. The full extent of Japanese real estate depreciation is yet unknown, but it has been estimated to be half of the previously inflated $16 trillion valuation, or $8 trillion. The force of this deflation apparently has not fully hit the Japanese economy.

Japanese businesses expect male employees to put their careers above family life. They say a good marriage is like air—essential for life but taken for granted. Business stress has begun to devastate Japanese family life. The official number of divorces is 179,000 annually, up 50 percent from 1970. But now the Japanese couples are adopting in-family divorces—called *katei-nai rikon*—which has separated more than 200,000 couples who still share the same living space.[3] The children of these fractured unions will, in my opinion, experience the same types of behavior that is evident in so many children from broken homes in America.

With all that, we are looking at a long-range future trend, not the immediate present. The odds of being murdered are 7 times less likely in Japan than in the United States, 2.7 times less likely to be raped, and 158 times less likely to be robbed.[4]

Three Keys for National Success

The lessons of the Japanese experience should be clear to all of us. For a people to succeed as a nation, their institutions, their customs, their education, and their personal lives must be founded on faith in God. First of all, they need a reality that transcends materialism and a consciousness that they are personally accountable to a higher power. Second, their governmental structures should be checked and balanced against abuse and limited to performance of the collective tasks that are beyond the scope of the individual, particularly including public safety and national defense. Third, their business endeavors should be based on a shared code of ethics, individual initiative and hard work, excellence, and a passionate desire to serve both workers and customers.

When these three ingredients are in place in a nation, the tide will begin to turn in its favor, but if one or more elements is missing, sooner or later trouble will come.

I don't want to overemphasize any immediate collapse of Japanese economic power, but as the tide slowly turns against the naked materialism of Japan, the tide of freedom is already beginning to run deep in another country that the *Economist* of London declared will have the largest economy in the world by the year 2010—mainland China.

I first visited this vast land in 1979. What I found amazed me. Wages were unbelievably low. A skilled artisan received a monthly wage equal to $28. The manager of a factory employing two thousand workers was paid approximately $70 per month. Yet somehow the government had managed to feed the vast population that was close to one billion in number. It seemed that everyone had at least one gray or dark blue Mao uniform and a place to live. The principal mode of transportation was bicycles, and it appeared that just about anyone who wanted a bicycle could afford one. There was a great deal of dirt and subsistence living, but nowhere was there the filth and squalor that characterizes some African and Latin American countries.

The Chinese people were very friendly, and I was struck by their ingenuous nature. They seemed like sweet, unspoiled children. And they were unbelievably honest. One illustration is etched in my memory.

When I was in Quandong (the old Canton Province), I visited the city fair and made arrangements to address the crowd from a small bandbox. About one thousand people crowded around to hear me. They were friendly and very responsive to what I had to say. When I finished, I told them that we would like to give them a part of the Bible in the Chinese language. They mobbed my associates to receive the Bibles. After the crowd had dispersed, my interpreter, who was from Hong Kong, came up to me with a very sad expression. He told me that during the crush of the crowd his expensive camera had slipped off his arm and was lost. I didn't feel very sorry for him, because I had visited his brother's house on the Peak in Hong Kong and had ridden in one of the brother's matching white Rolls-Royces. Surely a member of a family with wealth in excess of $150 million would not miss one little camera. But just then my musing was stopped short when a young Chinese couple approached my interpreter-friend. To his amazement they held out his camera and said, "Your camera slipped off your shoulder in the crowd, and we wanted to return it safe to you."

We were dumbfounded by this beautiful display of honesty and thoughtfulness, but that was the way it was in China wherever we went. Out of their poverty the Chinese people had adopted a code of conduct, especially toward visitors, that was exemplary. When my wife and I returned from the beautiful simplicity of mainland China to the tawdry opulence and commercialism of Hong Kong, we were genuinely shocked by the comparison.

Who's in Charge?

However, in 1979 every facet of economic life in China, save one, was under government control. Every time I visited a shop—or a factory—I asked the same question, "Who owns this place?"

The answer was always the same, "The government."

From the small hole-in-the-wall peddler, to a department store, to a small factory full of artisans carving jade, to a major industrial complex, the government owned and controlled it all. Only the small farms were allowed to sell their products directly, and their production was beginning to rival the much larger agricultural communes.

I visited the Quandong International Trade Fair where the newest Chinese wares were on display. Wherever I went, I looked carefully at their factory machinery, their weapons, their agriculture, and their systems for healthcare. From the newest to the oldest—whether in computers, or farm equipment, or military hardware—China in 1979 was at least twenty or thirty years behind the modern industrial economies of the West.

Thirteen years later, when I returned in December 1992, the new China I found was like another world. Their leader, Deng Xiao Ping, had begun a careful move to a market economy—first in the Quanzhou province, then Fukien, the two provinces nearest Hong Kong. Then the government allowed the creation of a massive capitalistic zone in an area called Shenzen directly on the border of the Kowloon part of Hong Kong—in an area known as the New Territories.

Given the chance to achieve without the shackles of government interference, the Chinese economy took off. The Quanzhou economy began growing at 20 percent a year—the fastest in the world. Deng visited the area, beamed his approval, and uttered the famous words, "To be rich is beautiful." Certainly from a standpoint of material prosperity, change had become beautiful.

Money from overseas Chinese is pouring into the mainland. Gordon Wu of Hopewell Holdings is building a $1.2 billion toll road from Hong Kong to Quandong. I met with the vice-chairman of Li Kaishing's Hutchinson Whampoa, which is investing hundreds of millions of dollars in Chinese companies and is getting a jump on the planned expansion of Shanghai as the successor port to Hong Kong. I visited with Hong Kong financier Robert Kuok, who told me that he had invested $500 million in the China World Hotel and Office Center in Beijing and that the project was already becoming profitable.

The people in Beijing seem happy, well-fed, well-dressed, and vastly more prosperous than I remembered. Our hotel was nothing short of gorgeous, although evidence of communism had not completely vanished. Each room had its own bugging device, equipped with its own tape recorder, which was activated when the room light was turned on.

Opening New Vistas

Our meetings with China Central Television were extremely cordial. They told us that there were two hundred million television sets in China. They sell twenty million more sets each year, and the officials were asking our advice as to methods of selling more of them.

Of course, the market size of China is enormous. There are 1.2 billion people there. Official statistics put per capita income at $400 a year. But independent studies put incomes, adjusted for black market activity and purchasing power parity, at $1,000 or even $2,000 per year. Multiply that by 1.2 billion and the result is a huge economy—behind only those of the United States and Japan—and growing at a rate that will surpass both of them in twenty years.

A great number of U.S. companies are pouring into China today. According to an August 2, 1993, article in *Forbes* magazine, Coca-Cola is currently building ten new bottling plants in China to add to the thirteen existing facilities. Because of their advanced products and technologies, American firms are gaining a huge market share—among them: Johnson & Johnson Band-Aids, Smith Kline Beecham, Contac cold medicine, Procter and Gamble's hair care products, and Bausch & Lomb contact lenses. Kentucky Fried Chicken will soon have outlets in all Chinese cities with a population of one million or more. Chris Strachan, managing director of United Biscuits China, was quoted as saying, "UB regards China as the greatest opportunity in the world today."[5]

From what I observed, few if any Chinese have any belief in Marxism. Certainly the cult of Mao Tse-tung is dead and gone, along with its founder. In my opinion the members of the Communist party hierarchy are holding on to power, on the one hand, for their own selfish reasons and, on the other hand, because they fear that their nation may break apart if they let go too soon.

The Oriental mind often seems inscrutable, and obviously there is a chance that they may change course. But for now it seems inconceivable that the progress of the economic freedom granted to the Chinese people can be reversed without causing a major upheaval. State control of economic life is being relaxed. Unquestionably, political reform must follow. But what of the third key ingredient for success—spiritual reform?

It is fair to say that communism demolished the hold of Buddhism in China and severely restricted formal Christian church life. With the communism of Mao Tse-tung no longer a factor, the Chinese of 1993, like the Japanese of 1946, will be faced with an enormous spiritual vacuum. However, from reports reaching me, since the massacre in Tiananmen Square thousands of university students have turned to faith in Jesus Christ. I regularly hear of powerful spiritual revivals breaking out in various parts of that ancient land. Estimates of the numbers of Christian believers in China today range between seventy-five and one hundred million. This is a mighty underground army that, despite the reports of barbaric persecutions, holds the key to ultimate spiritual and moral renewal.

The Chinese government has still not granted religious freedom, nor is it tilting in any way toward Christianity. But among the nation's intellectuals there is a yearning for democratic freedom, and to many of these people Christianity is seen as the antithesis of communism, and therefore, as in Russia, it has become a symbol of freedom.

There is no question that the tide is turning in China. The pillars of liberalism and atheism are falling. Common-sense free-market ideas are firmly in place. With its vast population, China has already become one of the economic giants of the world. As Christianity, democratic government, and free-market economics grow together in China, I foresee a time in the next century when China will replace not only Japan but the United States to become the greatest economic power on earth.

The Latin Miracle

I arrived in Santiago, Chile, to negotiate television airtime for our CBN programs right after the overthrow of Salvador Allende. Allende was an apparently nonthreatening theoretical Communist who was the first and only Communist ever elected with the avowed aim of introducing communism to a free society. Predictably, the world's liberal press lionized him, but almost from the outset it was apparent that the application of his theoretical liberal nonsense to real-life government was destroying the nation.

One airline manager in Santiago sketched out for me the situation that developed. Allende and his fellow liberals believed that free-market capitalism and traditional middle-class thinking were diseases that needed to be destroyed before the perfect communist society could be built. Therefore, he deliberately set about to destroy all of the existing institutions—particularly those concerned with the production and distribution of goods.

Of course, the outcome was predictable. The nation was plunged into economic chaos, with shortages of everything. First, inflation, then the black market, and, of course, the blundering attempts of government to "fix" all the things their destructive policies had caused. The combination of all these factors literally crippled the nation.

My informant told me with tears in his eyes of the suffering his family endured under Allende—how he was unable to obtain the simplest necessities of life—not even baby food for his hungry child. A free election had put Allende in power in Chile in 1970, but a military coup in 1973, led by General Augusto Pinochet, took him out.

Little was ever printed in the liberal press in this nation about the excesses and failures of the Allende government, but suddenly the media turned on the conservative regime of Pinochet with a vengeance. Western readers were barraged with a steady drumbeat of stories about "repression in Chile," "human rights abuses in Chile," "torture in Chile," "right-wing extremists in Chile." William F. Buckley reported with his usual wit that if Chile would just rename itself "the People's Republic of Chile," the world's press would begin to applaud it.

In truth, what Pinochet did may have seemed brutal, but he did apply common sense to a very volatile situation. He jailed about two thousand communists who were certain to be fomenting counterrevolutionary activity. Some were executed. For a limited time he instituted martial law in order to keep his economically prostrate nation from falling into total anarchy.

Slowly the new leader stabilized the currency, fostered the rebuilding of the economy, privatized state-owned enterprises, and stimulated exports. He restored representative-constitutional democracy and finally paved the way for the free election of a president in 1989 to replace himself.

When I arrived in Chile shortly after the coup, I expected from what I had read in the press accounts to find a police state with mass arrests, spying, repression, and brutal torture. Instead I saw attractive young couples strolling about in the balmy evening air, laughing, enjoying ice cream cones, holding hands, and embracing. I thought, *If this is torture, I know a few young fellows back home who wouldn't mind a couple weeks of it.*

A Model for Others

Now the whole world looks to Chile as the model of success, not only for Latin America but for Third-World nations in Africa and Asia. The common-sense solutions of Pinochet and his successors are nothing short of a miracle. Consider their accomplishments.

In 1992, Chile's economy grew at a rate of 9.7 percent following nine years of uninterrupted growth. Unemployment was at 4.5 percent, a twenty-year low. Exports were near $10 billion a year, 30 percent of the gross domestic product. The country's reserves of $8.9 billion were enough to cover the entire import bill for one year. Investment was growing at twice the rate of the economy, and savings were 18 percent of the GNP. Chile's per capita income is $3,000, roughly nine times that of formerly Communist Nicaragua. According to the *National Journal* on July 3, 1993, "compared with the rest of Latin America, Chile's economic superlatives are unending. Chile was the first Latin American country whose bonds were rated investment grade by Standard & Poor's and Moody's Investment Services."

The tide has turned in Chile. Liberal statism fell and was replaced by representative government. State ownership of business along with oppressive regulation of business has been replaced by a vigorous free-market, free-enterprise system. And the third essential ingredient is in place—a powerful expression of religious faith.

After Allende, 24 percent of the population were considered Pentecostal Christians. While newly published figures show a population of

11 percent Protestant and 89 percent Roman Catholics, such numbers do not indicate the high levels of charismatic and evangelical activity in Chile that crosses all denominational lines.

That high a percentage of dedicated Christian believers will normally translate into stable families, law-abiding children, hard-working honest workers, a bias toward education and responsible participation in government. It also means a lower incidence of alcoholism and drug abuse, less absenteeism, less crime, and a higher level of personal savings. Common sense tells us that a government should foster the religious values that produce such attributes among its citizens—and General Pinochet clearly fostered the growth of Christianity in Chile.

But all the furor surrounding the struggling nation of Chile points up the great danger we face in America today. Secular liberals in America who control the media, the universities, the judicial system, and all three branches of government think that they must destroy religious faith in our nation. And then in the absence of common-sense principles and popular morality, they must then spend billions of dollars to correct the social ills that their actions have caused. This is a national tragedy and a scourge upon the land.

Why are the American elites seemingly the only people on earth who are blind to the truth? Wherever you look, there are signs of enormous changes taking place. Space does not permit the description of the turning tide in Argentina, Mexico, El Salvador, Nicaragua, Vietnam, Zambia, Mozambique, Angola, and even Cuba, but clear evidence of dramatic change exists in each of those places. We can see now that the vision of freedom that spread from our shores in the 1980s is sweeping back even now. But we have to wonder how long the liberal agenda in Washington can stand.

The Tide Returns

What we must understand is that communist and socialist command economies and their handmaidens, atheism and secularism, are being rejected by the people in Western Europe, Eastern Europe, the Far East,

Latin America, and even in Africa. New leaders who are no longer willing to accept the doctrinaire nonsense of the Left are helping to bring these nations back to common sense.

Clearly these dramatic changes would not have happened without the deep-seated yearning in the people's hearts for faith in God and personal freedom, and I believe that a major impetus of the worldwide trend came from the clear-eyed, free-market conservatism of Ronald Reagan in America and Margaret Thatcher in Great Britain. This vibrant message went out from our shores and brought forth a revolution all over the world.

Through a quirk in the U.S. electoral process, a third-party candidate siphoned off enough votes from George Bush to give Bill Clinton a 43 percent plurality. Former President Richard Nixon told me that the change of only 470,000 votes out of the millions cast in a few states like Ohio would have brought Bush a second term as president.

There is no way that any responsible analyst can read the 1992 election results as a mandate for the radical liberal agenda that Bill and Hillary Rodham Clinton are attempting to put forward. They are certainly taking advantage of their moment in the sun, but even this will prove to be a momentary aberration in the worldwide trend that is bringing government back to its senses.

The tide of freedom that washed from America just over a decade ago is now bearing down upon our shores again. Can Bill Clinton stand against that tide?

3

Clinton Against
the Tide

$\mathcal{M}$Y WIFE DEDE AND I were having breakfast Wednesday morning, July 28, 1993, when the phone rang. The caller was Ralph Reed, executive director of the Christian Coalition. He was breathless with excitement.

"Pat," he said, "the tide is turning! Did you hear the news?"

I had caught his excitement and shouted back, "What news?"

"The returns are in," he exclaimed, "and Mike Huckabee just defeated Clinton's chosen candidate for lieutenant governor in Arkansas. Mike is a former Baptist minister and has attended our Christian Coalition training seminars. Clinton sent his top team to help the Democrats. They spent $1 million fighting Mike, but we distributed three hundred thousand nonpartisan voter guides in the churches, and Mike finished six thousand votes ahead. He's the first Republican to win a state office in Arkansas in thirteen years!"

I could scarcely believe my ears. Arkansas—President Clinton's home state. A race that put the president's prestige on the line. Yet an evangelical candidate backed by pro-family conservatives beat the president's candidate decisively.

The Arkansas defeat was humiliating for the president, but it was just one of a growing string of defeats for the liberal agenda. Clinton's ultraliberal candidate Michael Woo went down in Los Angeles before

Republican conservative Richard Riordan. U.S. Senator Bob Krueger was beaten two-to-one in predominantly Democrat Texas by the conservative Republican Kay Bailey Hutchison—a race that turned largely on Clinton politics. Earlier, conservative Paul Coverdell had beaten U.S. Senator Wyche Fowler in Georgia for a Senate seat. There was an obvious foment in the land, and a tide of disgust with radical liberalism was growing.

After just six months in office, Bill Clinton succeeded in turning what should have been a first-term honeymoon into the most unpopular first six months of any president in recent memory. Clinton campaigned as a moderate who cared about people—to use his words, "I feel your pain." But once in office, his advisers seemed intent on inflicting pain on mainstream America as they unloaded one far-out, left-wing initiation after another. Clearly, Clinton had determined to swim against the tide of freedom and morality that is cresting all over the world.

Celebrity Packaging

Yet Clinton's inauguration seemed to hold out a great promise for success. After a heated war of words that lasted more than a year, he led his party to victory in the November 1992 elections, and from far and wide the elite and fashionable came to bask in the glow of their success. It was a strange and unaccustomed sight for the old District of Columbia. Most of the time Washington is a relatively cold and austere city, magnificent but lacking the glamour of Beverly Hills, Palm Beach, or Cannes. But thanks to some all-star entertainment and glitzy packaging arranged by Linda Bloodworth-Thomason and her husband Harry, best known for their hot sitcoms, the climate of the capital suddenly changed.

With one eye on his "mandate" for change and the other on his public opinion polls, the president-elect danced his way through a lavish procession of inaugural festivities that made Pennsylvania Avenue seem, for all the world, more like Sunset Strip.

In places where dour politicians and lackluster bureaucrats customarily stood, flanking the president and first lady, suddenly there was an entire constellation of stage and screen idols. And the elite from Tinseltown and the media—celebrities who had contributed greatly to the Clintons' winning campaign—turned out in a splendid cavalcade through the nation's capital. They weren't just gawking at monuments and historic places; they were actually participating in cabinet meetings, strategy sessions on "marketing" the president's new "investment" programs, and high-level policy briefings previously reserved for heads of state.

State dinners literally sparkled with the rich and famous. Actors, singers, dancers, celebrity producers, and famous rock stars showed up. Network personalities and hosts from MTV brought the place to life, and the television cameras didn't miss a beat. Ronald Reagan, who had taken abuse for having been "just an actor," had never assembled such an illustrious contingent of stars.

Some wondered aloud if this was going to be the new look of American government. If Hollywood celebrities were, in fact, America's only royalty, then wasn't it fitting that they should find such honor at the seat of power, and from a president who also smiles, plays the saxophone on "Arsenio," and keeps the crowds amused with his Elvis Presley impersonations?

During the festivities, reporters found Hillary Rodham Clinton sitting for her portrait by country singer and photo buff Kenny Rogers. They also captured favorite singer Judy Collins sleeping over in the Lincoln Bedroom and Liza Minnelli darting off personal notes to friends on the White House stationery.

Picture the scene of Bill and Hillary Rodham Clinton dining with Paul Newman and Joanne Woodward at Galileo's in Georgetown. And later the Clintons entertained Billy Crystal, Christopher Reeve, John Ritter, and Lindsay Wagner. On top of that, Richard Gere and Richard Dreyfuss are reportedly on a confidential basis with the president. But perhaps most visible of all is Barbra Streisand, who has become a White House regular, camping out in the Queen's Bedroom. And there's always a place for Michael Douglas, who apparently stole the show at the inauguration spectacular. Streisand and Douglas have become such favorites that they're already advising the Clintons on everything from public relations to a military policy for Bosnia.[1]

The New Face of Government

In an incredible article for the *New York Times* in which she gives even greater detail of the Hollywood connection, writer Maureen Dowd observes that "The Clinton White House is extravagantly star-struck, and Hollywood's liberal luminaries, sensing an opportunity to be taken seriously and savoring the compatible politics, are flocking to Washington. Hollywood moguls and stars are pushing to move beyond their traditional roles as campaign ornaments and cash machines and become more substantive players as communications, image, and policy advisers."[2] So if this is, indeed, the new face of government today, is it the best profile of an administration that has demanded and received the largest tax increase in history in order to penalize the rich and soak the fat cats? And is it the image Washington wants to show the world?

Columnist Michael Novak, always strong on common sense, hasn't missed the irony of this Hollywood side of the Clinton White House. Writing in *Forbes* magazine, he says:

> Our new President is certainly a charmer. He has the bodily repertoire of a charmer, the eyes of a charmer and the smooth-as-honey speech of a charmer—and all of it works together beautifully. He wants very much to be loved, and you can taste with him his desire to succeed.
>
> For all of this, the nation should give thanks. Twelve years ago the nation was privileged to learn from the Great Communicator, among our many presidents perhaps the most persuasive ever. Now we have another extremely persuasive man, who wants to teach exactly the opposite lessons.[3]

But what a profound difference between those two presidents. Reagan was actually one of the great agents of the tide of worldwide freedom as he sought to limit government, to lower taxes, to return power to individuals both rich and poor, to emphasize moral values, and to create a climate of self-reliance and self-restraint. Clinton, Novak observes, has done his best to blacken the memory of his most recent predecessors—Reagan and Bush—and to portray the boom years of the 1980s as a scandal and a nightmare.

But the differences between the two men are more than cosmetic: They are very real. Novak adds, "Like Jefferson, Reagan preached limited government. Like FDR (he thinks), Clinton stands for the maximum feasible government. His aides often cite the systems of Germany and other northern European social democracies as their ideal. Reagan distrusted experts, particularly those who wanted to manage other people's lives. Clinton loves experts [and] surrounds himself with them."

It should not go unnoticed that the world that Reagan inherited in 1980 was suffering from double-digit inflation, intense public despair, shortages of every kind, and increasing international humiliation—the legacy of another Democratic administration. No one felt good in 1979 about being an American, though perhaps that was, after all, the real purpose. But the world Reagan and his successor gave back was upbeat, with rock-bottom inflation and interest rates at a thirty-year low. And despite constant resistance from the Democratic Congress, Reagan led the recovery that saw employment turn around 100 percent since the Carter years, falling below 5.5 percent, and America's prestige was at an all-time high around the world.

Under Reagan-Bush the United States won the Persian Gulf War, eased the specter of Vietnam, and, best of all, America won the Cold War decisively. It was Reagan's strength of character and the perceived threat of his military muscle that brought an end to the Iranian hostage crisis, which had been stalemated under Carter. And it was the resolve of Reagan's successor, George Bush, that led us through the fall of the Berlin Wall, the Iron Curtain, and the Soviet Union. When Clinton took office, America was the undisputed leader of the Free World. But what will it be when he gives it back?

The Way Things Really Are

The tide of human history was beginning to bring a blessing to America. Bill Clinton, as if caught in a 1960s time warp, is trying to return this nation to the discarded nostrums of socialism. The question before us all is this: Can Clinton successfully fight the tide of history?

When the president's popularity polls began to fall in February 1993, there were many factors at work. For one, he had promised the moon to his special-interest supporters, and they felt cheated when it didn't come out the way he said. For another, from his first days in office it was clear that he had an activist's agenda to redesign America after his own image. And that wasn't good news for everybody.

In a column for the *Fort Worth Star-Telegram*, a liberal newspaper in the heart of a historically Democratic district, Debbie Price wrote: "I don't know why we're so surprised about all these promises, made in the heat of election passion and now scattered around broken like the debris of a messy divorce. It was clear from the start that Bill Clinton is the Great Seducer. . . . Gennifer Flowers tried to tell us about old Bedroom Eyes." The sweet nothings Clinton whispered in America's ears didn't mean much, the writer surmised, once the candidate got what he wanted.

But there were plenty of other concerns to go along with the issue of broken promises. How would America feel about a middle-class tax cut that actually ended up being a tax increase for households earning more than $30,000 a year? Or how would they feel about lifting the ban on homosexuals in the military, trying to lift the ban on AIDS-infected Haitian immigrants, or making abortion on demand and federal funding for abortion his first priorities in office?

What would they say about the actions Clinton has already taken to bring the French abortion pill, RU-486—known to cause bleeding, severe systemic reactions, and even death in some patients—into the United States? And how about the shock of appointing a known liberal activist from the Children's Defense Fund, his own wife, to head the national task force on healthcare reform? Certainly the White House should have anticipated the controversy that arose when Hillary

Rodham Clinton convened her secret panel behind closed doors with no qualified medical personnel as members.

Furthermore, what should America think of a president who campaigned on a promise to put an end to the influence of Beltway lobbyists and then named former Democratic National Committee Chairman Ron Brown—who had himself lobbied for "Baby Doc" Duvalier and Japanese industrialists—to head the Commerce Department?

Suddenly there was a vast gulf of distrust between the president and the people. How could Americans reconcile the difference between Candidate Clinton who blasted George Bush for being "out of touch with the American people" and the newly elected President Clinton whose appointments to high government office not only self-destructed one after the other, but drew down the nation's rage upon his head. This president was not in touch with the people; he didn't seem to be in touch with reality.

Early in the new administration a dispute erupted over Zoe Baird's having employed an illegal alien as her child's nanny and then failing to pay Social Security taxes. And then came the nominations of Donna Shalala and Roberta Achtenberg, both of whom won the approval of Congress despite the fact that Shalala is widely known as the "Queen of Political Correctness" and Achtenberg is the radical lesbian who spearheaded the smear campaign against the Boy Scouts of America because they pledged, before God, to be "morally straight," and consequently refused to have homosexual scoutmasters.

Even Clinton had to acknowledge the accuracy of the charges against Lani Guinier, his ill-fated nominee for the Justice Department, when he discovered that she was the author of flagrant and questionable scholarship that had earned her the moniker the Quota Queen. And while the appointment and confirmation of Ruth Bader Ginsburg to the Supreme Court elicited no visible emotion, her background as a liberal feminist and ACLU attorney brought forth some anguish from conservatives.

Even the extremism of Shalala, Achtenberg, and Guinier pales alongside the outrageous mouthings of the nominee for Surgeon General, Joycelyn Elders. The national press is selective in its reporting of this woman, and the chairman of the Senate Labor Committee, Teddy Kennedy, would hardly find fault with any of her far-left utterances. Nevertheless consider what she advocates—positions that Clinton declares he supports "100 percent."

> According to Elders, an integral part of a comprehensive school-based health clinic today is that we have *sexuality education beginning in kindergarten*.
>
> *Arkansas Gazette*, 3 July 1988 (emphasis added)

> Elders supports providing condoms in school-based clinics: "I don't know any parent who wouldn't go out at midnight and try to find contraceptives to start their children properly."
>
> *Arkansas Gazette*, 3 July 1988

Between 1980 and 1985 there was a 10 percent drop in teen pregnancies in Arkansas. In 1986, Elders became the director of the Arkansas Department of Health. By 1990, the percentage of teenage pregnancies reached a ten-year high in Arkansas, according to the Arkansas Department of Health.

> Since 1989, there has been a 130 percent increase in syphilis cases among Arkansas teenagers.
>
> *Pine Bluff Commercial*, February 1992

> Elders told an abortion rights rally in Little Rock, "abortion foes need to get over their *love affair with the fetus*."
>
> *West Memphis Evening Times*, 22 January 1992

> Elders characterizes abortion foes as a celibate, male-dominated church, a male-dominated legislature, and a male-dominated medical profession.
>
> *USA Today*, 6 April 1993

> The Doc is Political Correctness on Wheels.
>
> *Arkansas Democrat-Gazette*, quoted in *USA Today*, 6 April 1993

Clinton has reached out to radical elements in society that have only been associated with the lunatic fringe—homosexuals, radical lesbians, raging socialists, the high priestess of political correctness, and now political correctness on wheels—to fill positions of great responsibility with the oversight of hundreds of billions of taxpayer funds.

The Reality Gap

Everything the nation learned about Bill and Hillary Rodham Clinton from the outset showed that something was missing. It wasn't just "the L word" but a deeper issue his supporters had been trying to evade for the longest time: It was a question of character. There was a dangerous "reality gap" between what was being said and what was actually being done; there was an even more worrisome gap between what the nation had expected of its leader and what it was, in fact, seeing palmed off on the public.

After even the third and fourth passes, the administration's budget plan merely convinced economists that the rhetoric about "investment" and "sacrifice" was the old liberalism dressed in new garments. And despite the arrogant boasts of the Democrats in Congress and the White House media handlers, the president's $16 billion "stimulus package" was debated, filibustered, and finally defeated. Prior to the inauguration, former Education Secretary William Bennett and Paul Weyrich of the Free Congress Foundation had worried candidly that Republicans were in for a long, bitter exile from power. But less than a month later they found themselves in a whole new ball game.

Today his opponents are saying that Clinton has done more for the fortunes of the Republican party than anyone could ever have dreamed possible. Just when it looked as if conservatives had lost control of government, an incredible succession of bad policies, media gaffes, and legislative blowups have rallied conservatives of every stripe back to the Republicans.

Writing in the *New Republic,* columnist Fred Barnes said, "Clinton has touched the hot button of every ilk of conservative—free market purists, social issue conservatives, right-to-lifers, anti-tax crusaders, the Christian right, deficit hawks," and the result is a powerful new coalition that promises to be a major force not only in the elections of 1994 and 1996, but right now, even before the dazed Democrats can get their feet back on the ground.[4]

Short takes from many highly visible conservative leaders give an indication of their expansive new mood. Haley Barbour, chairman of the Republican National Committee, recently said, "Bill Clinton's done more to unite Republicans in four months than I'll do in four years." Gary Bauer, president of the Family Research Council, told Barnes, "Clinton has tried to move on so many issues at once he's succeeded in reactivating the Reagan coalition." New York Representative Bill Paxon smiled: "There's never been a better time to run as a Republican."

Until the Clinton victory, the under-funded American Conservative Union (ACU) had always struggled to keep its head above the water. But ever since Senate Minority Leader Bob Dole signed a fundraiser in early 1993, ACU sources report adding up to six thousand contributors a day. From a membership of just thirty thousand in 1991, suddenly there are more than two hundred thousand today. ACU Chairman David Keene said that he sees a new sense of unity and purpose among conservatives. "We used to have communism," he told Barnes. "Now we have Bill Clinton."

But many other conservative groups are experiencing the same growth phenomena. The Family Research Council, headquartered in Washington and affiliated with Colorado Springs–based Focus on the Family, reports that it used to average about five thousand pieces of mail per month; since the Clinton election it's averaging more than fifteen thousand—so many, in fact, the organization is examining the prospect of expanding its quarters. And when William Bennett introduced the new study compiled by Empower America, the *Index of Leading Cultural Indicators*, on the Rush Limbaugh radio show, the 800-number at the Heritage Foundation, which was taking orders for the report, was flooded with more than seventy-five thousand calls.

At the root of Clinton's troubles is not his management style, which is atrocious. Nor is it his staff, which is young and inept. Nor is it even his unbelievable penchant for lying. The problems stem clearly from the fact that he does not represent the sentiments of America nor those of the world around us.

What is happening in America, like the rest of the world, is a desperate search for transcendent values and a moral compass for personal living, coupled with a clear understanding that less government (not more government) is the wave of the future. Although Americans are relatively tolerant about individual lifestyle choices, they clearly are opposed to paying other people to kill their unborn babies, and they are overwhelmingly opposed to special legal privileges for any group based on the way individuals in that group perform private sex acts.

Yet Clinton is determined to put forward time and time again initiatives that are anathema to his fellow countrymen. In the process his ability to lead diminishes and his opponents gain stature every day.

The Force

In July, David Broder, the nation's most respected political writer, penned an article in the *Washington Post* with these words, "speakers . . . readily acknowledged that the half-dozen moderate GOP groups that came together have nothing like the financial, organizational or communications network that the Christian Coalition and other religious right groups can muster."

Broder wrote, "[the Christian Coalition] has the names of 400,000 contributors and another 350,000 'activists' in its files and is 'on track' toward its goal of raising between $12 million and $14 million this year."

In the fall of 1989, a year and a half after the conclusion of my unsuccessful run for the presidential nomination of the Republican party, I acceded to the urging of several key advisers to start something that would give focus and direction to the tens of thousands of Christians who had entered politics for the first time during my campaign with a hope of ensuring a better future for themselves and their families.

After searching for months for an executive director of the new organization, the Christian Coalition, I met Ralph Reed during the inaugural ceremonies for George Bush. He had founded a splendid organization called Students for America. Ralph was as unusually talented individual, studying for a Ph.D. at Emory University in Atlanta. After his classwork was concluded, he agreed to become the executive director of the Christian Coalition as he was completing his doctoral thesis. It was truly an appointment with destiny for us both.

Using the donor file from my campaign, the Christian Coalition in three years has become, without question, one of the most effective, if not the most effective, grass-roots organizations in America. Evangelical Christians, pro-family Roman Catholics, and Orthodox Jews have labored in a somewhat desultory fashion to break the hold of the liberal left on the power centers of America. The excesses of the Clinton administration have been for the pro-family forces in America what an afterburner is to a jet. It simply put the movement into orbit.

The Christian Coalition has soared in membership and is adding 10,000 new donors a month. It has organizations in every state and about 860 active chapters throughout the United States.

Let's see how that translates into action. It is clear that most voters in the United States are apathetic. In presidential elections, scarcely 50 percent of eligible voters actually cast ballots. In school board races the numbers fall to 8 or 10 percent of registered voters. In a race for governor in a nonpresidential year, probably 40 percent of registered voters will turn out. About the same number will cast ballots in a congressional race. Fifty-one percent of those who vote is all that is needed for a majority.

Consider what this means. In a school board race in a city with a population of 500,000, there may be 250,000 registered voters, but only 20,000 will vote. This means that 11,000 people out of 500,000 will be sufficient to elect one or more school board members. In a state with 6 million residents in a hotly contested race for governor, about 1.6 million people will vote. This means that 801,000 people, or 13.5 percent, of the total population will elect the governor. However, in a closely contested, statewide race, any determined, cohesive voter block of 10 percent, or even 5 percent, of those voting can swing an election. So in this hypothetical gubernatorial race, 80,000 to 160,000 people could easily swing an election from Democrat to Republican or vice versa.

The simple truth regarding apathy, low voter turnout, and close elections tells us that the combined strength of dedicated Evangelicals coupled with equally dedicated pro-family Roman Catholics and Orthodox Jews is more than sufficient to decide any election for any office in the land.

All that is necessary is that church people understand clearly how each candidate stands on the major economic and social issues and then are encouraged to register and vote. It is so simple, it is frightening—not to the mainstream of America but to the liberal left that has held this nation in its grip for so long. This in turn is why a group like the Christian Coalition has experienced remarkable success in a very short time, and why it is beginning now and will become more and more the principle agent of the turning political tide in America.

Strength in Numbers

Contrary to the calumnies of its opponents, no one in the Christian Coalition believes the goal of political action is to take over in matters of religious faith. Nor do they have any interest in co-opting any other group's personal or moral beliefs. The coalition's clear mandate is to affirm and support America's historic and traditional political institutions, which happen to be founded upon ethical systems derived from (and strengthened by) Judeo-Christian values. The democracy conceived by George Washington, John Adams, and Thomas Jefferson was a system of principled administration of the public affairs of a nation of free men and women, with respect for the individual liberty of each citizen and tolerance for individual differences. That is the vision of democracy we all support.

Ralph Reed shared some of his personal insights on how the effort to build a coalition of people from all walks of life has gained such incredible momentum. One major reason for the growth, he believes, is that people feel their faith in the system has been betrayed, so now they are turning to the more practical and proven concept of strength in numbers. "The event which I believe contributed most to this rapid growth of the conservative movement over the past five years," he said, "was the 'Robertson for President' campaign. Even though that nomination eventually went to George Bush, the groundwork of today's organization was laid at that time, and we learned a lot of lessons the hard way.

"In that campaign," Reed said, "many people received their doctor's degrees in the school of hard knocks, and they learned what politics is all about. They learned how to play hardball, and they learned how to get beat up a little bit and keep on standing. And what we have discovered is that a lot of the business of good citizenship is about staying power—about seeing who can stay the longest, about who has more stamina, and who has the vision to do what it takes to win in the end."

Maybe this really is the biggest lesson that conservatives have learned since the tumultuous 1988 campaign. Ralph told me, "I was in a meeting with Jerry Falwell one time when he said, 'You know, when Christians lose, they quit. And when Christians win, they quit. They just quit. They're quitters.' Of course, Dr. Falwell had been through some bloody street fights himself, and often when he'd look around to see who was backing him up, there was nobody there. So I understood what he was saying, and I think that used to be true. But I assure you, it's not true anymore.

"In fact," he continued, "the Clinton presidency confirms everything we've been saying, which is that the pro-family movement's previous fixation on the White House was a mistake. To think that simply electing George Bush or Pat Robertson to the White House would somehow solve all our country's problems was naive. Even if your campaign had been successful in 1988, I believe you would have been incapable of turning the country around. There was no base of support at that time. That was the problem that plagued both Reagan and Bush. They had no foundation to build on, and even if a conservative does hold the power at the top, it's just not enough.

"And so what we have done," he added, "is to take the whole equation and turn it on its head. Instead of focusing strictly on high office, we have turned our attention to the local school boards, city councils, county commissions, zoning boards, and state legislatures, and we're seeing tremendous success. In New York City, for example, we fielded 130 candidates for school board positions, and between 55 and

60 percent of them were elected. The *New York Times* identified 88 candidates supported by our organization, 56 of whom won. So that would be 60 percent.

"However you add it up, more than half of all the pro-family candidates who ran for the school board in New York City—supposedly the most liberal city in America—were actually elected. Just imagine what that means to the process of governance in that city. Imagine what it will mean to have that many responsible, conservative voices helping to scuttle the liberal agenda that is attempting to make children into pawns of the state and to use kids as social experiments in their war against American society."[5]

These victories make news, and among those paying closest attention are the people on the other side of the fence. Despite the loss of the presidency by George Bush in November 1992, pro-family candidates were winning. In fact, People for the American Way, an avidly anti-Christian group, identified as many as five hundred pro-family candidates, 40 percent of whom were elected at the state or local level. "Actually," says Ralph Reed, "the correct figure is closer to a thousand pro-family candidates, 40 percent of whom won their races."

The lesson of such practical political action should be obvious. If conservatives can replace another four to five hundred liberals with pro-family activist candidates during every cycle and every year in every state, by the late 1990s that will mean a critical mass of about five to ten thousand locally elected officials. As those people begin to percolate up through the system, you will see pro-family statesmen in the office of governor, attorney general, state legislators, U.S. congressmen and senators, and the presidency. Then the bureaucracy will be changed, and along with it the entire liberal agenda. Can this be the decade when the political tide turns in America? I believe the answer is yes, because the mechanism is in place to make it happen.

The Meaning of Ethical Convictions

When people with sincere ethical convictions, who are dedicated to the welfare of the family and who have a deep love for this country move into public office, there will be an immediate improvement in the quality of life in this country. You can count on that too. But be assured, these people will not be trying to legislate their personal beliefs or their religion on others. As Ralph Reed teaches his people, "When you assume a public office, you have to act and speak and carry yourself in such a way that other people can receive you. If you are a Christian, for example, don't expect to use the language of the Bible study and the church in the public arena." We are, by design, a pluralistic society, and we must work together, despite our personal differences, for the mutual benefit of everyone. If Christians resort to Bible talk, as Reed describes it, "there's going to be a disconnect."

As I have written in my newsletter, *Pat Robertson's Perspective*, a political party is not a church. The purpose of a party is not to promulgate a doctrine of faith. Nor is its purpose to convert unbelievers. Rather, its purpose is to build a winning coalition of 51 percent, which by definition means gathering together people with similar ideology but not necessarily the same theological beliefs. People will naturally find many important issues upon which they do agree, and from that shared consensus comes victory.

Oscar Wilde once said that there are some people who tell you that you're going to hell in such a way that you want to get there as quickly as possible. That was part of the problem in the early days of the pro-family movement. Its adherents sometimes thought that its political involvement and civic involvement was for evangelism, but that was not wise. Christians must recognize that if they speak with authority, with conviction, and with consistent credibility, people may be drawn to them. It is their behavior that will be a light to others. That is evangelism by conscience and behavior, and that is fair. But there must be some difference between what a person of faith would do in the pulpit and in public office. That, despite the objections of the adversaries of faith, is the purpose of Christian political involvement. But I will come back to that subject in more detail further along.

Statistically Speaking

The good news is that the great mainstream of America believes in traditional values, not liberalism. Although the radical left has a very small and vocal minority out there—with gays accounting for just 3 percent and radical feminists only about 1 to 3 percent—they are actually a small, nonrepresentative sample of what this country believes. Furthermore, as I pointed out earlier, when Christians and other conservatives unite on an issue, when they are properly informed and motivated, and when they turn out the vote, they can sweep any election.

"Our survey, conducted by the Christian Coalition in February 1993," Ralph Reed proudly states, "reveals that 39 percent of the electorate in this country attends church four or more times each month. Approximately 30 percent of those are Roman Catholics, and most of the remaining 70 percent are Protestants. That means that from 30 to 40 percent of all the voters in this country are people who are in church on a regular basis.

"We also discovered," he adds, "that 57 percent of the entire population prays every day. About 40 to 45 percent of the population reads the Bible on a daily basis. Now that's not to suggest, by the way, that every one of them is an Evangelical or even a Republican. But they do have some core beliefs about their children, about education, about having a safe neighborhood, about having lower taxes, and other shared values and interests that we can appeal to."

I recently read a quote in a Family Research Council study that expresses this idea very well. "A conservative," it said, "is a liberal with a daughter in high school." That is a very wise insight. When it comes down to *our* homes, *our* children, *our* money, or *our* most cherished freedoms, we *all* become conservatives. But, in fact, this is the cornerstone of conservative political involvement. Those who are called "movement conservatives" care about the rights of other people, about protecting *all* our individual liberties, about guaranteeing *everyone's* right to compete in a free and open society, and in seeing that *all* are protected both by the state and from the state.

What the Christian Coalition is trying to do is change the context of the current debate over church-state issues, to put things back into their natural and historic perspective. Theological agreement should not be the determining factor. When John F. Kennedy was elected president, the majority of the country was not Roman Catholic. Only about a quarter of the country is Roman Catholic. But the country voted Kennedy in as president. In the Christian Coalition there is concern about school choice for all parents and their children, concern for lower taxes, limited government, a balanced budget amendment, and a line-item veto over the federal budget by the president. Besides that, the Coalition is against special rights for those self-proclaimed "minorities," such as lesbians and gays, and for common-sense restrictions on abortion.

As Reed puts it, "We support quality education and tougher laws against crime and drugs. This is such a mainstream agenda that it is held by the majority of the American people, yet the media have done their best to characterize us as dangerous zealots and book-burners. That is simply not the case, and more and more people are coming to realize that there is much greater danger, in fact, in the mass media, who are complicit in the hate and intolerance and the deterioration of moral values that has been eating away the soul of America. So that, too, is part of our challenge. We have to get beyond this hurdle of bias and fear and suspicion. We want to assure people that we do not want to legislate our theology. We want to legislate our public policy views, and that is the basis on which our coalition was formed."

Voices of Hope

Wherever you look today, there is a visible welling up of resentment for the legacy of liberal idealism and bureaucratic nonsense. For fifty years the halls of government have been jammed with political hucksters and "experts" of every description, pushing schemes that invariably enslave masses and further strip away pieces of ourselves that were invaluable to us. And that fact, as much as anything else, created an environment in which the November 1992 election would suddenly provide the opportunity for changes the radical left never imagined.

Part of the turning tide, I believe, can be attributed to the phenomenon of a broad-scale public awakening to reality, as if the nation were slowly rising from a long, troubled sleep only to find that it has given the reins of power to the graying Woodstock generation. From February to June 1993, the president's approval ratings dropped from 58 to 36 percent. According to a report in *USA Today*, Clinton's approval among business executives stands at 15 percent. And even with his sudden surge of popularity after the Iraqi retaliation bombings, public suspicion and discontent are unlikely to change much in the months ahead. People just don't buy the big-government, big-tax "solutions" anymore. The leopard has revealed its spots.

As Fred Barnes reports, fully 56 percent of the nation now feel that "the country is seriously off on the wrong track." And finding fault with the Clinton administration is not a very difficult or challenging task anymore; there's so much to choose from. But what the disaffected voters are really seeking is a voice of hope. Yes, they want to see government taking positive steps to turn around America's economic and ethical problems and taking substantive action for getting our house back in order, but most of all they pray for leaders with clarity of vision, with personal honor and integrity, to lead us across the formidable divide of a new century and a new millennium looming just ahead. Americans want leaders they can trust for the long haul.

What Americans really hope for is a return to common-sense leadership, where things are what they seem to be, and where men, women, and children can live together in peace and in harmony, free of the plague of experts that has flooded this country for more than half a century. This is one of the main reasons that we are beginning to hear new voices from middle America telling us that there is hope, that there is a right and wrong, and that the values this nation has always cherished are just and right and worth fighting for.

In his article for the *Wall Street Journal* entitled "What Ever Happened to Common Sense?" Irving Kristol writes:

One can expand indefinitely the catalogue of errors where expert theory has been allowed to dominate a clearly contrary reality. We hand out contraceptive pills to young girls because our experts tell us this will reduce teen-age pregnancies, but it seems to have little real effect. We de-institutionalize the mentally ill because it is supposed to be good for their psychological health, and then we are shocked that our streets are populated with homeless, helpless people. We permit philosophers and educators to assure us that there really is no necessary connection between religion and ethics, only to discover we then need "ethicists" to teach our students morality—only then to discover the "ethicists" can teach about moral beliefs in general, but not the difference between right and wrong.[6]

So when Calvin Butts, the pastor of the Abysinnian Baptist Church in New York City, lashes out against the violent and vulgar rap lyrics that have created such visible hatred among blacks, people listen and they applaud. And when David Brock's book, *The Real Anita Hill* (which details the radical feminists' plot to discredit Supreme Court Justice Clarence Thomas) makes it to the *New York Times* bestseller list despite the media's blockade of silence, the real people of America cheer even louder. And it is a portent of things to come when Linda and Richard Eyre's book, *Teaching Your Children Values*, runs to the top of the charts. Among the moral principles taught by the authors is the suggestion to encourage kids to ask, "Now, what would Jesus do in this situation?" when confronted by ethical dilemmas.

People with convictions were also gratified by the honesty and candor of Generals Norman Schwarzkopf and Colin Powell who, along with a number of enlisted and officer personnel, told a congressional panel that homosexuality and the military don't mix. And when Senator Jesse Helms pointedly asked a belligerent homosexual activist during the Senate hearings if he had sought professional help for his problem, saying, "It's not normal!" conservatives and members of the gallery gave him a standing ovation. Isn't it amazing how people respond to a little honesty?

Many others were cheered when the popular sitcom "Step by Step" ran its May 14, 1993, sequence in which a group of bright, trendy teenage boys and girls came to agree that waiting until marriage to have sex really is "the right thing to do." Most of us know that the lessons being taught to our children without parental consent are frequently harmful to our kids and destructive of our hopes for their futures. So the president of the local school board in Western Queens, New York, Mary Cummins, and a Bronx homemaker, Delores Ayling, spearheaded the battle against Joseph Fernandez—who had attempted to fire one of the New York City school boards so he could implement the radical pro-homosexual "Rainbow Curriculum"—responsible citizens had their faith restored when the women won and Fernandez was sacked. Sometimes good does come out of evil.

In accepting the outstanding citizenship award of the Conservative Political Action Committee in Washington, D.C., in April 1993, Cummins said that she never had a doubt about what had to be done. As a former teacher, she understood the implications of what Joseph Fernandez was trying to do to the children of New York City. Books endorsing lesbianism and homosexuality and programs to promote radical feminist objectives were just for starters. "It was a complete behavior modification program," she told the crowd at the Omni Shoreham Hotel. "It was a brainwashing program. All I had to see was one sentence that said, 'School is your family,' and I thought, *The next edition will say the state is your family.* So we went back at the next public meeting. I put a resolution in, and we threw the whole thing out." The courage of the citizens of the five boroughs of New York says a lot about the honesty and decency of grass-roots America. No matter how dark the night may seem at times, there is still hope because America is full of people like this.

In the conclusion of his article on common sense, Irving Kristol made the statement that it is precisely because the situation has been so bad for so long that we have reason to think things may yet come around. "Indeed," he said, "it is such an obvious mess that there is room for at least a modicum of hope that common sense will prevail." I would add that the victories of conservatives, on common-sense principles, in grass-roots issues from New York to Seattle is the strongest indication that hope is already on the way.

Changes No One Expected

These victories underscore the trend that is sweeping the nation. It is a cry for basic values and principles—the same cry for common sense that helped Richard Riordan defeat the liberal, pro-homosexual activist Michael Woo to become the first Republican mayor of Los Angeles in more than twenty years. It is the voice of reason that prompted the editors of the *Atlantic* to publish Barbara Dafoe Whitehead's twenty-page article proving, as the cover proclaimed, that "Dan Quayle Was Right" and the breakup of the family is really destroying our kids.[7]

When the Clinton crew began promising an era of change, they certainly never imagined what sorts of changes lay just ahead. They never imagined that, despite his presidential edict that military doctors must grant abortions on demand, almost every man and woman serving in the medical corps in Europe would refuse to obey, many because of religious and moral grounds. And they never dreamed that, just two months later, the government of Germany, considered by many American Democrats to be the ultimate proponents of "progressive" legislation, would decree that "life begins at conception" and that abortion on demand would henceforth be illegal.

No one would have guessed that the trendy, New Age Pacific Northwest would turn out record crowds for Billy Graham's 1992 Portland Crusade or that as many as fifteen thousand men, women, and young people would come forward to receive Christ. But incredible things are happening all over America, and it is overwhelming even to imagine where such changes may eventually lead. Consider the fact that prior to May and June 1993 graduation exercises, the American Center for Law and Justice (ACLJ) received more than seven thousand calls for legal assistance to ensure that students' rights to voluntary prayer would not be violated.

These things are not accidental nor are they incidental to all the other things we see on the news. In fact, they *are* the news. And the fact that they are seldom faithfully reported by the major media is not co-incidental either, since the major media seem primarily concerned with the "free speech" rights only for those who share their liberal beliefs. But the American people are growing more suspicious, and the media are gradually losing their stranglehold as the arbiter of political thought in America. More and more people are tuning to cable television, to CBN, or to their local Christian radio stations for news they can trust. Millions more are turning to Rush Limbaugh's funny and hard-hitting radio and television shows and sometimes also to CNN's Headline News for a clear version of the facts.

And finally, who would have guessed that thirty years after Madalyn Murray O'Hair succeeded in having prayer taken out of the public schools, her own son, Bill Murray, would be preaching the gospel coast to coast and praying for his mother's work to be undone? And who would believe that in a recent interview published in the *Austin American-Statesman* the grand dame of the atheists cause would say, "I think the window of opportunity for atheism has closed. Before the end of the century you'll have full-fledged religious ceremonies returned to public schools"? According to O'Hair, Christianity will become, in essence, the official U.S. religion.

O'Hair would never have made such a statement without the stunning series of court victories by the legal staff of the American Center for Law and Justice under its brilliant general counsel, Jay Sekulow. In truth Sekulow, arguing First Amendment free-speech rights for Christian students and pro-life protestors, has not lost a single court case in two years—a fact that is well known to the ACLU and its atheist allies.

A Hunger for "Meaning"

The press has made much of Hillary Rodham Clinton's commitment to what she has characterized as the "politics of meaning," and some clever battles have been pitched in print by those on either side of the issue. The term "politics of meaning" came into currency after the first lady's address to a University of Texas audience in which she accused Americans of being shallow pragmatists without a well-developed spiritual side.

Shortly thereafter, columnist Paul Gigot accused the editor of the journal *Tikkun*, Michael Lerner, of masterminding Rodham Clinton's ideas about "political meaning." In his dispassionate defense, Lerner acknowledged that the Religious Right has long held the high ground in this arena, since the whole area of spiritual values is a moral debate that the Left has persistently refused to consider. But in the end, the first lady's philosopher-"guru" expressed his belief that the Clintons would serve themselves and the nation best by damning the torpedoes from the Right, by disdaining the rancor of the media, and by perpetrating their liberal policies upon the nation without either regret or popular consent.

But perhaps the most interesting battle of all was waged in the *Washington Post* between Norman Lear, the outspoken head of People for the American Way, and conservative columnist Charles Krauthammer. Lear led first, claiming that America's future was being threatened by moral decay and spiritual emptiness. The culprit, he said, was capitalism with its focus on the bottom line; what we must rediscover is a reverence for that which is "unquantifiable and eternal." We must awaken "our capacity for awe, wonder and mystery, that place where acts of faith in something larger than ourselves prove ultimately satisfying in the fullness of time."[8] This, Lear felt, was what the first lady was actually saying in Austin, Texas.

Krauthammer's response mentioned that Lear had taken him to task for lampooning the naiveté of Rodham Clinton's "politics of meaning." What she had done, in Lear's view, was touch the spiritual longing in all of us—presumably the part that gives unselfishly and asks nothing in return. But passing over that hidden context, Krauthammer found it intensely odd that Lear of all people, a man who has bashed Christians and conservatives for years, should suddenly grab onto their tether and try to ride the "values" and "spiritual meaning" wave now that it has become a useful issue for liberals.

But Krauthammer pointed out that, first, conservatives, and especially conservative Christians, do not need to "rediscover" spiritual values. They never lost them. And second, it was Lear who had filed the friend-of-the-court brief in the case of *Lee v. Weisman* that helped persuade the court to declare even nonsectarian prayers unconstitutional at high school graduations. Krauthammer then went on to say:

> Pat Robertson has been encouraging his people to go out and say prayers at high school graduations regardless. The latest edition of People for the American Way's newsletter, *Right-wing Watch*, alerts subscribers to this dire threat to the First Amendment. . . . Mr. Lear is so embarrassed to talk about religion that the word does not once appear in his column. Instead, we get mush.[9]

If this were anyone but Norman Lear making such charges, Krauthammer writes, we might just take them as the remarks of "another Beverly Hills bubblehead pronouncing himself in the Age of Clinton. . . . But Mr. Lear is no ordinary Hollywood liberal." People like Lear have so little respect for spiritual values they see organized religion as simply another way to play the crowds. Spirituality is something warm and fuzzy and never the authentic worship of the Creator God.

Krauthammer then says, "Conservatives are not against spirituality in public life. But they see such stabs at it as Mr. Lear's vapid call for public discussion of our common spirituality as limp substitutes for the real thing." He adds that if Lear really wants to bring spirituality back into the debate, he should ask the court to reverse itself on the *Weisman* case and allow schools to post the Ten Commandments once again.

One fact that seems to emerge from all these various debates is the view that issues of faith and conscience definitely do matter to a growing number of people. And in the ongoing warfare between the Right and the Left, one common denominator is the desire to get back to things that really matter—back to common sense. Because so many liberals have rejected God and His role in our national life, it is doubtful they will ever grasp the truth. Their present failed theories are for intellectuals only. They never reach the hearts and minds of the people. History is making a clear statement: Without God's presence, life becomes empty, leaders lack a moral ground for their actions, and failure is certain. Where He is lifted up, people prosper, and there is liberty, moral order, and stability.

In the chapters that follow, I will look more closely at the condition of government today and the prospects for a common-sense "revolution." I will also discuss the role and influence of the media, the state of the church, the urgency of social issues as interpreted alternately by the Left and the Right, the opportunities in education, and some of the challenges ahead of us. Then we will examine the process of coalition building. Today the tide is turning. People are coming back to a common-sense vision for this country and for the world. But it matters little if the tide of history turns and we are unprepared to pursue that wave. Those who close their eyes to the onrushing tide, quite simply, will drown.

However dark the way ahead may sometimes seem, voices of hope and renewal are rising even now. All across America and around the world the trumpet blast of freedom is growing louder and clearer. For those who follow that call, the coming revolution may truly bring us to the threshold of the most thrilling chapter in the history of America.

4

The Cookie Monster

*H*AVE YOU EVER BEEN around a bubblegum machine when it broke and began to pour out candy? Or in Las Vegas when the silver dollar jackpot hit? If you have, you know the thrill, the shouts of glee as the lucky recipients rake it all in.

For the bubblegum vendor and the slot machine operator, the cost of the thrill is figured into his expense budget. He will make a profit regardless of the jackpots.

But what would happen if there were an enormous cookie machine spewing out an endless stream of treats to lucky people, and *you* had to pay the bill for it? No chance to make a profit. No percentage of the take. Just pay for the goodies given to others, every day, all day, all week, all year. More and more and more.

Well, like it or not, those who run our government think of it as the great cookie monster that gobbles your flour and sugar and then passes on the sweets to others. If it were only cookies, maybe we could stand it, but that's not the way it is. It is $1.5 trillion ($1,500,000,000,000) of your hard-earned wages every single year, and the government's appetite just keeps growing and growing, bigger and bigger and bigger.

Can you imagine how much $1.5 trillion is? Granted it is too vast for any of us—including the Congress—to grasp, but consider this image.

If you took a stack of crisp, new thousand-dollar bills and burned one every second, 60 seconds a minute, 60 minutes an hour, 24 hours a day, 365 days a year, without stopping, constantly burning thousand-dollar bills second by second, it would take 47½ years to burn up $1.5 trillion. Yet the U.S. government burns this much in 365 days. That works out to $171,000,232 every hour that you and I live.

Just think, yesterday in the twenty-four hours while you were working, eating, sleeping, watching television, or reading this book, the great big cookie monster in Washington went through $4,109,568,000 of America's hard-earned money—in *one day!*

And then we hear the nonsense about "investments," "contributions," and "shared sacrifice"—for what, to feed the government's cookie monster? How do you feel about sacrificing for amazing projects like the following: A government warehouse in Franconia, Virginia, holds a huge cache of perfectly good furniture. A few years ago the *Washington Post* broke the story that the bureaucrats were spending $250 million a year on new furniture instead of reusing what they had. But that was then, before the cookie monster swung into high gear. The spending for new furniture and decorations—hidden carefully in the overhead category of the federal budget—is estimated at $2 billion. One congressman requisitioned a $3,000 desk to replace his old one. Should we "sacrifice" so the cookie monster will be able to give $2 billion in new desks to bureaucrats?

Or how about $58 million in goodies to bail out the millionaire owner of the New York Yankees, George Steinbrenner, and his American Shipbuilding Company in Tampa, Florida? Or $25 million so the University of Alaska can study how to trap energy from the aurora borealis? Or $19.7 million for the International Fund for Ireland, which in the past has received money from the cookie monster for a golf video and pony trekking centers? Or $2 million to build Walk on the Mountain in Tacoma, Washington, to see distant Mount Rainier on one of the fifty-seven days a year when it is clear?

How about building a $35 million U.S. courthouse in Reno, Nevada? Or a $2 million restoration of the Liberty and Lucas Theaters in Savannah, Georgia? Or a plain vanilla overall grant of $260 million to

HUD for general goodies to spread around in various congressional districts? Do we really believe that we should be forced to work until the middle of May each year to earn the money to pay for this nonsense?

Perhaps these projects would excite your patriotic zeal more: $6.4 million for a Bavarian ski village in Kellogg, Idaho—$3.1 million to convert a ferryboat into a crab restaurant in Baltimore—$107,000 to study the sex life of the Japanese quail—$150,000 to study the Hatfield/McCoy feud—$1 million to study why people don't ride bikes to work—$144,000 to see if pigeons follow human economic laws—$219,000 to teach college students how to watch television—and the biggest blowout of all, $19 million to study gas emissions of cow flatulence.[1]

If those don't do it for you, surely these will: As part of $1.8 billion in government grants to Stanford University, $1,500 for liquor at pre-football game parties; money to enlarge the president's bed and $7,000 for larger sheets for the bed; $2,000 a month for fresh-cut flowers; and $64,000 for the upkeep of the deceased chancellor's residence.

But nowhere has the cookie monster been so lavish as in the field of agriculture. Any farm unit can get $50,000 just to help things along, and remember a farm "unit" is any individual or partnership who farms. The most egregious giveaway has come to be known as the Mississippi Pyramid. Here is the story. One farmer farmed six hundred acres and was entitled to $50,000. Then he and his wife farmed a unit on the same farm for $50,000 more. Then he and each of his four sons farmed units on the same farm, then the wife and each son farmed units on the same farm until this one family had talked the cookie monster into a perfectly legal $1.2 million jackpot.

The U.S. Department of Agriculture started at a time when six out of ten workers were farmers. The department had nine employees and a $64,000 budget. Now the cost of that one department is $62.7 billion, and it employs an estimated 150,000 workers at 11,000 field offices, roughly 84 percent of them in counties where there is no appreciable agriculture. All this at a time when less than 3 percent of the population are farmers.

This division of the cookie monster had one worker spending three years writing a nine-page manual, *United States Standards for*

Grades of Christmas Trees, and another spending three years on the standards of ketchup—the "new" thicker ketchup flows two centimeters less than previously. But worst of all, 40 percent of the $9.3 billion in grants to farmers went to the largest 5 percent of farms, including in recent years $9 million to Sunkist, $6.2 million to Blue Diamond Growers, and $5.1 million to the giant E&J Gallo Winery. Then, of course, the Farmers Home Administration is subsidizing wealthy real estate developers with loans at 1 percent interest.

For this we must "sacrifice" and grant congressmen pay raises for the burden they bear for throwing away our money.

How It Began

The United States of America was formed as just that—a union of sovereign states into what is known as a federal government. The U.S. Constitution replaced the early Articles of Confederation for the express purpose of forming "a more perfect union."

The concept behind our government was simple. The "Creator" gave each person "unalienable rights," out of which that person in turn gave limited rights to his or her respective state governments. Then the states in turn gave a portion of their rights to a central government that could accomplish wide-ranging tasks, such as the conduct of foreign relations and national defense, which no state could realistically accomplish by itself. However, the framers of our Constitution were careful to make clear that powers not granted to the federal government were reserved to the states and ultimately the people.

I recall reading in the writings of President James Monroe an extremely lucid veto message of a congressionally funded federal canal system. Monroe vetoed the bill because he did not believe, despite the demonstrated worth of the project, that the federal government under the Constitution was permitted to engage in such a program.

Our nation grew and prospered under the restraint of its leaders who refused to violate the separations and reservations of powers that the framers of the Constitution so wisely set forth to guide our nation.

Although the punitive laws against the Southern states that followed the Civil War and the passage of the post–Civil War amendments to the Constitution somewhat broadened the powers of the federal government over the states, there were two landmark periods of liberal thinking that dramatically reversed age-old precedents and brought our nation to where it is today. It seems to me, if the tide of freedom is truly to turn in this land, we must go back and reverse the mistakes that have now grown to haunt us. It is still far from certain whether such a return would ever be politically acceptable in our land, lacking an economic catastrophe, a natural catastrophe, or a major military catastrophe.

In my book, *The New World Order*, I discussed in detail the momentous years between 1908 through 1913 when Colonel Edward House, who clearly was committed to the Utopian one-world socialism of Cecil Rhodes and the British Roundtable, pushed through the two pieces of legislation that effectively collapsed federalism in the United States. As was clearly documented in *The New World Order*, Colonel House dominated the gentle Virginian Woodrow Wilson while doing all in his power to maneuver the United States into the key role in a world government to be ruled by a cabal of world bankers, industrialists, nobility, and men like House. The colonel's vision of himself was set forth in lurid detail in his own book, *Philip Dru Administrator*.

Without fully understanding what it was doing, the Congress was tricked into ceding control of America's credit, interest rates, and currency into a federally mandated national bank owned by the private banks. The Constitution clearly gave Congress the power to "coin money and regulate the value thereof." In this civil coup by a group of European and American bankers, the Congress turned over this enormous power to a nonelected national bank called the Federal Reserve System, modeled after the German Bundesbank or the British Bank of England.

This central bank could print money, based on nothing, which it loaned—at interest—to the Treasury. It also had the power to loan funds to member banks at a so-called discount window at low interest.

In turn, the member banks were free to loan this money back to the U.S. Treasury with no risk, but at higher rates of interest.

To make the dramatic expansion of government borrowing feasible, government revenues had to be expanded. The graduated income tax had been one of the key tenets of Marxism. Now Congress and the individual states, over the strenuous objections of wiser legislators, passed a constitutional amendment authorizing the direct taxation of every person's income by the national government. We have become so accustomed to this policy of confiscation that we fail to recognize just how unnatural and how dictatorial this policy really was at the time of its passage.

Thus, in 1913, the federal government was given the power to reach across state lines, violate the doctrine of the "reservation of powers," and tax people directly. There is now no more powerful, no more intrusive, and potentially no more abusive arm of the federal government than the Internal Revenue Service. The IRS has sweeping subpoena powers, search-and-seizure powers, and enforcement powers. Even Congress is afraid of it, because the IRS has the power to learn everything about everyone's financial transactions—even those of the president and the members of Congress.

Retribution for Dissent

I read several years ago that a group of congressmen were introducing a bill to curb the powers of the IRS. Suddenly, twenty of these public servants were put through extensive IRS audits. When a taxpayer and a really tough private attorney are fighting the IRS in court, one of the IRS tricks would be to put the taxpayer's counsel through a grueling income tax audit to divert his attention from his client's case.

With expanded and secret control over the nation's currency, credit, and borrowing, and with the ability to extract by force ever-increasing amounts of tax money from individuals and corporations, the machinery was in place to begin the incredible growth of the monster across the Potomac. However, as so often is the case, the central planners were stymied in 1929 when the nation plunged into the most devastating economic depression of its history. Businesses were devastated, and unemployment soared to 25 percent. The memory is still etched in the minds of those who lived through that period of gaunt, disheveled men standing in long lines at some emergency soup kitchen waiting for a bowl of soup and a couple of pieces of bread. Scratchy old 78-RPM records are still around of Bing Crosby singing the heart-rending ballad of the once-proudest work force on earth: "Once we built the railroads, made 'em run on time. Now the work is over: Buddy, can you spare a dime?"

After a brief correction, America could have pulled out of recession. Instead the government responded then just like some in government are acting today. Punitive taxes were levied on the "rich," tariffs were raised on imported goods, and a tight money policy was initiated that saw the broad measure of money fall by 25 percent. Only the strong religious roots of the American people, plus the escape valve that a large farm population gave to their relatives in the cities, prevented a violent revolution.

Instead, the country experienced a political revolution. We elected an immensely popular president, Franklin D. Roosevelt, who so dominated a docile and panic-stricken Congress that his first hundred days probably saw more laws enacted to expand the power of the federal government than in any other time in American history. Desperate people didn't care about the niceties of states' rights or limited government. Nor did they care about the differences between the free market, socialism, or communism. They wanted jobs and food and shelter, and they wanted them right away whatever the cost.

The New Deal gave it to them, in spades. The contemporaneous critique of the early days of the New Deal in the *Saturday Evening Post* article by former President Herbert Hoover that I mentioned earlier is fascinating:

> An enormous extension of bureaucracy is inevitable. Already a host of new government bureaus and nearly twenty thousand commissions have been established with authority over every trade, and in nearly every town and village. *We have witnessed this host of government agents spread out over the land, limiting men's*

honest activities, conferring largess and benefits, directing, interfering, disseminating propaganda, spying on, threatening the people and prosecuting for a new host of crimes [emphasis added].

President Hoover saw the evil coming in his time. How could he possibly have conceived the growth of the monster in the sixty years from 1933 to 1993?

In 1933, the government spent $4.6 billion in one year—we spend that now in one day. By 1940 the total was $9.5 billion. By 1965 it edged over $100 billion to $118.2 billion. By 1980 government spending had hit $590.9 billion, and that nearly tripled in thirteen years. In 1932, we had 605,000 government employees—by 1940, 1,053,000—by 1965, 2,538,000—and now 3,041,149.

Our total population in these sixty years has grown by 100 percent, but the number of government employees has increased 500 percent. Federal spending in nominal terms has risen 3,260 percent. Spending is one thing; debt creation is another. In 1933, the U.S. government had accumulated only $22.5 billion in debt in the first 157 years between the Declaration of Independence and then. By 1940, in just seven years under the New Deal, the debt had more than doubled to $50.7 billion. By the end of World War II, just five years later under the same New Deal, it had risen 11.5 times to $260.1 billion.

Under Lyndon Johnson's Great Society and during the Vietnam War, it climbed to $323 billion. By the end of Jimmy Carter's presidency, the national debt was hovering just below $1 trillion, a fiftyfold increase from 1933. Under Ronald Reagan, the total debt of our nation tripled in eight years, and George Bush added $1 trillion more. By mid-1993 the direct debt of the federal government is a staggering $4.4 trillion, almost 2,000 times as large as the national debt of 1933.

Plenty of Advance Warning

If the Grace Commission and industrialist and author Harry Figgie are right about the "hockey stick" climb of the national debt, our national government will owe $13 trillion by the year 2000, our currency will be nearly worthless, foreigners will treat our government bonds as high-interest junk, the U.S. economy will resemble Argentina of 1980, and the standard of living of every American will first be wrenched through a deflationary depression and then through a murderous hyperinflation.

This is why the tide must turn here and fast! So what do we as a nation do to dismantle the out-of-control cookie monster and to return to some form of responsible, limited government? The first answer is easy. We must, as a people, recognize that only God has unlimited resources and that secular government can only obtain for us the "pursuit of happiness"—it can never "guarantee happiness." John F. Kennedy had it right when he admonished the nation to "ask not what your country can do for you." We must understand that government does not create wealth, it wastefully redistributes wealth. When it distributes more than it takes in, you and your children must pay it back with interest.

The class warfare that liberals love to throw around about "taxing the rich" to "provide for government services" is a lie. Peter Grace told me in 1983 that if all the income of America's millionaires were confiscated each year by the government, the money received (assuming they would keep on earning taxable income) would fund the government for just eight days. Big tax dollars will always come from those earning $30,000 to $75,000 a year—the great, defenseless middle class. It is hardly "liberal" to confiscate the money of the wage earners and small businesses of America to pay for the vote-buying extravagance of pork-barrel congressmen.

Second, government needs to be managed along the same lines as any failed, bankrupt business. If the officers and directors of any bankrupt public company had looted trust accounts, falsified income projections, misstated by deliberate trickery the growth rates of expenses and deficits, slid major expenses off balance sheet contrary to sound accounting principles, used corporate funds to bribe special shareholders to gain and hold office, and then had lied repeatedly to the public about their own plans for the direction of the company, such directors and officers would have been prosecuted and jailed for SEC violations, criminal fraud, embezzlement, IRS violations, and the catchall charges of mail fraud and wire fraud.

Yet the U.S. Congress and its various staffs, plus the chief executive, the director of the Office of Management and Budget, and their staffs are guilty of every one of these acts—repeatedly and deliberately.

The people of the United States need to bring a civil indictment to the polls against these people on a bipartisan basis. It will not be enough merely to elect a majority of candidates from the Republican party if those candidates are implicated in the crimes of those they replace. George Bush was a good friend of mine, but the record shows not only the breaking of his historic no-new-taxes pledge, but a proliferation of federal regulatory excesses under his administration and the largest share (25 percent) of the American gross national product ever spent by the federal government in peacetime.

Frankly, when it comes to federal spending and growth of bureaucracy the only difference between the typical Republican and the typical Democrat is that the Democrat wants to speed the growth of government without regard to efficiency and the Republican wants to slow the growth of the monster to make it efficient.

As an aside, talk of budget cuts by both Bush and Clinton are nothing but shamefully deceptive falsehoods. Here is how the game works. Assume that an agency is spending $1 million this year. Government economists forecast that its service demands will increase by 10 percent next year for a total of $1.1 million. The budget boys of the administration and Congress decide that they will *slow the rate of growth* to 7 percent instead of 10. Then they announce that they have "cut" the budget by $30,000. There is no cut at all. There is an increase of $70,000. All of the highly publicized budget packages of spending cuts are really increases, and the accompanying taxes are increases. The rhetoric to explain what they are doing is outright lying. The game of government continues by "cutting" to take more of your money to pay for ever-increasing government spending.

Remedial Surgery

No bankrupt business is going to regain its health by improving the "efficiency" of bloated staffs and outdated product lines. There needs to be radical surgery. Unprofitable product lines are discontinued, certain staff functions are discontinued, plants are closed, layoffs occur, and redundant functions are eliminated. The new managers simplify communication and speed the decision process. A basic mission statement is adopted, and the enterprise is recapitalized by restructuring the company's debt, an infusion of equity, and a new burst of cash flow from operations greater than the reduced level of expenses. The U.S. government needs to execute every one of these sound business practices—fast!

Third, we must stop trying to make the muddled snare of regulations, bureaucracy, agencies, punitive laws, entitlements, and waste from Roosevelt's New Deal and Johnson's Great Society more efficient. Like a company emerging from bankruptcy, the federal government needs a new set of priorities. We should urge a sunset provision (or time limit) on vast numbers of laws, regulations, and penalties that serve to impede the private sector of our nation. All regulations should be made understandable, and the volume of regulations should be cut by no less than two-thirds.

We should abolish wholesale and without regret those departments and agencies that are no longer key to the survival of America. To name a few, the Departments of Education, Energy, Housing and Urban Development, the National Endowment for the Arts, the Legal Services Corporation, and large sections of the Agriculture Department. The Postal Service should be given to its employees with the present guarantee of exclusive delivery of first-class mail extended for five years only. After that time, it must compete with others for its business. If it fails after that, it fails, and something more efficient from the private sector should take its place.

A review should be made of every grant, subsidy, consulting contract, and building project currently authorized by the government. Any one that is not essential to our nation should be canceled. All grants and subsidies to the middle class should be abolished.

All but five of the government's VIP airplane fleet, which cost $2 billion to purchase, should be sold, and the enormous government civilian air support facilities should be sold or abandoned. The same should be done for the fleet of 340,000 government-owned and operated vehicles, which cost $3 billion to purchase and $750 million a year to maintain.

The information systems of the government are horribly antiquated, costly, and inefficient. An efficient computer network of efficient machines would save at least $18 billion every year.

The bureaucracy should be reduced by attrition, retirement, and layoffs by at least one-third. For those who remain, there should be a provision for promotion, bonuses, and merit raises for efficiency comparable to that offered in private business. Job security for bureaucrats should be the same as that in business. Above all, the bureaucracy must have instilled in its employees the concept that they exist to serve the people; the people do not exist to serve them.

I might add the process of "double dipping"—retiring from one branch of government at a generous pension and then working for another at a generous salary—is wrong, and it should stop. If retirees can get employment in private industry, that is fine, but being retired and active for the same business is an anomaly that should not continue.

Regulation and Suspicion

I was told by one of the key procurement officers for the Air Force that the Department of Defense could save upward of $60 billion by changing its procurement methods. All that would be necessary would be to change the overregulation that comes from the distrust of free enterprise and personal initiative by the liberals in Congress. For instance, if we assume that a civilian hammer can be purchased for $9 retail and wholesale for perhaps half that, why should the same hammer cost the military $450? Because Congress and its bureaucracy were not willing to trust the free market to supply good hammers at reasonable prices. So elaborate specifications were devised to describe a military hammer, and each one had to be custom machined under the cover of contracts that required a team of skilled lawyers to negotiate. Yet military and civilian hammers do the same thing—drive nails.

Why not trust the procurement officers to make their best deal purchasing hammers and every other item that is available out of existing civilian stock? Overregulation caused this absurdity. It creates manuals that expend seventeen pages just to detail the specifications of a military fruitcake. What utter nonsense! Why not let the mess officers buy the same fruitcakes the rest of us eat from the same sources at quantity prices? After all, most American homemakers can bake one from scratch with only a one-page recipe.

One of the keys to successful business management is the concept of empowering the lowest levels in the corporate ladder to have responsibility and make decisions. But that means freedom, and freedom and responsibility are anathema to liberalism. So instead we take power and merit rewards away from capable workers who are concerned with waste, then we mandate gross bureaucratic bungling and nonsense by incompetent time servers, and then spend $593 million between October 1990 and March 1991 for the audit, inspection, and investigative activities of the newly created Defense Contract Audit Agency. As Paul Beckner put it, "*Imagine spending a billion dollars a year to eliminate waste* at the Department of Defense."

We spend $31 million on a fighter plane that should cost a third that much. Why? Because government insists on specifying every detail of the finished product *and* how it is put together. Wouldn't it be a much better practice to tell the manufacturer what performance specifications were desired, then let the manufacturer work out the best, fastest, and cheapest way to arrive at the goal?

In business or in private charitable organizations the function of the board of directors is clear. The board has the ultimate authority over the purse strings and is charged with approving income and expense budgets and appropriating the necessary funds to cover the ongoing expenses and capital purchases. The Constitution gives the Congress the same power, and I believe our country would be well served if we had a current expense budget, on the one hand, and a capital budget, on the other, for permanent facilities that would depreciate over a number of years. That deprecation would then be charged each year to operating expenses. There should be no borrowing at all to meet the current budget and only highly restricted borrowing to pay for productive long-term infrastructure projects.

Term Limits

In the private sector, the board of directors is charged with picking a chief executive and other key officers. Although the board is charged with the duty of setting broad policy guidelines and drafting any changes in the governing constitutions and bylaws, plus the obvious oversight and audit of operating practices, it is not good form for a board of directors, certainly not a committee of the board, to try to usurp the authority of the chief executive or to micromanage the smallest details of the enterprise.

Private board members usually serve for a limited time. In Regent University where I am chancellor, the board members serve for three-year, staggered terms and are eligible for reappointment after a one-year hiatus. This means that the entire board of trustees turns over every three years, but at any time two-thirds are experienced members and one-third is new. By this system we have a continuous flow of capable board members who are constantly bringing insight and fresh concepts to the mission and administration of the university.

Now consider the governing board of our nation, the Congress. What was intended as a part-time task for citizens has now become a full-time job for career politicians who live full time in Washington, read the *Washington Post* every day, and who, with the passage of time, have completely lost touch with America.

In the 1960s Congress was relatively uncomplicated, with a few major committees such as Appropriations, Finance, Foreign Affairs, Commerce, Banking and Currency, and so on. Through seniority, a group of relatively courtly Southern Democrats—of whom my father, A. Willis Robertson was one—held the chairmanships of almost every major committee.

Today that is all different. We now have 300 committees in the House and Senate, including standing, select, and joint committees and their subcommittees, each with a chairman, staff, office, and related perquisites. According to Martin Gross, in 1950, the staffs for all House committees numbered 180. In the early 1960s there were only 700 staff members in the House and Senate combined. That number is now 3,700, a 500 percent increase during a time when our population grew only 37 percent.

All those committees and chairmen have to find something that will attract television time. So they pass unnecessary laws, hold unnecessary hearings, begin unnecessary inquiries, and start unnecessary investigations. I remember hearing from John Lehman, then Secretary of the Navy, that he personally had to defend his budget before thirty-one separate committees of the Congress.

Common sense tells us that, like the rest of government, the board of directors is out of control. The answer very simply is term limits—two six-year terms for senators, three two-year terms for members of the House. Congress must be reorganized and simplified even as we would like to see the rest of government simplified.

With term limits—members going in and out—the governing body would not be fixated with long-term power, because its members' term of power would be short. Congress now exempts itself from most of the onerous regulations it lays on the rest of us. With term limits, congressmen and senators would know for certain that they would soon be living under the laws, regulations, and taxes that they imposed. With that prospect, we could expect a significant rollback.

A Glimmer of Hope

This cookie monster may never be curbed, short of utter collapse, but there are very encouraging signs on the horizon. Term limits for politicians are strongly favored by a majority of Americans. The public supports the idea of giving the president a veto over individual appropriation measures—the so-called line-item veto. In fact, the editorial staff of the *Wall Street Journal* insists that the president already has such power and urged George Bush to use it.

Of course, the nation is very close to forcing Congress to approve a balanced budget amendment to the Constitution. Such an initiative was beaten down by the Democrat-controlled Congress in the latter days of the Bush administration, but the concept is very much alive. I would be willing to propose that the salary of Congress be docked in proportion to the deficit and raised when it is balanced. That may sound silly, but small personal financial incentives have a powerful impact on public policy.

There are a growing number of people with influence in government who support the idea of replacing the unbelievably complex income-tax system with a simple 19 percent flat tax. One national magazine recently featured a member of the Ways and Means Committee that writes the tax bills. He is himself a CPA and a lawyer, yet he is unable to fill out his own personal tax form. When the people who conceive the laws cannot figure these things out, something is terribly wrong with the system, and it must be fixed, posthaste.

The whole entitlement mess started by Lyndon Johnson must be drastically overhauled. Social Security is headed for a crisis of unimaginable proportions in less than twenty years unless we adopt some form of compulsory, private retirement system for younger workers now. If we fail to take pro-active steps, the young men and women who are currently paying into Social Security will end up with nothing but worthless IOUs at retirement time.

How do we deal with such intractable problems? The American people know something is wrong—very wrong. They say they want change. But more than 51 percent of them receive some payment or subsidy from the government. Are they willing to put the long-range good of this nation ahead of their own immediate benefits? Will they begin regarding government as what it was intended to be, instead of what it has become? Are they smart enough to see through campaign hype and realize that it is their nice, friendly liberal congressman who is causing these problems—not somebody else—and vote him or her out of office?

Again, there is no doubt the tide is turning, but will the average man and woman in America respond in time to this moment of opportunity?

5

A Crisis of Law

> It is not mere coincidence that the twilight of the gods has brought on the age of lawyers. . . . As traditional sources of social norms—families, schools, churches—weaken, law seeps into the vacuum. As laws, regulations, rules, contracts, mediations, arbitrations, and negotiations multiply, so do lawyers. Antipathy toward lawyers expresses resentment of the need to rely on people without whose arcane skills (and vocabularies) we frequently cannot function. Doctors, too, are like this but most patients still feel that doctors generally are on their side, and are providing something they need, whereas lawyers seem increasingly parasitic.
>
> George Will, *Newsweek*, 26 July 1993

SINCE THE DAYS OF EGYPT AND ASSYRIA there have been crooked judges and corrupt lawyers. One of the more famous parables of Jesus Christ concerned an "unjust judge who neither feared God nor man." His statement, "woe unto you lawyers" indicates that problems in the legal system are neither new nor unique to the United States. I know a former inmate of the Florida prison system who, prior to his release, was visited by a state circuit court judge to request that the now-reformed jewel thief come back to Miami to resume his craft once again for organized crime.

There isn't a streetwise criminal anywhere not familiar with the phrase, "The fix is in." Cases are fixed, judges are bribed, political hacks get elected or appointed to the bench, prosecutors are compromised, pleas are bargained; yet by and large our system of criminal justice is reasonably fair and equitable. No, the stuff of scandal is not the real problem. The real problem of law in our society goes much deeper. Consider these cases.

A grossly overweight man with a heart condition decided to mow his lawn on a hot day. As he pulled a few too many times on the starter, he keeled over dead. His widow sued the lawn mower manufacturer for damages, alleging that the design of the lawn mower was faulty and caused her husband's demise. A jury awarded her substantial damages.

One man set up a loaded shotgun in the bedroom of his farmhouse. During the night a burglar attempted a break in and was shot in both legs. Later, the burglar sued the man and collected a $30,000 award.

A burglar attempted to enter a Southern California school through a skylight. Before he could gain access to the building, the skylight broke and he fell to the floor below, permanently injuring himself. He sued the school for having a defective roof and collected some $275,000 in an out-of-court settlement.

Rewarding Stupidity

In one case, a jury ordered an outdoor restaurant to pay $3 million to a patron who was stung by a bee. In another, a girl who had been raped by her father was awarded a $2.4 million judgment against her parents because her mother had failed to protect her from abuse. In another case, an inebriated man who tried to board a moving bus at a point between bus stops sued the city of New York and won $619,000 because the bus failed to stop in time. In another case, a despondent man threw himself in front of a subway train and then sued the city and won $650,000 because the subway driver failed to stop in time. Even more bizarre, a woman in Philadelphia sued her doctor because she said a CAT scan he prescribed had interfered with her psychic powers. Was the case thrown out of court? No, of course not. She was awarded nearly a million dollars.

In a report cited by the *Wall Street Journal*, researcher Mark Pulliam is quoted:

> A system that was designed to compensate tangible and serious injuries at the expense of culpable parties has been transformed into a mechanism for redistributing income from large corporations and insurance companies to self-styled "victims" and contingent fee lawyers, often in the absence of any blameworthy conduct.[1]

Cases like these are so absurd that they offend the common sense of any thinking individual. But why are they happening? The answer is very simple. Some decades ago, professors, judges, and practitioners of law began subscribing to the concept that all truth was relative. Charles Evans Hughes of the Supreme Court had made the cynical statement, "We are under a Constitution, but the Constitution is what the judges say it is."[2] This, of course, opened Pandora's box. There were no fixed rules, no standards. The Constitution of the United States, other constitutions and statutes, and judicial precedent were considered subject to the evolution of the social prejudices and concerns of whoever was sitting on the bench at any given point of time.

Certainly for the new activist judiciary an appeal to time-honored biblical standards, even the historic standards of the common law, was out of the question. All that really mattered was how judicial decisions could implement the liberal agenda to right the perceived wrongs of society, enshrine individual rights of politically correct "victims," and punish the "wealthy exploiters of the masses."

As things stand now, anyone can sue anyone else for almost anything. Obviously there is some degree of order in our civil jurisprudence, but any litigant will tell you that there is no way to predict the outcome of any case with certainty, nor is there any way to predict the amount of money a jury will grant a plaintiff. Cases proliferate, lawyers proliferate, and craziness seems to rule in some courts over common sense and reason.

The very idea of justice has become a joke to most people. Lawyers and judges no longer elicit the kind of respect they once did. More often today they are the butt of coarse jokes. Why is this happening? What has gone wrong to change our perspectives on the legal profession? What has happened to the idea of law and order? Is there any reason to hope for a common-sense solution to some of these problems?

In *The Litigation Explosion*, Walter K. Olson describes the crisis in America's civil courts in this way:

> For all the many successes of American society, our system of civil litigation is a grotesque failure, a byword around the world for expense, rancor, and irrationality. America's litigation explosion has squandered immense fortunes, sent the cream of a nation's intellectual talent into dubious battle, reduced valuable enterprises to ruin, made miserable the practice of honorable professions, and brought needless pain to broken families. It has been a spiral of destructive recrimination, with no end in sight.[3]

The situation is equally desperate in both civil and criminal law. But despite the many attempts to regulate the legal profession and to establish stronger controls and greater accountability within the profession, it is the lawyers themselves, through powerful lobbies and advocacy groups, who have consistently beaten back the regulators. Working from inside the system, attorneys have been able to frustrate even the efforts of the executive and legislative branches of government.

The Need for Sane Laws

The tort reforms and other corrective measures advocated by former Vice-President Dan Quayle in his speech to a national lawyers conference in 1991 never materialized. The administration's plans were so violently attacked by spokesmen for the plaintiffs' bar that the federal government's momentum was derailed. However, there is good news from the states.

In the August 2, 1993, issue of *Forbes* magazine, David Frum penned an article entitled, "Sanity Is Back in Style," which presented some clear evidence that the legal tide is turning in at least some of the states—a tide that sources claimed had been building for several years and predicted would expand in 1994. Here are some of his findings:

- On March 4, Governor Ann Richards signed a major product liability reform statute that requires plaintiffs who want to claim that a product's design was unsafe to show that there was a safer alternative design available that was both economically and technologically feasible. And lawyers will find it harder to pull out-of-state litigation into Texas courts.

Mississippi's new law is a "model product liability code." It provides that:

- A product's design will not be considered defective if it could not be fixed without compromising the product's "usefulness or desirability."
- The manufacturer will not be liable if the danger posed by the product is known or obvious.
- Punitive damages may be awarded only if the defendant is proven to have acted with actual malice.

North Dakota has restricted product-liability suits and has limited punitive damages to no more than double compensatory damages or $250,000, whichever is greater.

Arizona's new law exempts personal-injury defendants from liability if the plaintiff's injury was caused by his own drunkenness. Arizona also abolished "joint and several" liability, preventing plaintiffs from extracting their entire award from the richest defendant when multiple defendants are at fault.

Tort reform also appears imminent in Massachusetts, which looks likely to eliminate damages for defective design unless the plaintiff can prove an alternative design was "commercially and technically feasible." In New York, Governor Mario Cuomo's proposed action against medical malpractice abuse has recently been approved by the state legislature. Punitive damage reform is being considered by the state legislatures of

Wisconsin and New Jersey. Michigan's legislature is now considering a bill to control medical liability. More is coming next year, but there is still a great need for vigilance.

Walter Olson correctly observes that the problems in the structure of the law are intractable, but they are also symbolic of a deeper failure in our philosophy. "This practical failure," he says, "is born of an underlying moral failure. Our law has ceased to attach moral significance to wrongful accusations." In other words, the law has lost the moral connection between truth and justice. Principles that derive from the Ten Commandments and from a code of Christian morality are no longer deemed "legal" in America. Men and women today prefer to do "that which seems right in their own eyes,"[4] and the entire nation pays a terrible price for this arrogance. There is little certainty in the courts today, and the law is no longer an inviolable standard. American jurisprudence has become a nightmare.

Common-Sense Solutions

So how do we deal with these problems? Here are a few common-sense solutions to the avalanche of crime and civil suits that have descended upon our society:

1. At present anyone can sue anyone else for any reason that the would-be plaintiff's attorney can concoct. I personally was sued—following a private, loving, and prayerful spiritual counseling session—under a nineteenth-century dueling statute because the plaintiff, himself a lawyer, alleged that the statements I said about him in counseling were "insulting words" under the state statute (and, therefore, by inference, likely to result in a duel!).

Not only did his attorney file this absurd lawsuit, but a state circuit judge refused to dismiss it. Only during an intense examination of the plaintiff during a sworn deposition following months of legal maneuvering did the plaintiff's attorney acknowledge how foolish the entire proceeding was and agree to "non-suit" the case. The case went away, but along with it went between $10,000 and $20,000 in legal fees paid by CBN's insurance carrier to defend me.

The case ended, but there was no penalty or sanction whatsoever against one individual for trying to use the legal system to hurt someone else. Yet in this one case there were numerous pleadings, counterclaims and answers, scores of pages of sworn depositions, time-consuming legal research, hours of valuable time wasted. There are federal sanctions and selected state sanctions against frivolous lawsuits, but the difficulty of obtaining sanctions and the modest amounts of money assessed under sanctions makes their use virtually meaningless.

But there is a simpler and better way—the English common law system. Simply put, under English law a plaintiff who brings a legal action and loses in court must pay not only his own attorney's fees but also the attorney's fees of the party that he sued. Under our legal system, a plaintiff using an attorney who works on a contingent fee basis has no risk whatever if he loses. Under the British system a plaintiff must have a legitimate, provable claim that would stand up before a jury, or else he would be foolish to commence a costly legal struggle. I dare say that this one very simple, common-sense solution would cut the incidence of civil suits brought in America by at least one-third.

2. Under the current, imprecise, anything-goes standards of jurisprudence, juries have been allowed to run amok. Cases are no longer decided on established legal standards but on the concept that a jury is free to find liability where none should exist and then to assess damages that do not merely compensate an injured plaintiff but are designed to "punish" a defendant.

The Supreme Court had the opportunity in 1991, in the case of *Pacific Mutual Life Insurance Co. v. Haslip,* to limit the insane punitive damages being assessed by juries all across America. The original jury had awarded the claimant punitive damages of $800,000, but the case was appealed. By refusing to throw out the *Haslip* verdict and by vacating six separate cases before the district courts, the Supreme Court effectively upheld the idea of excessive damage awards.

Again, in 1993, the Court had another opportunity in the case of *TXO Production Corp. v. Alliance Resource Corp.* Here it had an unprecedented chance to restore some sense of balance to tort litigation by undoing a judgment of $19,000 in actual damages and an outrageous $10 million in punitive damages that had been upheld by the supreme court of West Virginia. The district court's reasoning was so distorted, the proceedings even include the ruling justice's comment that there are two kinds of corporations that end up in court: those that are "really stupid" and those that are "really mean." The Court upheld the jury's assessment of the $10 million damage award in this case because the defendant had been "really mean."

When Law Becomes Predatory

Our standards of excessive compensation are wrong and, in my opinion, they are both unconstitutional and contrary to biblical standards. According to biblical standards, a person who inflicts a monetary wrong on another must pay the amount of the actual financial loss plus 20 percent. This is a rule that is not subject to the desires of juries to punish the wealthy.

Before the liberal judicial revolution, the measure of contract damages was considered to be the amount of the loss actually suffered by the plaintiff less recoveries that were obtained or should have been obtained to mitigate damages. In tort injuries the damages to be paid to an injured person included medical expenses, loss of earnings, some reasonable allowance for pain, suffering, loss of limbs, and disfigurement, and reasonable attorney's fees. In cases of wrongful death, legislatures often specified the monetary limits of recovery.

The Old Testament concept of "eye for eye, tooth for tooth, lash for lash" was not an invitation to vengeance. Instead it was intended as a limitation of tort liability. In other words, if a man accidentally or maliciously knocked out another man's tooth, a court could not order him blinded or maimed in retaliation. In a crude sense of parity, the judge could order his tooth knocked out—but nothing more. In the Sermon on the Mount, Jesus Christ introduced a better way that went beyond lawsuits and tort damages—it was a call for judgment based on peace, love, and forgiveness.

In tort cases the plaintiff had to prove some type of negligence or wrong for which the defendant was responsible, and then the plaintiff was required to prove his damages. Of course, the jury was free to award more or less money than the plaintiff asked for, but within the scope of provable facts guided by reason and common sense.

Many people are familiar with the highly publicized case decided in a Georgia court in January 1993 in which plaintiffs Thomas and Elaine Moseley sued General Motors because an accident involving an older model pickup truck with a side-mounted gas tank resulted in the death of their son, Shannon.[5] This was the case in which the producers of an NBC news program had rigged a crash and explosion to demonstrate what might have happened. The network had to apologize to the entire nation for its behavior, but the jury was apparently undisturbed by the resulting flap. The plaintiffs proved their case, winning $4.2 million in compensatory damages, and then they were awarded an additional $101 million in punitive damages by the jury.

When asked why they had made such an outrageous award, members of the jury said that they wanted to send a message. To me their message is perfectly clear. It says to General Motors and every other large manufacturer the same thing that all the other outrageous verdicts have said—"Stop making automobiles and airplanes and other vital equipment because the risk of loss at the hands of out-of-control juries is simply too great to bear!"

If you analyze this verdict a bit closer you see how ludicrous it is. If a person works for forty-five years at a salary of $40,000 per year, his or her lifetime take-home pay after taxes would be roughly $1,350,000. By what stretch of perverse logic could that person be justified in extorting from the American economy under the guise of justice a tax-free sum equal to seventy-five times his lifetime earning potential? But then the real shock comes when we realize that the injured plaintiff does not receive the entire sum. His attorney, who had no injury and who suffered no pain, will receive, under a contingent fee arrangement, somewhere between $33,000,000 and $40,000,000 for part-time work over a three- or four-year period.

No nineteenth-century robber barons, no Chinese warlords, no Barbary Coast pirates even came close to the rapacious greed that characterizes the plundering of America by what is called the "plaintiffs' bar." Today the courts' average judgment for damages exceeds $650,000, and the average cost of liability insurance for manufacturers has risen as much as 1,000 percent over the past twenty years.

The Meaning of Malpractice

I sat next to an insurance company executive on an airplane who told me he no longer deals in malpractice insurance because the risk is too high. As an example, he told me about a former client, a firm of plastic surgeons, who was charged a premium of $3.5 million a year for malpractice insurance. In order for those people to stay in business and make a living for themselves, they have to charge their patients an extra $3.5 million a year. That means, above and beyond their normal fees for treatment, they had to come up with another $292,000 every month. And we wonder why medical costs are so high?

I read recently that as many as 25 percent of the obstetricians in this country have chosen to close down their practices rather than pay the high cost of malpractice insurance. The American College of Surgeons estimates the cost of "defensive medicine" at over $100 billion. It isn't hard to realize what an incredibly wasteful burden this places on the healthcare industry. A burden, I might add, that is borne by every American. Doctors are doing unnecessary tests, making unnecessary referrals, and bringing in unnecessary specialists for expert opinions. They must treat their patients not only for disease but also for the courts of law. There certainly must be a way to punish the frauds who butcher people in the name of medicine, but unless we can bring common-sense limits to malpractice litigation, the nation's healthcare costs will never be brought under control.

We also hear of businesses practicing "defensive manufacturing," "defensive innovation," and even "defensive marketing." Trying to run any operation always looking over your shoulder is both dangerous and stifling.

Just imagine how this litigious environment escalates the cost of doing business. Who pays the tab for the insurance, the quality problems, and the inefficiency that inevitably results? You do. These costs always come back to the consumer, regardless who is involved in the legal actions.

When Lawyers Abuse

Before I give the impression that I'm libeling the entire legal profession, let me be quick to say that my father was a lawyer, my son is a lawyer, and I have a law degree and am chancellor of a university with an American Bar Association–accredited law school. Most of these outrageous cases are not handled by good, honest lawyers. When people with spurious claims go after a surgeon or a healthcare provider, seeking huge damages, they seek out a flamboyant "hotshot" with a reputation for getting multimillion-dollar awards. We are not talking about a responsible attorney who is trying to help people legitimately.

Lawyers are compensated two ways. One is the contingency fee method, usually computed at 35 to 40 percent of the recovery. The other method is compensation by the hour—usually anywhere from $100 to $300 per hour. Whether he is in court, sitting in a deposition, doing research, or talking to a client on the phone, the meter is running. The longer a case, the more complicated it is, the more the lawyer gets paid. So it is to the lawyer's financial advantage to keep the parties apart, keep them belligerent, and escalate the cost of litigation as high as possible. It takes a strong and very righteous anger to do otherwise.

Why have depositions, discovery, motions, countermotions, claims, counterclaims? They all result in billable hours. I remember one simple trademark case in which we were represented by the most prestigious law firm in the state. They assigned four lawyers, each of whom billed separately and seemed to duplicate each other's work. By the first day of the trial our bill had already hit $150,000, and I had had enough. I personally met with the defendant. We had a cordial meeting. I asked how much it would take to settle the case. It turned out the figure for a completely amicable settlement was $100,000, but our lawyers and the defendant's lawyers received $200,000 in fees to do what it took me fifteen minutes to accomplish.

Lawyers who exploit these situations for their own gain are like vultures preying on the suffering of others. Yes, some claims are legitimate and necessary, but the situation has gotten out of hand and allowed unnatural and adversarial relationships to develop throughout our society. The underlying rationale is, "Everybody's doing it, so let's get ours; after all, the damages are being paid for by the insurance companies, and they have deep pockets." But what these people don't understand is that insurance companies make their money from individuals and corporations, and since they have to stay in business, they raise their rates. It's a vicious cycle, and it affects the pricing of every product.

Common sense is twofold. First, there have to be caps on the extent of punitive damages in tort actions. Excessive litigation has threatened certain industries to the point that they cannot function. The small plane industry, for example, has just about gone out of business in America. They're still producing commercial and military aircraft, but general aviation—the small Cesnas and Piper Cubs—are no longer being made. The risk is simply too great. If a private plane crashes for virtually any reason, the victim's families don't just sue the pilot, they also sue manufacturers and everyone else connected with the case. As a consequence, the manufacturers do not want to participate any more. Why should society be denied general aviation aircraft because of the exploitation of the law?

Unreasonable Regulations

We recently learned that the cost for environmental pollution is assessed against anybody in the chain of association, even those who may subsequently lease a property where a toxic spill has occurred in the distant past. A company I am familiar with, called Airplanes, Inc., wanted to lease a fixed-base operation at the airport in Elizabeth City, North Carolina. This was to be a small hangar with fuel facilities adjoining a Coast Guard base. A few years earlier, however, the Airport

Authority of Elizabeth City, which ran the airport at that time, had installed fuel tanks that had rusted through and leaked.

According to the law, anybody who subsequently took over the facility, even a lessee who had no responsibility whatever for the leakage, would be financially responsible to clean it up and to take care of damages to any adjacent property. Naturally, Airplanes, Inc., chose not to get involved.

When the United States was founded there were three crimes under federal law. Today there are more than three thousand. Most of these crimes did not spring from any easily understood universal moral law, such as those prohibiting murder, theft, kidnapping, or perjury. The new crimes sprang from the desire of special interests to force people to conform to the dictates of an all-encompassing, liberal welfare state.

Ordinary citizens can be sent to jail for intending to violate disclosure regulations by withdrawing $5,000 in cash from their bank accounts legally on two separate occasions without filing a disclosure form. They can also be harassed and sued for "parking" securities, making a mistake on a government-mandated form, making a mistake of fact before a congressional committee, or just spreading top soil on their yards if they happen to live in a "wetlands" area. Citizens can go to jail for traveling to the wrong country, failing to pay taxes, paying the wrong amount of taxes, failing to tell a government agency confidential information, telling a government agency incorrect information, hindering a government investigation, giving too much money to a political candidate, receiving an audio tape of a telephone conversation, giving a bank an incorrect financial statement, possessing various types of controlled substances, selling vitamins with incorrect labels, hiring the wrong kinds of workers, failing to destroy surplus agricultural products, and on and on, ad infinitum.

When No One Is Safe

The regulations of big government are so all-inclusive, it can be said with great certainty that, given enough time and provocation, unscrupulous prosecutors could obtain an indictment for some technical violation against any citizen in this country anytime they want to.

But potential criminal liability is only the tip of the iceberg. Government regulators, backed up by hordes of government lawyers, are actively bedeviling and second-guessing large corporations, small businesses, farmers, hospitals, doctors, universities, private shopkeepers, and everyone else who is productive in our society. Think of the bewildering array of regulatory agencies—the IRS, the SEC, the FAA, the FEC, the FCC, the ICC, OSHA, the NLRB, the EPA, the EEOC, the FDA, the FTC, the FERC, and now more ominously (after the Branch Davidian incident in Waco, Texas, in early 1993) the ATF, the DEA, and the FBI. Add to these the regulatory mechanisms of the Labor Department, the Department of Health and Human Services, the Agriculture Department, the Commerce Department, the Education Department, the Department of Housing and Urban Development, and the Treasury Department, all backed by the criminal enforcement powers of the Justice Department, including the United States Attorneys and literally thousands of government lawyers. The current cost to the private economy for complying with government regulations, demands, and civil enforcement of the various bureaucratic arms of the federal government has been estimated to range from $485 billion to $650 billion per year.

I have firsthand knowledge of how this insidious regulatory system works. Responding to a critical story in the *Washington Post*—considered by many to be the official press arm of the liberal welfare state—in July 1986, the Exempt Organization Branch of the IRS began an audit of a citizens organization called the Freedom Council, which had been started and financed by CBN. From there the audit spread to CBN itself, and thirteen field agents of the IRS, plus their supervisors, took up residence in our offices.

During their inquiry, interesting things came to light. The lead agent was committed by his ex-wife to an alcoholic treatment center. Before he was taken off the case, he was guilty of repeatedly breaking the IRS code of silence (which is in itself one more on the long list of federal crimes), and in the process he indirectly accused the then Secretary of the Treasury of another federal crime.

One of the "impartial" IRS staff members who took my deposition was a hulking woman wearing a large belt buckle with NOW emblazoned on it, indicating that she was a member of the militant anti-Christian, pro-abortion National Organization for Women. Yet it was this totally biased woman who was given the privilege of later writing a scathing indictment of the Christian Coalition, the American Center for Law and Justice, and several other organizations that I had founded to preserve Christian freedom and religious values in America.

Fortunately her statement of the facts was so distorted and her knowledge of the law so limited that it was easy to refute her vicious assertions. But how could a federal agency with such awesome power, professing impartiality, have sent such enemies of religion to evaluate a major Christian ministry?

This "audit" began seven years ago and it has still not been concluded, although negotiations are under way with fairer and more intelligent people at the Washington office of the IRS. We expect a satisfactory conclusion this year.

At the date of this writing, CBN's outside legal and accounting costs to provide information to the IRS and to refute its misstatements of fact and mischaracterizations of applicable law have exceeded $4 million. In the process, they have consumed thousands of hours of precious staff time and have diverted many of our key personnel from their core mission. But multiply what has been done to us by what has been done to hundreds of thousands of others, and it becomes abundantly clear what a hellish nightmare the agencies of the bureaucratic welfare state have created for the productive sectors of this nation. In the mode of Ayn Rand's classic novel *Atlas Shrugged*, the productive taxpayers of this nation are ready for a major revolt.

But I must add that if neither the Democratic party nor the Republican party is willing to take this challenge and throw off the shackles of the socialist welfare state, then a third party is sure to arise, like that of Ross Perot! Short of a third party, what is the common-sense solution to the problem? In dealing with bureaucrats I have learned one simple truth: For an IRS investigator to report "no fault" in an investigation subjects the investigator to discipline and, in some cases, even a possible congressional inquiry. Whereas finding fault and prosecuting or persecuting those parties under investigation is not only safe, but it is often the road to promotion.

Reversing the Equation

The way out of the dilemma is easy. Reverse the equation. Make it beneficial to say "no fault," and make it painful for a bureaucrat to harass a citizen. Very simply, as I suggested for civil cases, force the government to pay the reasonable legal and accounting fees that citizens and corporations incur as a result of government-initiated civil and criminal regulatory actions. Then deduct those payments directly from the sums appropriated by Congress for the bureaucratic activity authorized.

Just think of it. Every time a government bureaucrat begins to harass a member of the private sector, his agency's budget would be cut by the victim's costs. Later, one or more bureaucrats would be fired because the agency's funds were depleted. This would be an ongoing mechanism. The fewer enforcement cases, the less need for costly budgets. The more failed enforcement cases, the smaller the agency would become.

But someone might ask, What about the drug dealers, tax cheats, industrial polluters, monopolists, and the Mafia—in short, what about the bad guys? Again, the answer is simple common sense. When those people are found guilty, assess either civil or criminal fines and forfeitures that would be more than adequate to cover the expenses of both parties, plus enough extra to defray the costs of trying criminals who have no money. These sums, of course, would be credited to the budget of the agency winning the forfeiture.

Democrats in Congress want the taxpayers to pay the costs of all federal elections. That would only guarantee that incumbents stay in office, and it is a bad idea. But payment by the government of the cost of regulatory harassment is a good idea that would improve the economy and limit abuses.

There is one final common-sense approach to criminal law and the treatment of offenders. At the present, our legal system permits private individuals to sue other individuals for various civil wrongs. However, if you or I are criminally attacked or robbed, we as victims have no real voice in the proceedings. The case is no longer John Q. Public, victim, versus Public Menace, defendant. Instead it is the state or the United States versus Menace. The victim has little or no voice in the trial, plea bargains, or sentencing, and except in a few special circumstances, the victim gets no compensation for what has been done. Perhaps even more tragically, because of the extreme overcrowding in our nation's prisons and the newly accepted philosophy that, since there are no rights and wrongs, rehabilitation and not punishment should prevail, tens of thousands of chronic, often violent felons get little or no jail time and are released on probation or parole. According to an article entitled "When Criminals Go Free" in the March 1993 issue of *Reader's Digest*, the Los Angeles probation system is so overcrowded that sixty-five thousand probationers roam the streets at will, reporting in each month by postcard.

Violent offenders are free to hunt down their former victims or to prey on unsuspecting members of the public. According to Charles Murray, co-author of *Beyond Probation*, common sense began to evaporate as "*elite wisdom* [my emphasis] had shifted to a consensus that punishment was pointless, and often the best thing to do was leave the offender on the street."[6]

According to the article, nearly two-thirds of all convicted criminals in the United States end up on probation. The folly of this extreme example of humanist nonsense is shown by two studies: one from the Justice Department of seventy-nine thousand felony probationers, of whom 43 percent were rearrested within three years, and a California study that showed that two-thirds of probationers studied were either arrested or in violation of their probation within one year.

Regaining Our Bearings

Because we have lost our moral compass, we have abandoned the only true rehabilitation, which is spiritual conversion. Without a reliable compass, without standards of right and wrong, and without trustworthy methods of judgment handed down by an all-wise God, law enforcement, in effect, surrenders the prisons, the probation, and the streets to criminals. But there is a better way. Since the prisons are schools for crime, nonviolent juvenile first offenders should be given probation, but only on the condition that they do something to make it up to their victims, face up to what their actions have caused, and then perform whatever work is necessary to make restitution.

Second, in all criminal cases victims should be included as a party, and a major part of every sentence should include some form of restitution to the victim. How better to make the punishment fit the crime than for a criminal to serve at some clearly defined task until his labors have paid back to the victim some part of the damage done? Then it would no longer be a criminal who hurt a defenseless "mark," but one human being accountable to another for his actions.

Beyond this, sentences should be reasonable and fair and then carried out fully. Except for what is called "good time," the principle of parole and probation for dangerous criminals should be abolished. The public needs to be safe from violent acts, and criminals need to know that punishment will be swift, certain, and unpleasant.

Finally, keeping an inmate in prison for a year costs roughly the same as a year of full tuition and board at Harvard University. Common sense would tell us that society does not need to be victimized twice by repeat, violent offenders—first, through the injuries that they inflict and, second, through the cost of protracted and repeated incarceration. For the repeat, violent crimes perpetrator, the death penalty is entirely appropriate. We need not be ashamed to say that the goal of criminal justice is not just rehabilitation, or even deterrence, but punishment as well.

Multiplying the Damages

In his book *Straight Shooting,* Boston University President John Silber pointed out that during the 1980s American law schools were churning out more than 35,000 new lawyers every year. In one year we graduate more lawyers in this country than the total number of lawyers in the nation of Japan. There are already more than 750,000 practicing attorneys in this country, and some statisticians suggest that if the trend continues there will be more than a million before the turn of the century. Dan Quayle remarked on the irony that while this country makes up just 5 percent of the world's population, we have 70 percent of the world's lawyers. At the rate we are going, John Silber joked, by the year 2074 every man, woman, and child in America will be a lawyer!

In the United States there is one lawyer for every 365 ordinary citizens. Contrast that with Western Europe, where the ratio is one lawyer per 1,500 citizens, or England where it's 1,250 to one. This incredible deluge of men and women in the legal professions prompted former Chief Justice Warren Burger to say, "We may well be on our way to a society overrun by hordes of lawyers, hungry as locusts, and brigades of judges in numbers never before contemplated."[7]

So what has all this legal expertise accomplished? We have become the most litigious society on earth, and it is costing this nation a fortune. Silber offered this estimate of the cost:

> Although no adequate study has been made of the total cost of our current legal system, such a study would have to include not only direct costs but also the costs to other professions, to institutions, to industry and to government in opportunities foregone, initiative lost, time wasted, enterprise destroyed. And it would be folly to assume that this crippling hidden tax on our economy could be less than $200–$300 billion a year.[8]

Further, the author noted that while the gross national product (GNP) of this country increased by 179 percent between 1972 and 1983, the value of legal services and private attorney's fees increased by 259 percent. The cost of law in this nation, according to these figures, grew at a rate almost one and a half times faster than the entire GNP.

Government, of course, employs a great many lawyers, and the amount of legislation and litigation created by the bureaucracy has grown proportionately as the number of lawyers and "experts" has increased over the past half-century. When the *Federal Register* (the record of official transactions conducted each year by the executive branch) was first issued in the mid-1930s it contained just 2,411 pages. Today it contains more than 60,000 pages and is growing at a rate of 1,000 pages every year. If that does not seem imposing, just remember that every page represents another case or action or source of expense to the government. Throughout the government there has been a multiplication of the number of incredibly expensive, highly time-consuming, personnel-intensive legal proceedings. Among these is an average of more than 60,000 lawsuits being waged by the federal government at any given time in the 1990s.

There are many reasons why these things should concern us. Common sense says that we should learn to live in peace and settle disputes amicably without having to resort to legal actions, but we have lost our rudder. American judicial practice no longer relies on its historic sources of authority.

The Roots of Radicalism

Until modern times, the foundations of law rested on the Judeo-Christian concept of right and wrong and the foundational concept of Original Sin—that humans are capable of wrongdoing by nature. It was the belief of traditional law that without suitable social and moral restraints and a strong legal code, society would inevitably degenerate into chaos and anarchy. Modern secular sociology, however, shuns such biblical teachings in favor of an evolutionary hypothesis based on the ideas of Darwin, Freud, Einstein, and others. This view, often called "secular humanism," takes the view that man has evolved from the slime and that with time and ever greater freedoms, mankind will ascend to the stars. These ideas, which are contrary to the Word of God, have led directly to the bitter conflict and social chaos of our day, and furthermore, they have somber implications for the future health of the justice system in this country.

The legacy of the 1960s is still with us today. The free-love, anti-war, psychedelic 1960s proclaimed not only the right of dissent but the right to protest against and defame the most sacred institutions of this nation. Patriotism, liberty, and the national flag—the symbols of America that millions have died for—were rendered meaningless. Liberal activists still claim the right to burn the American flag and to desecrate our national shrines and emblems. And these things are being upheld by the courts! Free love, the rise of pagan cults, and the New Age movement have all thrived in this atmosphere of defiance. And what may prove to be the greatest holocaust in history—the abortion movement—is one of its most sinister expressions.

On the one hand, politically correct rulings without any sort of legal precedent have been handed down by the nation's high courts. On the other, anti-family and anti-religious bigotry are still on the rise and being upheld by courts at every level. While all this is happening, crime is raging in our streets. It is apparent that we have lost our legal and moral moorings because we have lost contact with the very touchstone of law and order.

In his classic work *The Roots of American Order*, the distinguished Heritage Foundation scholar Russell Kirk wrote:

> Without Authority vested somewhere, without regular moral principles that may be consulted confidently, Justice cannot long endure anywhere. Yet modern liberalism and democracy are contemptuous of the whole concept of moral authority; if not checked in their assaults upon habitual reverence and prescriptive morality, the liberals and democrats will destroy Justice not only for their enemies, but for themselves. Under God, the will of the people ought to prevail; but many liberals and democrats ignore that prefatory clause.[9]

There is little doubt that this is the root cause of the crisis of law crippling this nation. The problems within the justice system—as in the problems with American liberal democracy in general—actually began with the liberalizing policies of some of our second-century leaders.

Justices of the Supreme Court from the mid-1800s through the mid-1900s deliberately set about to redefine the role of the Court and to change the meaning of "individual rights." In the 1960s, the ultimate example of civil rights was called "self-expression." This ideology, sustained by the courts, ultimately led to the radical judicial activism we see today, to the abuses in the way the courts assess damages in consumer grievance claims, and to the more recent attempts to establish constitutional precedent through judicial action.

Justice by Fiat

There is a strong movement today among activists to wrest legislative powers from the Congress and give that power to the courts. We have seen many examples where the Supreme Court, for example, has overstepped its bounds and actually rendered judgment with the force of law. In such cases, the Court is not interpreting the law but actually enacting it by fiat. This is a miscarriage of justice that has not escaped the notice of groups such as pro-abortion activists who fear the will of the people on this issue. The case of *Roe v. Wade* which legalized abortion on demand was a judicial fiat. Those in the pro-abortion movement who can see the possibility that this ruling will be overturned are already looking for other ways to defeat the will of the American people.

But the founders of this nation foresaw a time when one branch of government might attempt to gain control of the others. That is why, in the Constitution, they specifically ordained a balance of powers between the executive, legislative, and judicial branches. Not to be restrained by a mere document, however, judges and lawyers for many years have attempted to turn the bench into a political soapbox and to change the laws to suit their own social and political beliefs. Writing in the *Wall Street Journal*, Appeals Court Justice Alex Kozinski said recently, "Judges who get into the habit of playing legislator find it tempting to start treating all laws—including the Constitution—as merely a springboard for implementing their own sense of right and wrong." Anyone looking at specific examples of such judicial activism would be horrified by the results of this type of abuse by the courts and the irresponsible actions it has encouraged.

Before he was named to the Supreme Court, Justice Antonin Scalia wrote, "We live in an age of hair-trigger unconstitutionality." The results of the general abuse of law has actually encouraged massive misuses of the system and an exponential multiplication in civil litigation. Instead of the "crisp and specific interpretation" of law in previous generations, we now have what author Walter Olson calls "fuzzy new standards," which, in essence, guarantee that everything eventually ends up in court. As with Justice Sandra Day O'Connor's "evolving standards," greed and exploitation thrive in this environment. We are still dealing with their consequences.

At the same time, the outcry against crime, criminals, and criminal abuse of the legal system is growing louder by the day. Product liability claims, the consumer protection code, and the litigious atmosphere within the civil courts is only one part of the story. The battle in the criminal courts is, if anything, more intense, and this situation has helped foster a climate of open warfare between entire sectors of our society.

Even with the largest justice system in the world, no one is safe on our city streets. With more than eighteen million lawsuits transacted in this country every year at a cumulative cost in excess of $300 billion annually, we are no safer in our homes than the villagers of some primitive tribal nation. In fact, we are not as safe. During the Persian Gulf War it was reported that American soldiers serving in Saudi Arabia and Kuwait were less likely to be injured or killed in combat than they would be on the streets of their own hometown. Equally true, we would be safer traveling in the most primitive villages of Africa or Southeast Asia than our neighborhood shopping malls.

The Cry for Change

Americans want change, not to more liberalism, but to common-sense criminal justice. They want to see realistic sentences meted out to criminals and punishment carried out in full without releasing recidivists and prison-hardened thugs onto our streets.

Returning to the tried and tested standards of justice is at least a first step to getting our legal system back on track. But where do we look for guidance? To what standard should we return? Russell Kirk wrote:

> Some people in the twentieth century have come to understand afresh how the lust for power is rooted in the corrupt nature of mankind. If that lust is not restrained by religious sanctions for morality, then it will be kept in bounds only by force and a master.[10]

But he also said that the law and the prophets gave clear ethical meaning to human existence; that is why the order of modern society is founded upon them. All the sins of man that Amos denounced are with mankind still: ghastly violence, corruption of justice, oppression of the weak, selfish indulgence, hypocrisy, and ruinous complacency. Although thirty-three centuries have passed since Moses heard the voice of Jehovah, mankind in general has not succeeded satisfactorily in ordering either soul or commonwealth. Yet without the principles of order made known by the law and the prophets, modern man could not recognize any standards for individuals and nations.[11]

The standards of justice set down by God in the Mosaic Law and further detailed in the teachings of Jesus, most notably in the Sermon on the Mount, have been foundational to Western-style justice. These standards indicate the seriousness of judgment and the importance—reflected in Judeo-Christian custom—of fair and impartial applications of the law in society. But secular humanism disdains the authority of religion, and secularist judges have become a law unto themselves.

The liberal courts of the 1960s and 1970s, particularly the Supreme Court under the late Chief Justice Earl Warren, probably did more to redefine the law in terms of personal liberties than any court before or since. Constitutional scholar Harvey Mansfield, Jr., writes that this whole concept of self-expression is focused inwardly, on the rights of the individual to the exclusion of the rights of the group—a doctrine that came into being during the era of the Warren Court. "Those who are 'into' self-expression," he says, "do not care whether they gain their point by persuading a majority." Of course, the judicial precedents that have come from this movement could never have passed a legitimate legislative challenge; therefore, legal reformers and special-interest groups have legislated their will through the courts. Mansfield writes:

> It is no accident that most of the policies associated with these values have been begun by parts of the government not directly dependent on an elected majority. Above all, the judiciary through both the Warren and the Burger Courts has initiated a series of major policies and sustained them, without apology, against majority opinion and the protests of elected representatives. The judiciary has acted, it claims, only in response to urgent calls for justice from the Constitution, which coincidentally has been developing toward the values of self-expression at a pace far exceeding the ability of a majority to keep up with it.[12]

The first major changes to the legal system arose in the mid-1800s, in part from the slavery question and related civil rights issues. Appropriately, the prohibition of slavery led to an amendment of the Constitution. However, extenuations and extrapolations from these basic principles helped to open the door to other issues never conceived of by the men and women of that day, and this has helped create what we now recognize as a nation of victims. It is an environment that actually encourages litigation, provides virtual license for certain kinds of character assassination and name calling, and breeds a dangerous splintering of society.

Judging Without Evidence

Consider the following examples of judicial idiocy. In Florida, a forty-eight-year-old man sentenced to life in prison for raping a thirteen-year-old girl with muscular dystrophy was released when the Second District Court of Appeals ruled that the rapist had been convicted with the wrong charge. The charge, "sexual battery of a helpless person," was deemed unfair in the court's opinion since the girl had screamed for help and tried to push the man away. Instead of the maximum thirty-year sentence, the rapist served only a few months for battery.

A Philadelphia mother was cleared of murder charges in the smothering death of her infant daughter. Judge Lisa Richette cleared the woman because, as she explained, the child had lingered in a coma before she eventually died, and the court was not convinced the mother was guilty of "murder." Later the mother told detectives she was glad to be rid of her kids, saying: "Now I can go out and do what I want. It's all about freedom."

Such cases of semantic legerdemain are no longer rare. They reach from the bottom to the top of the legal system. In New Jersey, the supreme court decided that a robber convicted of purse snatching had been wrongly sentenced since he slipped the purse off the victim's arm quietly and did not actually "snatch" it. Even more shocking, the Pennsylvania Supreme Court vacated the death sentence of a convicted murderer because the deputy district attorney had cited the Bible in his closing arguments. The prosecutor, not the murderer, was severely admonished by the justices and a new sentencing was ordered. Later, the U.S. Supreme Court upheld the ruling.

Be assured these are not rare or isolated examples. It was Justice Sandra Day O'Connor, after all, who delivered the majority decision of the Court in the *Hudson v. Macmillan* decision, referring to "evolving standards of decency that mark the progress of a maturing society." What does this reflect about the High Court's own moral and ethical beliefs? In these words, which she incorporated from an earlier 1981 decision, Justice O'Connor betrayed the sentiments of the Supreme Court, that it is empowered to interpret law and justice beyond the purview of the Constitution. Too often, as *Forbes* columnist Thomas Sowell has said, the evolving standards of judges are actually "the Zeitgeist of the anointed imposed on an electorate which has rejected it." In effect, the justices held that they are free to go into uncharted ethical territory in determining how Americans should think and behave, even if that should mean violating certain "unalienable rights" of the citizens.

This is dangerous territory, but consider the body blows to law enforcement that have already taken place in this nation since the controversial *Miranda* decision of 1966. Obviously, we applaud a requirement that police officers give fair warnings and not exploit or otherwise coerce confessions from those being questioned. But the further judicial restrictions on police procedures have actually helped to erect a vast superstructure of limitations on law enforcement, impeding the apprehension, retention, and ultimate prosecution of criminals. Crime has reached epidemic proportions, much of it perpetrated by repeat offenders. Yet it is a fact that criminals with shrewd lawyers can be back on the streets within minutes of arrest while their victims may never recover from their losses. Although some changes are being made, the entire structure of the legal system is weighted for the criminal, not for the rights of law-abiding citizens to be safe in their homes and possessions.

Signs of Change

The situation sometimes seems hopeless, but there are signs of change on the horizon. Thanks in large measure to the actions of responsible conservative activists and Christian groups such as the American Center for Law and Justice, based on our CBN campus in Virginia Beach, we are beginning to see a movement back to common sense in the courts. Not because the courts have gotten smarter, but because our lawyers have gotten tougher, building rock-solid cases based on constitutional law and historic judicial precedent. Here is a sample of what I mean.

All across America, Christians have slumbered while groups such as the American Civil Liberties Union, American Atheists, and People for the American Way have been waging a vicious war on our traditional values and the free expression of our religious beliefs. Judges and lawyers, intimidated by the threats and strong-arm tactics of these groups, have repeatedly caved in to the pressure, and they have virtually stripped this nation of any visible evidence of faith or belief in God. But not everybody is taking it lying down.

Take Rita Warren, for example, who not only displays a nativity scene in public each year, but she does it in a conspicuous public place: on the steps of the U.S. Capitol. For twelve years now she has obtained a permit to display a life-size crèche with shepherds, wise men, the holy family, and the infant Jesus for the world to see. Despite the best efforts of the ACLU and the atheists, Mrs. Warren also plays recorded Christmas music, including "O Come All Ye Faithful" and "Joy to the World," and she displays a small sign that says, "Happy Hanukkah."

How does one woman prevail against the powerful forces aligned against her? She stands with her display at all times. Except for brief trips to the rest room, she is there; through rain and snow and cold and remarks both pro and con, she is there. Thus the crèche is considered a part of her right of free speech. "As long as she is there, this is regarded as her being on public property saying things," admits the legislative counselor for the ACLU. "In this case, those things happen to be about religion." Mrs. Warren is a living tribute to what one person can do.

But young people are getting involved too. In Tallahassee, Florida, for example, fifteen-year-old Jennifer Beach has filed suit against the county board, its superintendent, and the administration of Raa Middle School where she attends. The suit alleges that school authorities acted unlawfully, violating her right of free speech and free exercise of religion, when they stopped her from handing out copies of the Christian newspaper, *Issues and Answers*. Her attorneys were from the Liberty Counsel, a nonprofit, religious civil liberties education and defense organization founded in Orlando in 1990. The suit states that the rights of free speech are protected by the Constitution and the Bill of Rights, and students may not be discriminated against simply because their views are religious.

With a rousing standing ovation, the citizens of Bloomingdale, Michigan, applauded the school board's decision to appeal the ruling of U.S. District Judge Benjamin Gibson that a painting of Jesus be removed from a hallway of its high school. Of the 120 people who attended a public meeting to discuss the ruling, those who spoke were unanimous in urging the school board to continue the fight to keep the picture on the wall, which had been in the school for more than thirty years. No one spoke in support of the court's decision to remove it. "I am deeply saddened that we have lost this first battle with the ACLU," said Bloomingdale resident Barb Strong, "but we haven't lost the war."

Standing Up for Their Rights

In North Carolina, more than five hundred parents and local ministers came out to support the rights of students in the Iredell-Statesville School District to form student-led Bible clubs and to have a student-led prayer before football games and other sports events. Officials who had first demanded that such activities be stopped became conciliatory when confronted with recent Supreme Court rulings on these issues and with the mass of citizens who promised to resist any anti-religious policies they enacted.

In Westminster, Maryland, it is teachers who have joined together to protest the discrimination against Christian values in the public schools. As a move to counteract the unbalanced positions of the local teachers union, abetted by the National Education Association, they have formed the Christian Educators Association to provide a forum for teachers who support the belief that Judeo-Christian values are an essential part of American education. Teacher Bob Foster reported that the new group was formed because members believe Christianity has been "systematically removed from education and replaced with secular humanism."

The legislature of the state of South Carolina approved a motion to allow a moment of silent prayer at the beginning of the school day. Of the 124 members of the state house of representatives, 88 were official co-sponsors of the bill. The measure requires schools to set aside one minute at the beginning of each school day "to allow for voluntary silent prayer." But Steve Bates, the executive director of the South Carolina ACLU, vows his group, aided by dissenting Democrats, will defeat the bill when it comes before the state senate.

Josh Perry, president of the student council at Houston High School in Memphis, Tennessee, and editor of the school newspaper, did not ask for permission to speak his faith. At graduation ceremonies, he welcomed a crowd of more than a thousand, asked them to stand and recite the Pledge of Allegiance, and then surprised faculty and administrators by his remarks on the deterioration of morals in the schools, followed by an invitation to join him in prayer. The entire auditorium erupted in applause.

In his prayer, Perry said: "Father, as we start this graduation ceremony we call upon Your strength. The strength that built this nation, the strength that crushed communism in the former Soviet Union, and the strength that will guard our footsteps and be with our families and friends that we will soon leave behind." He then added, "Father, we realize that an intentional omittance and denial of Your almighty Word is the sole reason for the adverse changes of the last forty years. We beg now for Your forgiveness and humbly ask that You would re-establish America as the world's educational leader."

School Superintendent James Anderson did not call for any response to the student's prayer, but he sent word that no other school graduations should include prayers. Even though the Kirby High School graduation exercises were held in a local church auditorium, Class President Darlita Brooks was told she could not pray. Instead, in her remarks to the students, parents, and faculty, she said, "Always keep God first. Everything is possible through Him," which drew the applause of the crowd. Afterward one woman remarked on the irony of the situation. "Here we are in a church and we aren't allowed to pray. . . . Why do we have to submit to the 1 percent who don't want to pray?"

In Florence, Alabama, high school senior Drew Jamieson ignored the warnings of school officials and teachers not to pray because, he said, God should be involved in this important occasion. "I did not do it to bring focus upon myself as a religious student," he said, "but to stand for God." Originally, Jamieson was supposed to present the school flag and make a speech. But early in his remarks he began to pray; then, spontaneously, as the graduate was completing his own prayer, a group of students in the audience stood up and recited the Lord's Prayer. Strong protests came from the ACLU and school administration, threatening not only lawsuits but future penalties against students.

It was a similar scene in Princeton, Indiana, where the salutatorian's request for a moment of silence produced a spontaneous and emotional response as the crowd began reciting the Lord's Prayer. No one was sure who uttered the first words, but by the second phrase practically everyone in attendance joined in. At the conclusion of the prayer the crowd cheered and rose for a standing ovation, while the school board and administrators remained seated.

Graduates in nearby Oakland City, Indiana, were specifically forbidden from offering any sort of prayer at their ceremony, so when Kena Liniger stood up to read a poem, she explained that the poem was to take the place of the prayer she had originally planned. But when she finished the reading, she said, "I just want to thank God for getting us all here and for all the friendships we have had, and I just hope He keeps us all together," and the senior class jumped to its feet in another standing ovation.

Order in the Courts

In Louisville, Kentucky, attorney Vincent Heuser was whisked off to jail for reading his Bible in silence during the trial of an abortion protester. Two hours later, Judge Kevin Delahanty ordered Rowena Hegele jailed on the same charge: reading the Bible in a courtroom. The following day the two filed a petition with the circuit court to restrain Judge Delahanty from prohibiting silent reading of the Bible in the courtroom. The Constitution, they pointed out, guarantees the "free exercise" of religion, and the judge's actions were a violation of their rights. Now the onus is on Judge Delahanty to defend his actions against Heuser and Hegele.

In Newport Beach, California, Police Sergeant Richard T. Long brought charges against the ACLU of Southern California for violation of his civil rights when he was ejected from an ACLU-sponsored community seminar. During a session on police practices, Long, who was out of uniform, was singled out by the ACLU speakers, berated, and forced to leave the premises. After a long and costly lawsuit, lasting more than twelve years, Officer Long was finally awarded a $635,000 settlement against the ACLU.

In Washington state, CRISTA Ministries successfully defended the right of a subdivision, Intercristo, to screen and hire personnel based on religious preference. The ACLU claimed it was illegal for Intercristo to ask applicants seeking jobs with Christian organizations about their religious beliefs. But the courts disagreed, and both parties to the suit were required to sign documents recognizing that CRISTA and other Christian organizations may not only ask about religious beliefs but, in fact, make these matters of preference in hiring prospective employees.

In New Jersey, Richard Smith, a twenty-year employee of the state department of health, has filed a civil rights complaint in the district federal court, charging that he has been harassed, interrogated by superiors, and transferred because he opposes and has expressed resistance to New Jersey's condom distribution programs. The suit, filed by Communications Workers of America on Smith's behalf, names the state's health commissioner, Frances Dunston, and the assistant health commissioner for AIDS prevention, Douglas Morgan, and seeks an injunction against the health department, plus compensatory and punitive damages and lawyers' fees.

In Texas, again over the objections of the ACLU, inmates assigned to a Christian rehabilitation program in the Tarrant County jail have won the right to continue their programs using biblically based materials. The so-called God Pod came under fire when a Fort Worth attorney representing the ACLU learned of the objections of some inmates who were not included in the program. The inmates had contacted the American Jewish Congress and then the ACLU, who brought the original complaint. Chaplain Chris Athey, who administers the program, reports that since the publicity brought about by the ACLU actions, he has received calls from jails in New York, Chicago, and Denver, and a fax from a chaplain in Germany, all inquiring how they can launch Christ-centered programs in their facilities.

The Hammer

In chapter 1, I wrote of a telephone call from Jay Sekulow, general counsel of the American Center for Law and Justice, announcing a major victory. I get a lot of those calls these days because Jay keeps on winning cases. In the old days of the "flower children" they sang a song, "If I had a hammer, . . . I'd hammer out freedom all over the land." In my opinion, Jay, Executive Director Keith Fournier, and their brilliant associates are God's hammer ringing out freedom all over the land.

I founded the American Center for Law and Justice in 1990 to fulfill my heart cry over the sorry state of religious freedom in our land. Before then, believers had been terrorized by the American Civil Liberties Union, which had set as its mission the destruction, under the guise of "liberty," of every public expression of faith in America.

The ACLU was founded in 1920 by Roger Baldwin for the purpose of defending convicted Bolsheviks. At least three of the founding directors were influential in domestic or international communism. Baldwin wrote in 1935 that he wanted to make America a "workers state" (read that as *Communist*). For a time, during the so-called Red Scare when government was making it hot for Communists, the ACLU voted to ban known Communists from its governing board, but later that policy was rescinded.

Bolstered by incredible amounts of pro bono legal work from large law firms, and even larger contributions from socialists who have grown rich and fat on capitalism, the ACLU played a significant role in destroying American public affirmation of faith while opening this country up to an onslaught of pornography and crime. Former Attorney General Edwin Meese called the ACLU a "lobby for criminals." Predictably, participants in the smut industry have been among the organization's most generous contributors.

During the past three decades the ACLU has postured itself as the defender of free speech and freedom from religious oppression. It gained widespread support by seeming to support some fragile little atheist against the terror of Christian bullies. So our strategy at the American Center for Law and Justice was to unmask the ACLU for what it really is—an advocate of crime, pornography, atheism, and socialism—and to put the ACLU on the side of the government against the free speech rights of Christians and other believers.

This is precisely what Jay Sekulow and his brilliant associates have accomplished. They defended the right of a Messianic Jew to distribute literature in the Boston subway—and won overwhelmingly. They defended the right of Christians to pass out literature at Stone Mountain,

Georgia, and won by a unanimous decision of the Georgia Supreme Court. They defended Christians who wanted to pray in Houston, Texas, in an arbitrary "gospel-free bubble zone" and won a unanimous decision from the Texas Supreme Court.

They went to the U.S. Supreme Court to defend the right of the Long Island church, Lamb's Chapel, to show a family film by James Dobson at the local high school—and won unanimously before the highest court of the land.

They defended abortion protesters against prosecution under an ancient Civil War-vintage Ku Klux Klan act and won again, on a five-to-four vote of the U.S. Supreme Court.

In a mass mailing to fifteen thousand school districts all across America, they told the school officials and administrators that student-led prayer around the school flagpole is legal—and more than a million students turned out to pray at "See you at the flagpole" celebrations.

They advised schools that students have a right to voluntary prayer or expression of faith and threatened immediate action against any school that denies the First Amendment rights of students. In 1993, at least seven thousand high schools had student-initiated prayer at their graduation ceremonies.

The ACLU has fumed and fulminated, but they know they have been outflanked and outfought by the American Center for Law and Justice, which has not been defeated in a single case in two years.

For People of Goodwill

In an editorial in a Christian publication, Rob Gregory of Focus on the Family wrote these words that bear repeating:

There was a time when students at a school function would have comfortably and appropriately opened a dinner meeting with prayer, and not thought twice about it. There was a time as a nation when we didn't celebrate the little bones the Supreme Court threw our way in the area of religious freedom, but reveled in the greatest religious freedom in the world's history. There was a time when we came to moments of great importance—like high school graduation—and naturally thought of our dependence on God, regardless of whether or not we know Him personally. Today all of that is fodder of the odd and unusual.[13]

It's true the fight is not over, but at least on some issues it seems that the ACLU is not only defeated but deeply divided internally. The tide has turned. Now the American Center will not only be fighting in every federal judicial circuit for the rights of schoolchildren, it will soon begin employing the weapons of the feminists' sexual harassment suits in a new war to stop the incredible discrimination and harassment against Christians both in the public and private arena. Several illustrations are noted in the appendix.

The task to change our judicial system is enormous. The American Center is doing a fantastic job, but as a nation we must all work to establish a solid and broadening body of case law setting forth judicial precedents in every area of American liberty. There must be an expanding base of common sense and conservative reason in legal periodicals and journals.

Remembering that judges are usually appointed by the president or by governors and ratified by the Senate and the various legislatures, we must bring resources to bear on the electoral process to elect people of goodwill who believe in common sense.

With the wind of virtue, the strong will of the people, and the reassurance that our cause is just, we shall prevail. The wind is at our back, and the tide is turning.

6

The Fifth Column

*T*HE MONTH IS JULY. In a shabby house in Hoboken, New Jersey, three swarthy men speaking Farsi sit huddled with a fourth, a recently naturalized radical Islamic priest. The three are pyrotechnic experts and have just arrived from Teheran via Toronto from whence they traveled overland into the States. Their mission is specific. Create panic in New York City, America's financial capital. With them is a briefcase containing $1 million in crisp, new hundred-dollar bills and a shopping list of materials. The cleric quickly takes a thousand hundred-dollar bills and the list, kisses the men on both cheeks, and leaves. During the next week the living room of the old house begins to fill up with timers, mercury switches, blasting caps, containers, and assorted chemicals.

The three Iranians work tirelessly, scarcely eating or sleeping. At the end of the second week, they are ready. One after another, three nondescript Ford vans pull into the driveway, each taking aboard one Iranian, then loading up and heading toward one of the tunnel or bridge links between New Jersey and Manhattan.

Shortly after dark, each van takes its separate route slowly and methodically, making stops at six locations in Manhattan, eighteen stops in all, leaving off packages and unobtrusively taking one of three predetermined routes back to New Jersey. At 11:30 that night, right after the late-night television news and when most New Yorkers are already in bed, the fires begin. Within half an hour they are raging out of control. Soon it seems the whole city is ablaze.

Fire trucks from all five boroughs are alerted, then each is assigned one of the eighteen target areas. With sirens blaring and lights flashing, the firemen draw close to their assigned sectors, attach their giant fire hoses onto the fire hydrants, and begin pouring jets of water on the raging infernos.

Then, as if from nowhere, automobiles and vans marked with assorted press emblems pull up. The occupants don firemen's protective gear, then holding double-bladed fire axes firmly in their hands, they advance toward the firefighters.

Thinking they have come to help, the firefighters welcome these new allies in their fight to rescue Manhattan from the worst conflagration in history. But imagine their looks of horror as these reporters and newspeople head not for the fires, but the fire hydrants. With quick blows from their axes they sever the fire hoses and watch with satisfaction as the streams of water fall to a mere trickle and then stop completely.

The seasoned firefighters look at them in shock, then anger. Tears come to their eyes. "Can't you see Manhattan is being destroyed?" they yell above the roar of the flames. "Why in God's name did you do that? Can't you see that you have taken away the city's only hope?"

The newsmen reply with confidence, "We disagree with the idea of fighting fires with water. We have the word of many respected experts who say that gasoline is far better. And until you load your hoses with gasoline, you will fight no more fires as long as we are around."

The Meaning of the Parable

I used this very parable to introduce a speech to the annual Mid-Atlantic Regional Meeting of Radio-Television News Directors. I went on to explain, "The cities of our nation are on fire. Delinquency, drug addiction, and violence are epidemic. Families are falling apart. Huge numbers of children are being born out of wedlock. Our schools are crime-infested scandals. People of faith have the answers from the Bible that will put out the fires in our cities, but when we try to pour on the water of faith and morality, the liberal press ridicules our efforts and cuts our hoses. Then it sprays gasoline on the fire instead."

Scandalous as it may seem, this accusation is absolutely true. Virtually every effort of people of faith—whether Evangelical, Roman Catholic, or Orthodox Jew—to restore the moral climate of our nation has been ridiculed, denigrated, and opposed by the liberal press. The words "fundamentalist," "extremist," "intolerant," "narrow-minded," and "right-wing fanatic" come easily to mind. Not only do the liberals mount a press attack against morality, they applaud legal, educational, or religious concepts that destroy lives, families, and cities.

Who are those who dominate the media and what do they believe? According to the famous 1981 Lichter-Rothman survey, they are mainly white (95 percent), male (79 percent), college-educated (93 percent), and considering some incomes top $3 million a year, very well paid. Four out of five have been raised in relatively affluent business or professional homes.[1]

Some 50 percent list their religion as none, and 86 percent never go to church. Compare that to 94 percent of the general population of the United States who have some form of religious faith and the 42 percent who attend church each week.

At least 44 percent of the media in America describe their views as "left of center." And 94 percent voted for Lyndon Johnson, 87 percent for Hubert Humphrey, and 81 percent for George McGovern and Jimmy Carter. Only 17 percent of reporters and editors in a 1985 Los Angeles Times poll described themselves as "conservatives"; 55 percent as "liberal." In a 1988 survey commissioned by the American Society of Newspaper Editors of twelve hundred reporters at seventy-two newspapers, 62 percent of the respondents said that they were "liberal" or "Democrat."

On social issues as well as religion, the media elite in no way reflect the mainstream population of America: 90 percent of the media favor abortion rights, 97 percent think that the government should not regulate sex, only 25 percent think homosexuality is wrong, 45 percent "strongly disagree" that there is anything "wrong" with sodomy, 85 percent would permit homosexuals to teach in public schools, 54 percent see nothing wrong with adultery, 80 percent want strong affirmative action (presumably including job quotas to help blacks), and 81 percent feel that environmental problems are serious.

Many current and former members of the press have not only made campaign contributions but have actually worked for key liberal Democrats. For example, according to the Media Research Center, David Burke, president of CBS News, was chief of staff for Senator Ted Kennedy. Tom Donilon, CBS, worked for Joe Biden's 1988 presidential campaign. Richard Dougherty, NBC, worked on the 1972 McGovern campaign. Dotty Lynch, CBS, was a pollster for Gary Hart's 1988 campaign for the presidency. Walter Shapiro, *Time*, was a speechwriter for Jimmy Carter.

Former Reagan/Bush speechwriter Peggy Noonan, in her book, *What I Saw at the Revolution*, mentioned the cheers in the CBS election central when Reagan was trailing Carter and the hushed, deadly silence when he won. The press overall voted 68 percent for Walter Mondale over Reagan in 1984, the year the American people gave Ronald Reagan one of the biggest electoral college landslides in history.

And the media view on the Cold War years tilted not just toward Democrats but toward Marxism. Here is what they said:[2]

Despite what many Americans think, most Soviets do not yearn for capitalism or western-style democracy.

Dan Rather, "CBS Evening News," 17 June 1987

Many Soviets viewing the current chaos and nationalist unrest under Gorbachev look back almost longingly to the brutal days under Stalin.

Mike Wallace, "60 Minutes," 11 February 1990

Yeah, one thing I don't like is he's [Yeltsin] shut down *Pravda*. Not that I'm any big fan of *Pravda*, but I think that is flirting with censorship.

Eleanor Clift, *Newsweek*, on the McLaughlin Group, 24 August 1991

Media Lockstep

It is obvious, once the media leaders take a line, virtually everyone walks in lockstep. Usually the *New York Times* sets the pace, then the *Washington Post,* then CBS and the other networks, then the wire services. They become a formidable phalanx of liberal views. But now, more and more, the most trusted major television news source is CNN.

According to an excellent summary in the June 21, 1993, issue of *National Review,* "Such unconscious bias would not be a concern in a newsroom marked by a diversity of opinion, because conservatives would tend to check the prejudices of liberals and vice versa. When, however, the media elite is monolithically liberal, then journalists in the newsroom reinforce rather than correct each other's biases. *They eventually come to confuse their opinions with external reality*" (emphasis has been added).

A March 31, 1993, story in the *Los Angeles Times* sets out the incredible decline in the public's trust of the media. For the past eight years, polling by the Gallup Organization has revealed a solid 44 to 50 percent of the American people who do not believe the media get their facts straight. British historian Paul Johnson was quoted by the *Times* as saying, "The general view of the media is almost entirely negative: It is associated with ignorance, lies, malicious invention and scurrility. *Most people despise the media*" (emphasis added). Johnson was talking about the British press, but the American press generates much the same reaction.

Ed Turner, executive vice-president of CNN, told the *Los Angeles Times* two weeks after Johnson's remarks were published, "[Thirty-five years ago] we were then highly regarded. We were looked up to. We were subjects of admiration, sometimes even awe. *Now we are often despised*" (emphasis added).[3]

The *Times* printed a poll of its own showing that respondents have become more disenchanted with the news media than ever before. Principal reasons cited were (1) giving more coverage to stories that support their point of view, (2) too much emphasis on negative news, (3) revealing too much about the private lives of public people,

(4) too concerned about getting a good story and "they don't worry very much about hurting people."

Van Gordon Sauter, former president of CBS News, says the news media have become "a tremendous advocacy" group. "Look at *Newsweek* magazine. Look at *Time* magazine. The subjectivity that just runs through them I find absolutely stunning. If you look at the *New York Times*, the *Boston Globe*, the *Washington Post* . . . the liberalism of these papers manifests itself in their news columns, not just on their editorial pages."

Could it be that the public, having been victimized by a left-wing press so totally out of sync with its ethics, its morality, its politics, and its religion, is finally saying enough? Or will the liberal press correct itself without its own version of Watergate? Whatever the outcome, the tide has begun to turn against the liberal media of America.

An Epidemic of Violence

Even worse than the news side of the media, the entertainment side of the media—music videos, live concerts, daytime television and sitcoms, and motion pictures—has reveled (maybe a better word is wallowed) in profanity, cruelty, violence, and every form of illicit sexuality. And along with this nonstop diet of smut and violence comes repeated characterization of Christians as narrow-minded, intolerant, and depraved psychopaths.

Broadcaster Ted Turner's widely publicized claim before a House subcommittee on June 25, 1993, that television is responsible for the epidemic of violence in this country brought a crescendo of responses from both the Right and the Left. The CNN chairman said that television executives who air violent programs are "guilty of murder as far as I can see." Turner accepted his share of blame for the violent fare offered by his own stations. But *U.S. News & World Report* reminded its readers that Turner's way of competing with network Super Bowl programming in January was with "a day of unnecessary roughness, personal fouls and sudden death," highlighting a full day of Chuck Norris, Clint Eastwood, and Jean-Claude Van Damme films. The magazine labeled Turner a hypocrite.

U.S. News & World Report also reported that "fully 96 percent of the 70,000 people who recently responded to a write-in survey by *USA Weekend* said Hollywood executives glorify violence and an equal number said they had switched off a show before it ended because of its violence."[4] *Forbes* magazine reported on a 1992 survey from *USA Weekend* in which the "overwhelming majority" of those polled agreed with the statement: "Hollywood no longer reflects—or even respects—the values of most American families."[5]

Evidence of the public's frustration with the fare being offered by Hollywood can be seen in the kinds of viewing choices people make. It is also reflected by the fact that box-office revenues continue to fall to the point that theater attendance today is less than 25 percent of what it was in 1946. A recent study by California-based Paul Kagan Associates shows that between 1984 and 1991 R-rated films earned on average $11 million less per film than PG films. PG films were found to be three times more likely than R films to gross more than $100 million.[6]

There are many conspicuous examples of the public's increasing aversion to the garbage spewing out of Hollywood. Sex-singer Madonna's highly publicized, highly touted movie, *Body of Evidence*, grossed just $14 million, which by Hollywood standards made it a classic flop. That put it in company with Woody Allen's *Husbands and Wives* and the film *Henry and June*, about the novelist Henry Miller's sex life, as box-office disasters. At the same time, the lovable family movie, *Home Alone*, featuring child star Macaulay Culkin, grossed more than $280 million in the U.S. market, and *Home Alone II*, the sequel, earned $171 million—as *Forbes* magazine reported, nine times what the average R-rated film can expect to make—and nine times more likely to appeal to today's movie viewers. But even though the facts make it perfectly clear, some Hollywood producers and writers keep turning out filth in the name of "art" and for the sake of their destructive liberal ideals.

Some of the other films the public loved were Disney Studios' *Aladdin*, which earned more than $195 million in domestic sales, *Beauty and the Beast* at $145 million, and *Sister Act*, at $140 million. These were all clean, wholesome family movies. It was as if the audiences were saying thank you to the producers of movies where, as one writer put it, "The audience hadn't been forced to fidget and squirm through yet another scene of gratuitous sex or violence."

An Underground Agenda

The nature of the stealth campaign being waged against traditional values in this country is much like others we have seen in other times and places. When the city of Madrid was being attacked in 1936 during the Spanish Civil War, military advisers told the Nationalist commander, General Emilio Mola, that his four columns of infantry would never be able to rout the entrenched Loyalist forces in the capital. But Mola told them not to worry; he already had a "fifth column" in the city—by which he meant the hundreds of supporters working underground to bring down the government from within and cripple the opposition.

In his book, *The Fifth Column in America,* author Harold Lavine used the same term to describe the men and women in our own government (and in other places of influence) working covertly to further the agenda of socialism and Marxism. Even though Lavine's book provoked a flurry of reaction, it did nothing to rid the government, the universities, or the media of left-wing influences.[7] In fact, thanks in large measure to the 1954 Joseph McCarthy hearings, it may only have strengthened the resolve of the left-wing extremists within the system.

In any event, today that fifth column is stronger than ever. Only today it is no longer a mere column; it is an army working at cross-purposes with the traditional goals and moral values of the American people. With an even greater influence than the government are those within the print and electronic media, in radio and television broadcasting, the movies, and in the field of education, whose central purpose is to change the entire context and structure of American culture and to bring about a permissive, liberated, socialist society—a "new order of the ages."

Whether it is in television, films, or mainstream newspapers and magazines, the media have been essential to the Left's campaign to manipulate public opinion and assault the moral values of this nation. For more than forty years the popular media—especially network television and those newspapers and magazines owned and operated by people who support the goals of the Left—have been the fundamental agents of social change in the United States.

More than educational decline, more than the crises of rising poverty and welfare dependence, and more than any other celebrated event, the media have unparalleled influence upon the public welfare of this entire nation by controlling what people see, what they think, and how they feel about themselves. Even in their own literature there is evidence of their guilt about their role in conducting massive campaigns of disinformation. One such campaign is discussed in detail by pollster Barry Sussman in his book, *What Americans Really Think*.[8] Others have been documented in the book *Feeding Frenzy*, by University of Virginia Professor Larry Sabato, dealing with the philosophies and practices of attack journalism.[9]

For all their hypocrisy, howling at everyone else from government to the church about what's going wrong in America, the media clearly must share the blame for the moral decline of this society. The fact that they either totally ignore or belittle important initiatives from the traditional mainstream—which they call "the right wing"—callously distorting and misinterpreting facts to suit their own liberal perspectives, is a clear indication of their prejudicial stance.

In 1990, as the current turn of events was taking shape, William F. Buckley wrote in the *National Review*:

> Whatever else is responsible for the breakup of the family, it is inescapably the case that the official prejudice against religion in education has played a large, perhaps even a decisive role. The Playboy Philosophy, explicitly regnant in the Sixties, may have appeal to the younger generation as the key to hedonism, but hedonism is not the key to happiness, and wretchedness that blights so many families—white certainly, but predominantly black—has much to do with the nakedness of the public square, in which for

generations there were men and women who spoke the language of duty and morality, of loyalty and obligation.[10]

If the American people could simply look objectively at what has come out of the secular media in the past ten years they would be horrified. The cover story in the May 1993 *Atlantic Monthly* magazine was a twenty-page article on the disaster associated with the breakdown of traditional family values. In that major feature, entitled "Dan Quayle Was Right," the author showed how the family is being torn to pieces by the liberal agenda—just as the former vice-president said in his now-famous battle over the "Murphy Brown" television show.

But who can forget the way he was pilloried by the media? Dozens of times on network television, Murphy Brown was portrayed as a heroine, standing up for the dignity of the single mother against right-wing oppressors. Dan Quayle was the arch-villain, the butt of countless cruel jokes. The *Atlantic* article helps to right that wrong, somewhat belatedly. But the truth is that the media have an agenda to bring down the moral foundations of this nation. The Dan Quayle debate was just one stop on that disastrous ride.

The Naked Square

With ever greater zeal over the past three decades, the Left has continued its harangue on the separation of church and state as justification for eliminating religious issues from public view. Oblivious to the irrelevance of these arguments, and at the same time refusing to acknowledge that no document of state, let alone the Constitution, has ever proposed such a concept, those on the Left have tried to convince the American people that our founding documents warned of the dangers of mixing politics and religion. They have thus misled millions and worked against the public interest by damaging the commitment to ethics and moral values that come only through religious belief.

This deceptive trend was defined by Richard John Neuhaus in his book, *The Naked Public Square*, which analyzed the machinations of the Left in attempting to strip American culture of its forum for moral debate. Still, the debate continues.

Addressing these issues, William F. Buckley says that the church-state clause in the First Amendment has been used as an instrument of enforced secularization. But he adds:

> The time has come, for those who deplore present trends and wish to resist them, to invoke their knowledge of history sufficiently to proclaim that fanatical interpretations of the separation clause of the First Amendment are unrelated to protecting the public from the illusory threat of an established religion. And to go further, to note that the effect of the fanatical interpretation of the separation clause has been to insulate two generations of urban youth from exposure to an ethos whose advocates would have been celebrated as prophetic benefactors of the lower class, if only what they spoke hadn't been spoken under the aegis of the Bible. Conservatives should be adamant about the need for the reappearance of Judeo-Christianity in the public square.[11]

One of the best perspectives on the anti-America agenda of the Left comes from two Berkeley radicals who were at the center of the civil disobedience movement throughout the 1960s and 1970s. Peter Collier and David Horowitz were editors of the radical magazine *Ramparts* and supporters of the Black Panthers, Students for a Democratic Society, the drug culture, and many of the underground movements of the time. Somewhere along the way, Collier and Horowitz woke up to the implications of what they were actually doing, and that began a process of turning away toward a more centrist, common-sense perspective.

In their riveting book, *Destructive Generation*, they write that the sixties was a time when "the 'System'—that collection of values that provide guidelines for societies as well as individuals—was assaulted and mauled."[12] Their faith in the politics of dissent began to fail them as they realized that the flowers they had planted had suddenly turned ugly and malignant. "The decade ended," they wrote, "with a big bang that made society into a collection of splinter groups, special interest organizations and newly minted 'minorities,' whose only common belief was that America was guilty and untrustworthy."

In the conclusion of the book, Collier and Horowitz say that they are still in a period of transition—in "the middle of the journey." But what they now believe is "that the radical future is an illusion and that the American present is worth defending; and that we were part of a destructive generation whose work is not over yet." Then they add these stirring words:

> In the middle of the journey, we feel none of the reassuring certitude we felt at the beginning. Then, defeats were merely momentary setbacks, preludes to the final victory; then, time seemed clearly to be on our side. It is difficult now not to feel almost the exact opposite—that the losses America suffers in the world may be permanent; that the clock is running on democracy and freedom.[13]

As you might imagine, such words brought a barrage of protest from the Left. Not because the authors' words were untrue, but because two of their own had broken confidence with "the movement." When Collier and Horowitz came on our show, they said that they have been repeatedly vilified by the media, by academics and intellectuals in the major universities, by many of the stalwarts of the Democratic party, and even by their own friends. But now that they have come face to face with the implications of the radical agenda of the Left and have seen how it cripples those who are touched by it—and how it works like a destructive fifth column from within the system—they are committed to telling the truth as they know it, whatever the implications may be.

What I find especially moving in their story is the honesty and integrity of these two men. I can understand how they fell into the lure of rebellion and unrestrained freedoms in the sixties. Yet not many of their peers from that era have recovered from the fatal attraction. The fact that two have come forth to tell the truth is not only remarkable but also a rare and valuable insight into the thinking of the Left.

In the conclusion to the book, the authors say for all to hear that this fifth column of the Radical Left is still in our midst, more powerful than ever, and still working for much the same goals. They say:

> The resilience of the Left is primarily a result of the fact that it has built its political religion on liberal precepts; its luminous promise—equality, fraternity, and social justice—is in fact preeminently the promise of the progressive Idea. If the blood-stained reality of the Left is indefensible within the framework provided by liberal principle, its ideals nonetheless seem beyond challenge.[14]

At least its advocates will not tolerate any challenge, and those who speak up, as these authors would attest, are sure to be maligned, ridiculed, and discredited. Though they have an enormous arsenal, the principal weapon of the Left has always been invective.

A War of Words

I know what it means to be attacked by the media. I spoke in Los Angeles recently to the annual convention of the National Religious Broadcasters about the liberal assault on our values. I said that we must mobilize prayer and community support in defense of the values we hold. The next day an article in the *Los Angeles Times* reflected rather accurately what I had said, but the rewrite by the Associated Press, by someone who had not attended the convention, editorialized the story to suit the rewriter's own prejudices.

When the AP story ran nationally, it said that Pat Robertson called on the religious broadcasters to use their stations to "wage war in defense of family values," which, the story added, "*fundamentalists* generally define as being anti-homosexual and anti-abortion"—*fundamentalist* being a code word in the press for Islamic terrorist.

Of course, that was not what I said, nor was it even what was implied. Furthermore, no sincere Christian is about to suggest that Christians are interested in a "holy war." I immediately wrote my friend Lou Boccardi, president of the Associated Press, and told him that never in my life had I considered family values to be anti-abortion or anti-homosexual. "What they are," I said, "is the love of a man for his wife, the love of a wife for her husband, the nurture and care of children, and a stable home in a stable society." That's what I was talking about in my speech.

But the AP rewriter didn't really care what I had said or what I meant. I can only assume that the anonymous writer believed that evangelical Christians don't care for the poor, or for children, or for families. In his mind, Evangelicals are a narrow-minded group who are against abortion, against women's rights, and against gays. He held the liberal viewpoint and was using the nation's major wire service as a tool to deliver it, not presented as an editorial, but as hard news.

If that seems extreme, read what went out on the Associated Press wire from Chicago writer Sharon Cohen on May 17, 1993:

> In the quiet of middle America, the faithful of Operation Rescue protest and picket abortion clinics.
> In the tumult of India, half a world away, hundreds of Muslims and Hindus die during a week of riots when a sacred mosque is destroyed.
> Two news events, one common bond: Both are tied to fundamentalism, one of the world's fastest growing religious movements.[15]

Now you have it. In the eyes of the Associated Press, American Christianity, which springs from the Protestant Reformation, is fundamentalist. And Christian Fundamentalists, radical Muslims, Hindu extremists, and fanatical Zionists are all the same—bloodthirsty lunatics. The AP writer spouted the rhetoric that a trained observer could immediately identify as a derivative of the radical, feminist, homosexual agenda. Throughout the story, fed to every major newspaper in America, the news seethes with the rhetoric of the Radical Left, specifically comparing Evangelicals and other members of the Christian Coalition to Iranian mothers who sent their twelve-year-olds "to become human land-mines" for Ayatollah Ruhollah Khomeini back during Iran's seven-year war with Iraq.

Taking News Seriously

I have seen this kind of prejudice masquerading as news on many other occasions. When the vote was coming up before Congress on whether to sustain the ban on homosexuals in the military, I told viewers of "The 700 Club" that they ought to call their congressmen and express their point of view. I did not tell them how to vote, but I gave them the telephone number and said to let the people in Washington know how they felt. That day the Capitol switchboard was swamped with more than 430,000 calls. It was the largest number of calls they had ever received. Those calling were overwhelmingly in favor of keeping the ban.

The *Washington Post* began to look into what was happening, and published a front-page story about it. The *Post* said that it had learned that "televangelist" Pat Robertson had asked his "followers" (most television talk show hosts have viewers—in *Post*-speak I have "followers") to call in, and this explained in part the avalanche of calls. In the story, the reporter said that these "followers" of Pat Robertson and Jerry Falwell are "poor, uneducated, and easy to command."

That was one of the most arrogant, prejudicial, and bigoted statements I had ever read. Even people at the *Post* who disagree with us philosophically had to admit that the statement was totally unprofessional. But rather than fire off an angry letter to the *Post*, I simply showed the story on the air and told our audience, "They're talking about you, folks." We put up the address of the *Post*, and for the next three to four days it was inundated with letters and faxes and telephone calls from people who were furious.

What the editors found was that these people did not fit the stereotype they have imagined. Evangelicals and "Fundamentalists" are a cross-section of America. They include doctors, lawyers, and people in business; they are homemakers, teachers, nurses, laborers, store managers, truck drivers, and people in every other line of work. Some of the people who wrote the *Post* had master's degrees and incomes well over $50,000. They said, "We have had enough of this!"

The *Washington Post* did a short followup. The managing editor, Robert G. Kaiser, said in print, "We really screwed up." He further admitted the offending statement was not supported by any basis of fact, because the *Post* has no research to indicate that the statements made by the writer were accurate. But the writer of this front-page story, Michael Weisskopf, refused to back down from his liberal bias. "I try not to have to attribute every point in the story if it appears to be universally accepted. You don't have to say, 'It's hot out, according to the weatherman.'" The story passed through several editors before reaching print. Not one of them questioned that statement.

These two examples zero in on one clear fact: There is unbelievable arrogance in the newsrooms of America. Journalists feel that anybody who does not share their liberal point of view must be narrow-minded, poor, uneducated, and sheeplike. In the 1930s, African-Americans in the South were classified by bigots as "niggers," not worthy of respect; today it is evangelical Christians who are considered by the liberal media as "niggers" and not worthy of respect. Despite their protestations to the contrary, such blatant prejudice makes the liberal media truly the most bigoted group in American society today.

The Associated Press did a story in early 1993 that identified me as a "Religious Right activist." They and other members of the press continually try to paint me as some hard-line *fundamentalist* storm trooper because that fits their stereotype. If they had even bothered to look, they would have discovered that I used to be a staunch member of the Democratic party. I was once a civil rights activist in the ghettos of New York City and even headed Adlai Stevenson's 1956 presidential campaign on Staten Island. Because today I oppose big, wasteful government, they claim I lack compassion for the poor. A closer look would reveal that my family and I once moved to Bedford-Stuyvesant, one of the worst sections of New York City, to work with the poorest people there. But if the media's aim is to stigmatize and marginalize what Christians are saying, then they leave out all the facts that don't fit the negative stereotype.

The Spiritual Agenda of the Left

It is important for people to recognize that those who are working for the dissolution of our society have a spiritual agenda. They are not merely attempting to dismantle the historic cultural values of this nation and move us toward a homogenized world. They also want to destroy Christianity and Bible-based religion. It is a clear part of their agenda, and they have already moved a long way in that direction. The Christian Coalition is one of the few groups that is both effective in the political sphere and at the same time knowledgeable about the philosophical bases of our freedom. Its field reports demonstrate the degree to which the Left is on an ideological manhunt to discredit and discomfit Christians in political office. So the anti-Christian media want to discredit them.

I was visiting with a potential candidate for the presidential nomination in 1980 and asked him his view of secular humanism. He didn't even know what the term meant. He had to ask me to define it for him. Until people come to grips with the philosophical and contextual underpinnings of what is taking place in our culture, they will not have a chance of bringing about the kinds of positive change and reform we must have.

In the past couple of administrations there was no clear-cut enunciation of the potential danger from the Left to our individual freedoms. Frequently, I suspect, they were just putting legislative Band-Aids on social problems, trying to handle one little skirmish at a time. But they were glossing over the greater war that was going on all around them.

If you look back at the campaign that brought Bill Clinton to the White House, starting in the spring of 1992 and all the way to the election, the CBS Evening News hammered day after day about the bad news of the economy. "The Money Crunch" they called it. Then, within a few weeks of Clinton's election, on November 30, 1992, the *New York Times* ran a front-page story with the headline, "Is the Clinton Expansion Here?" What nonsense. How could a newly elected candidate not yet in office have any effect on an economy influenced by events that took place months before?

What we were seeing was the delayed effect of the loosening of credit by the Federal Reserve Board and the natural effect of economic policies still in place from the Bush administration. But the media were dying to give the credit to their chosen leader. Robert Lichter and

Stanley Rothman are currently doing an in-depth analysis of media bias in the coverage of the 1992 elections, and their findings should be very instructive. But whatever they find, it is perfectly clear that the media selected the economy as the number-one issue, black-jacked the Bush campaign into dropping the family-values issue, and then proceeded with their drumbeat of bad news to convince voters that Bush had fouled up the major issue—"It's the economy, stupid!" To say this played into Bill Clinton and James Carville's hands would be the understatement of the age.

Selective Hearing

A few months ago, a reporter came up to me in Pittsburgh and said, "You always seem so nice; I don't understand why you were so hard in your convention speech to the Republicans in Houston."

I said, "What do you mean?" She said, "Your speech was so full of anger."

I said, "Did you hear it?" She hesitated, then said no. I said, "Have you read it, then?" Again, she said no. So I asked, "Then how did you know I was so hard?" She said, "I read about it in the newspaper." And what had she read? Pat Robertson was a hatemonger and had given an anti-homosexual speech.

Early in 1993, after the debris of the elections had been cleared away, the leadership of the Republican party was looking at various candidates to head the Republican National Committee. One of them was my friend, John Ashcroft, a very distinguished man who previously had not only headed the nation's attorneys general but the nation's governors as well. Imagine how shocked I was to read in *Business Week* that Ashcroft had delivered "a blistering anti-homosexual speech" at the Houston Convention. I heard that speech. He didn't even mention homosexuals. He didn't mention anything at all about sexual orientation. He did talk about families and children. But the liberal media has become so warped that to talk about healthy families is to be anti-homosexual. A talk about morality and families and creating an environment where families can flourish is translated by these people as a "blistering homosexual speech" with no explanation of the spin they are putting on the news.

Then there are the closet homosexuals who hide behind the cover of respected newspapers. A couple of years ago, a columnist joined our local paper and began vicious, almost irrational, attacks against me. He railed against everything I stood for. I could never figure out why he was so angry until a member of my staff obtained the listing of his name along with members of the local chapter of Queer Nation.

Why won't he come out and say, "I'm a homosexual, and I don't like anyone who thinks homosexuality is sin"? Instead, he attacks me frequently on unspecified grounds. I think it is basically unfair for people who are Marxists or socialists or feminists or homosexuals or lesbians to pretend they are objective journalists so they can use the cover of their trade to assassinate the character of people who disagree with their social, religious, or political views. But it happens all the time, and it is one of the reasons that the media are losing credibility so rapidly these days.

The Media Turns

This book is primarily about the turning tide and not about how bad liberalism is. I would be remiss not to point out that, from my perspective, the media's attitude is beginning to turn. I suspect it may be that their disgust and dismay at Bill Clinton is causing thoughtful journalists to explore other political options, particularly traditional, conservative ones. I also feel that journalists who are constantly gathering facts from the world around us see the tragedy of broken homes, out-of-wedlock babies, an ethical jungle, and some of the same failures of liberalism overseas that I pointed out in the first chapter of this book. Not all journalists have made the switch, mind you, but some of the most thoughtful ones appear to be looking our way.

Nothing gets the respect of journalists faster than victories by an unlikely underdog. When Christians who have been either ignored or stigmatized begin to play a major role in elections, the leading-edge journalists want to know why. That is why I was asked to attend a very lovely and very cordial luncheon with the senior editorial staff of the *New York Times*. They were interested in evangelism in Russia, church beliefs in America, my personal plans, and how I perceived the Republican party and Ross Perot. They truly wanted to understand why it is an insult to mislabel a religious leader or to mischaracterize Evangelicals. In short, the *Times*, an extremely liberal paper but considered America's finest, is sincerely trying to report the news fairly.

The fact that evangelical Christians now number more than fifty million, and other conservative or pro-family Christians can add at least twenty million more, makes it clear that the press coverage of this numerically significant bloc in our society has been woefully inadequate. Larry Barrett, the senior political writer for *Time* magazine, penned a splendid article for the prestigious *Columbia Journalism Review* entitled, "The Religious Right and the Pagan Press." In it Barrett made these insightful comments in the July-August 1993 issue:

> Because much of the movement's rhetoric and many specific goals strike us as extreme, we overlook instances in which popular sentiment, measured by our own polls, agrees with the conservative view. . . . Among the "media elite," the study found exactly zero practitioners professing to be fundamentalist, born again, or evangelical. . . . It is an easy call to recognize that we need a broad sensitivity check . . . whatever we think of its agenda, we must get ourselves to church, if only as observers.[16]

But there is more. The Rush Limbaugh phenomenon has seized everyone's attention. To think that a conservative radio talk show host speaks to more people every day than all those who subscribe to *Newsweek* and *Time* combined is another dose of reality for all the liberal media out there.

Working Inside the System

That's still not all. My "700 Club" television program has a combined weekly audience of about seven million viewers. Our reporters are insightful, thorough, and balanced. They are on the spot with cameras and microphones at the same national events as everyone else. When a fair-minded and accurate television organization like CBN News is giving a story careful coverage, complete with video footage, it makes it very difficult for someone else to try to distort the truth. In addition to television, our United States Media Corporation has launched *Standard News*, which has assembled a superb group of broadcast journalists whose Washington News Desk is as good as there is.

Our intermediate goal is two thousand radio stations taking the audio news and two thousand radio and television stations and weekly newspapers taking the printed news. I believe that the new conservative mood in the country is demanding an alternative national news wire to compete with the Associated Press. We expect to become that alternative.

We are finding dozens of superb reporters to work for us who are tired of trying to "cook the news" to please the politically correct liberal biases of their peers or their bosses. There are hundreds, if not thousands, of fine owners of television and radio stations and newspapers who are not interested in slanted propaganda, but who would jump at the chance to receive honest, unbiased, professionally presented news at a reasonable price.

I recently read reports of a study showing the tremendous decline in the influence of daily newspapers—the most liberal segment of the news media. Among respondents under age thirty-five, only 30 percent had read any part of a newspaper, including the sports section and the comics, the day before. Only about 50 percent watched one of the evening news shows.

I believe that the tremendous illiteracy that has come to America—because of the failure of schools to teach children how to read—will have an increasingly devastating impact on the print media, just as the immediacy of live coverage of events by CNN is making it increasingly difficult for *Time, Newsweek,* and *U.S. News & World Report* to compete and stay in business.

Initially conservatives will cheer this trend because their enemies in the news media will have a continuously shrinking platform from which to manipulate the thinking of the public. However, in the long run, the trend will be devastating because it means that the young will be enfranchised to vote but increasingly without a sound basis for making political judgment. Heaven help us if Arsenio Hall and MTV become the new arbiters of political expression among a major segment of our nation.

Trying to Make a Difference in Hollywood

Chuck Norris was featured on "The 700 Club" recently because he is doing something we believe is very important. His 1993 movie, *Sidekicks*, is a family film about a boy with asthma who daydreams about helping Chuck Norris out of all kinds of tough situations. He daydreams that he is the hero who arrives just in the nick of time to save Chuck's life. Before it is over, he actually gets to be Chuck's sidekick, and they become good friends. It is an action-adventure film, but it is wholesome and, most of all, there is a lot of warm, good humor. That's what people are looking for.

Chuck has decided he wants to make a difference in the lives of children, and he told Ben Kinchlow, my co-host, that he has set up five demonstration projects with about a hundred students in each. Some of these are in some of the toughest inner-city schools, but Chuck's kids are taught self-respect, respect for others, and important principles of discipline and responsibility. It changes their lives.

He wasn't sure the idea would work at first, but when he came back to visit some of the schools after the programs had been going for a few months, he was shocked at what he discovered. Some of these schools had armed guards outside the gates and chains on the fences. In the gym where he spoke to the kids, there were lots of rude, loud, disrespectful young hoodlums. Things were different with the kids in the Sidekicks program. These young people were respectful and quiet and demonstrated incredible poise. Chuck was thrilled to see that the program was working. It was making a visible difference.

Today that program is one of many reaching out to the inner city and touching the lives of kids who desperately need something to believe in. This is an example of a man who made a fortune in violent movies but who wants to give something back to the people who supported him. I think programs like this, programs that take a serious interest in helping young people discover the values of respect and decency, are very important, and we want to encourage them.

What we have learned from Michael Medved, author of the incredible book, *Hollywood vs. America*, is that the little clique of producers and writers in Hollywood who come up with so many of the major films think they have to make "a statement" and that they are somehow cowardly if they are not making statements that shock society and bring down the taboos against bizarre sexuality and overt violence. So now, when you begin to see people turning away from sex and violence, and the American people saying, "We don't want any more of this," Hollywood would do well to notice.[17] When audiences begin to turn away from this violent material and the grossly sensual stuff on television, preferring to watch something more wholesome, it is a major trend.

Unfortunately, the average person in America still doesn't have the slightest idea what secular humanism is all about. For many people, secular humanism is confused with human goodness or humanitarianism. They do not realize the secular humanists are atheists with a well-defined and dangerous agenda. The essential core of this liberal philosophy is a hatred of God and religion. Its adherents also hate our Western civilization, which is based on Christianity, and they want to tear it down. They believe that man, the noble savage who lives within, is being smothered by social conventions and the hypocrisy of modern civilization. They want to liberate mankind from our Western values, and tragically they are succeeding.

I watched an environmental special on television not long ago, the purpose of which was to exalt a tribe of primitive Indians as if they were the ultimate example of virtue and wisdom. The whole idea of this kind of humanistic thinking is preposterous. Is this what rational people believe? Do they want to live like jungle dwellers? Is that what mankind has been aspiring to for the past six thousand years?

The common-sense reaction would be to see these primitive tribes in South America, the Philippines, and New Guinea and recognize what we all might be like in our natural state—naked, unlettered primitives. These tribes are not ahead of anybody; they are centuries behind. They are in an arrested state of social development. They are not less valuable as human beings because of that, but they offer scant wisdom or learning or philosophical vision that can be instructive to a culture that can feed the entire population of the earth in a single harvest and send spacecraft to the moon.

To see primitive tribes living on roots, berries, and monkey meat should show us how remarkable the achievements of Western civilization truly are—we have achieved a brilliant tradition of liberty, individual freedoms, and ordered democracy. We should reflect on all the incredible medical advances, communications systems, highways, and industrial progress science has achieved for us and how our culture has helped to reshape the destiny of man, offering people of every race and tribe a standard of living beyond anything men could have dreamed just a few years ago. This is the logical response.

Except for our crimes, our wars, and our frantic pace of life, what we have is superior to the ways of primitive peoples. Of course, thinking people can learn from anyone, but liberal philosophers and half-baked intellectuals want to convince us that Western civilization is worthless and exploitative and that the savages of the jungle are the giants of human progress. How can any responsible people buy into such nonsense? I confess, there is much to be said for a simple, pastoral existence— that's why we enjoy taking vacations to the mountains or the beach. But which life do you think people would prefer: freedom in an enlightened Christian civilization or the suffering of subsistence living and superstition in a jungle? *You choose*.

Wasting a Precious Resource

In an essay on the growing secularization of society, author, theologian, and lecturer Carl F. H. Henry expressed his concern that television and the media have not used their great technologies to strengthen and build up the American character but to weaken it. He writes:

The mass media, with their brilliant use of graphic arts and cinematic skills, sustain the interest in swift-paced materialistic lifestyles and unstable family patterns that subtly place mind and conscience at moral risk. Instead of enriching the intellect, the media impoverish the soul through a steady diet of sex-oriented, violence-prone, and trivia-weighted entertainment. Scientists who have researched the effects of exposure to present-day television say that it promotes a 20 percent decline in creativity, reduces persistence in problem solving, increases sex-role stereotyping, and accelerates aggressive behavior.[18]

Henry illustrates the consequences of the "dumbing down" of American culture in education, in the arts, and in many other areas of the society. Neither public television nor the commercial networks have done much to enhance the virtues and values of our culture, but Henry also notes that the apparent intellectual drift is accompanied by a deliberate infusion of anti-Christianity. He says:

> Public television, moreover, seems more interested in novel modern religious fads than in the constructive impact of historic evangelical Christianity. Religion editors—some of them agnostics—more eagerly publicize radical protest movements than depict the ministries sustained by traditional churches about which they sometimes know very little. It is noteworthy that commercial television and many daily newspapers as well now face a declining audience despite the notable tilt toward a *Playboy* mentality and exposure.[19]

But there are also strong indications that the cult of humanism is already beginning to change forms. Moving from a sort of pantheistic faith in human potential, the doctrine of humanism has begun to express a radical naturalism that is gaining greater currency now in public education, politics, the media, literature, and the arts. "Secular humanism," Henry writes, "which for a generation has covertly supplied liberal arts learning with its governing metaphysics, while securing its own favored position by emphasizing tolerance of all views except theistic alternatives, is now giving way to unabashed naturalism."

Common sense alone says that such intellectual blindness and stupidity have to go. Such ideas, first conceived nearly three centuries ago by Jean Jacques Rousseau, could only flourish in the ivory tower, totally removed from reality. It is the opposite of what the French Enlightenment claimed to be—it is more like "un-enlightenment"—and it is just one more expression of the doctrine of liberal, anti-American multiculturalism.

It is precisely this kind of politically correct stereotyping that needs to be exposed to the light of day. Christians may have been among the first to say out loud how stupid the politically correct movement is, but there are many others, even within academia and the media, who are speaking out against it today.

The tactics of these politically correct brainwashers are the tactics of the Gulag, of Auschwitz, and of the Chinese Communist labor camps. The propagators of political correctness (PC) may be Americans driving BMWs and living in five-bedroom homes, but they are idealistic totalitarians dressed up in academic robes. There is virtually no freedom of expression left on the campuses of our great universities today, thanks to the architects of PC.[20]

The very idea that a student or faculty member cannot say whatever is on his or her mind should be an outrage. It defies the entire heritage and purpose of the university in Western society. These people play on racial tensions, not to bring harmony to our society, but to increase anger and division between peoples. However, if the person who is being spoken against is an evangelical Christian, then there are no limits. None whatsoever. But protection is coming. We are beginning to examine some of these cases from a legal perspective, and you're going to see much more protection in the future for Jews and for Christians.

Family Entertainment

Laying aside for the moment concern for religious and political agendas, we also can observe in the 1990s a powerful demographic and technological trend that should alter dramatically what comes out of Hollywood in the future. The postwar baby boom generation, the so-called pig in the python, has now matured. The very popular television series "Family Ties" showed two former hippie rebels who had become stable parents with teenage children. In a phenomenon described by New York demographer Faith Popcorn, the baby boomers are turning to home and family in a process she calls "cocooning."

Their home life is their center, and one of their top priorities is sharing entertainment at home with their children. Regardless of their adult preferences, there are few parents who want to sit down with their eight- and ten-year-olds to watch a dirty movie or a steamy soap opera. These people will not only monitor their children's television viewing, they are not about to buy their children violent or sexually explicit videocassettes.

The economics of the situation are clear. Films are financed from domestic theatrical releases, sale of foreign theatrical rights, network or cable rights, U.S. and foreign videocassette rights, local television syndication, and so on. The profit or loss in any entertainment venture depends on audiences to buy tickets and videocassettes or to watch on television. If wholesome family fare draws families to theaters or causes them to buy or rent videocassettes or to watch broadcast television or cable at home and buy the products advertised, rest assured that more will be produced.

Family products are "in" because that's where America is. Today's film powerhouses—Lucas, Spielberg, Disney—all cater to family audiences, and they make hundreds of millions of dollars in the process. Even Time Warner, which published Madonna's book, *Sex*, and whose HBO unit often broadcasts disgraceful programming, has now started a family entertainment division. Now that such remarkable success is being achieved with computerized special effects, digital animation, and live-action animation, I see a proliferation of this film form that lends itself so readily to clean family programs.

I am personally pleased that International Family Entertainment, of which I am chairman, has met with such remarkable acceptance. Our Family Channel now has fifty-eight million subscribers in the United States alone, increasing acceptance by national advertisers, and a cumulative weekly viewing audience that exceeds the total number of subscribers to *Time*, *Newsweek*, the *New York Times*, the *Washington Post*, the *Chicago Tribune*, the *Los Angeles Times*, and a hundred more small newspapers combined.

My son Tim is the chief executive officer. He recently aired the splendidly produced, color, animated series of "Peter Rabbit" in prime time on the Family Channel. The nation's film reviewers, who must have included a number of family-oriented people, literally went wild in their praise of the series, which has now been nominated for a prime-time Emmy Award.

We have recently acquired the Mary Tyler Moore studio, which currently produces the wholesome situation comedy "Evening Shade." This studio not only gives us control of a library of some of the finest dramatic series and situation comedies ever produced for television, it also gives us the production capability and sales distribution to get some truly outstanding series into the American and international television arena.

Our efforts are meager compared to that of the giants that are moving into Hollywood like Telecommunications, Inc., U.S. West, Sony, and others. Billions of dollars will be spent on fiber optics, channel compression, interactive television, home shopping, video games, and new entertainment forms. All of this means ending the monopoly of the tiny group of ideologues that have dominated Hollywood for the past thirty years. It means a greater fragmentation of the marketplace and a radical realignment of power in the entertainment industry.

A Return to Faith

One of the optimistic signs within the turning tide is the return to faith we are witnessing all around the globe. African, Asian, and European newspapers are reporting a massive resurgence of religious faith worldwide. It's certainly true here in this country. However, the danger we face in our culture is "syncretism," which is the sort of mindless blending of ideas about God that are neither Christian nor Jewish nor Eastern nor anything in particular, but rather a mishmash of fuzzy feelings about life and the hereafter.

It is a "religious" way of thinking about life that includes angels, spirit guides, horoscopes, and other things with about as much depth as the doctrine of Santa Claus. Sadly, this is about the level of religious knowledge of many of the children in this country who have been cut off by secular society from the faith of our fathers. Yet even in the darkest corners of America—in the homes of the privileged elites—there is a growing realization that something profound and important is missing. People are beginning to search for that missing ingredient—the reality of God.

At the same time, many people are moving away from filth and violence, away from self-destructive nihilism, and away from the sheer hopelessness reflected by the media. My co-host, Ben Kinchlow, told me about a conversation he had with his son about a Mad Max movie. They were sitting in the family room watching this movie together, not saying much, and then Ben's son turned to him and said, "You know, Dad, there is no hope in these movies." Ben said that comment hit him like a flash of light. That is the message missing from these movies, all of them. *People want hope.*

There is an important common-sense message in this as well. When you give people hope, you give them life. When you take away hope, you condemn them to disappointment, hopelessness, and despair. That is the message of religion, of course, the ultimate hope in a personal relationship with your Creator. The Christian message is that Jesus Christ is the source of hope, and He is.

Retaining Our Citizenship

If human beings are made in the image of God, which we are, then we need to realize that God means something in our lives. In his treatises on the *City of Man* and the *City of God*, the fifth-century cleric Augustine showed that we actually live in two worlds, in the civic and secular culture and in the religious and spiritual culture. Popular culture in our time has almost lost its connection with the City of God, and as a consequence the City of Man has become increasingly dangerous and inhospitable.

Liberals in our society are very concerned about poverty and despair in the world, but they have failed to recognize that sorrow, hopelessness, and despair are the inevitable result of the impoverishment of our souls. We are not culturally destitute and morally bereft because we have lost our passion for the City of Man, but because we have lost our vision of the City of God.

As Charles Colson pointed out in an address to a conference in Florida on the culture wars, the elites of our culture have been doing everything in their power to secularize American society for the last fifty years. These people wield tremendous influence in law, government, education, and the media, and they have succeeded to the extent that we are now confused, empty, and guided simultaneously by lusts and some vague notions about "spirituality," yet lacking any sort of moral compass. Society is out of control. Ethical behavior is quickly disappearing, and we have come very near the point once expressed by Chairman Mao: Morality begins at the point of a gun.

Colson reminded his audience that no society in recorded history has ever survived without a strong moral consensus and there has never been a moral consensus that was not founded upon religious truth. He said, "Recovering our moral code—our religious truth—is the only way our society can survive. The heaping ash remains at Auschwitz, the killing fields of Southeast Asia, and the frozen wastes of the Gulag remind us that the City of Man is not enough; we must also seek the City of God."[21]

When we have finally been stripped of all moral restraint and the only interests we entertain are prurient, we can be certain that there will be little left of this civilization worth saving. The legacy of deliberate destruction we have witnessed in these pages so far is a grim reminder of the dangers to society and to each individual in it when the Creator God is no longer visible in public discourse, but it is also an assurance that there is a greater work to be done if we are only willing to take up the challenge. With God's help, we may yet see a rebirth of moral restraint and wholesome family values in this country. With strength of purpose and moral resolve, we may yet see God's blessing upon this land.

In the chapters that follow, I will be looking at several areas where the battle has been raging and where signs of change are now visible. So, from the darkness of liberal deconstructionism and disaster, we turn now to some others areas where we are beginning to see a return to common sense.

7

He Made Them Male
and Female

*P*AGE ONE OF THE *Wall Street Journal* of Friday, July 23, 1993, carried this encouraging headline, "Stay-at-Home Moms Are Fashionable Again in Many Communities," with the subhead, "Former Professional Women Bring Competitive Edge to Bake Sales, the PTA."[1] The featured woman in the story was a thirty-nine-year-old former insurance manager who is "living the life she vowed to avoid"—decorating cookies and working as a volunteer for the PTA of her two daughters' school.

According to the *Journal*, in pockets of middle- and upper-middle-class America "full time motherhood has become downright chic." Now the women are not being asked, What is politically correct? but What is MC or "maternally correct"? Women are no longer ashamed to be "just" a housewife. Now they are the CEOs of their households. Yankelovitch Partners Monitor showed that by 1991, 56 percent of the working women in America would quit their jobs if they didn't need the money, up from the prevailing 30 percent of the past two decades.[2]

Kathy Peel, a charming and vivacious fellow author with Word Publishing, is on the staff of *Family Circle*, whose readership is twenty-six million. Kathy was recently asked to speak at a Helene Curtis-sponsored seminar to the lifestyle editors of thirty leading women's magazines on the topic of how women in the nineties can balance the competing time demands of career and family. She wrote me, "It was quite an experience to hear comments by liberal-minded editors such as, 'We're beginning to see that running the home and raising children is a very big job,' and 'perhaps we should rename the full-time housewife or homemaker a "family manager"—giving her more value.'"

Then Kathy enclosed a press release from Good Housekeeping Institute containing these words: "In the nineties, people are striving for a simpler life with less extravagance and a smarter, value-driven lifestyle. Kids are 'in' and the focus of life is on family and the home," said Amy Barr, women's consumer trends expert. "These issues have recently reached Capitol Hill and promise to play an important role in the presidential elections—which will ultimately elevate the status of the Family Manager," says Barr.

In the same news release was this tidbit: "The Department of Commerce estimates that American women's unwaged work in the home is worth over $1 trillion a year to the U.S. economy. Members of Congress have initiated the unremunerated work list of 1991 to place a dollar value on unpaid housework and include it in the gross national product."

Return to Family Values

A publication called *The Boomer Report,* aimed at the baby boom generation, ran in its October 15, 1992, issue the news that "most social scientists are now saying that nothing works as well as a nuclear family for raising kids and creating a healthy society, and when asked if they intend to marry, 80 percent of high school seniors said yes in 1989, up from 74 percent in 1975."[3]

All this confirms precisely what our Family Channel executives and researchers have been discovering. The acquisitive generation of the eighties is becoming the at-home generation of the nineties. Traditional family values grew sharply and significantly between 1989 and 1991. In that short span, the proportion of Americans who said respecting their parents is one of the most important values grew from 38 to 47 percent, a remarkable jump of 9 percent. This trend toward traditional values, family life, clean entertainment, simpler lifestyles, and religious faith is accelerating rapidly. This is clearly not some moment of paradise on earth, but it does represent a swing back to the norm of American life in the 1950s.

But there has been one major difference between the fifties and the nineties. Women have proven that not only can they perform many tasks as well as men, they can do a great many of them better. When, from time to time, I would be asked on a survey to name the outstanding political leader outside of the United States, my first choice was invariably a woman—Margaret Thatcher. To me her leadership was nothing short of phenomenal. But deep inside, I thought Maggie had to be some sort of anomaly.

The old chauvinist in me didn't really come around until I watched LPGA champion Dottie Mochrie demolish several of my longtime senior golf heroes, Jack Nicklaus and Arnold Palmer, along with current PGA great Fred Couples as well. Then I watched the women's division of the French Open tennis tournament late one night in my hotel room in Kinshasa, Zaire, where I saw the ladies hit backhands like cannonballs and serves at a hundred miles per hour.

Yes, the ladies have proven their mettle. Elaine Garzarelli can analyze the stock market as well or better than most men: Betsy King, Nancy Lopez, Dottie Mochrie, and their compatriots can hit golf balls just as accurately as male professionals. Ruth Bader Ginsburg can undoubtedly adjudicate as well as any male judge. Women can write, produce, legislate, administrate, and sell as well as their counterparts. Thirty years ago few believed in their ability, but now few doubt it. So if women want the chance, they are certainly entitled—and for doing equal work with men they certainly should receive equal pay!

A repeat guest on my television program, Rachel McLish, won the national women's body-building competition and, to put it mildly, is a superbly conditioned athlete. Rachel wouldn't touch steroids, but the fact is that women can, if they so desire, take steroids just like some men do to deepen their voices and build up muscles as sinewy as any male bodybuilder. Most of us have seen enough evidence of that in photographs and on our television screens.

In addition to all these competitive abilities, however, God has given women an ability that no man has and for which no woman has any need to compete with a man. Only a woman can nurture within herself a creature made in the image of God. Only a woman can take the child that is born, mother it, and shape its destiny for its entire lifetime. By shaping their own sons and daughters, women shape the entire destiny of their nation and, in some cases, their world. For that matter, only a woman was chosen to bear the Son of God, Jesus Christ.

Lessons from History

In college I took a course centered on the British historian Arnold Toynbee. This famous academician projected the rise and fall of nations based on the challenge of environmental factors and the response of various peoples to that challenge.

In the Bible there is a brief analysis of the kingdoms of Israel and Judah from the time of King David and his son, Solomon, all the way to the Babylonian captivity—a period of roughly four hundred years, which is twice as long as America has had its present government but is roughly comparable to the age of America dated from the first landings and settlements by British Colonists.

External factors, certainly environmental factors, are either not mentioned or are secondary in the biblical account. The narrative is simple: Such and such became king, his mother's name was so and so, and either he followed the way of the Lord and the nation was blessed, or he "departed from the Lord and went after heathen gods," in which case God sent a warning and then judgment.

Sons of righteous kings were not necessarily righteous. Sons of wicked kings were not necessarily wicked. The key ingredient in shaping the religious faith of the king was the king's mother. That is why the mothers are very carefully listed. It seems clear to me that the order is simple in the pages of holy history: Mothers shape kings—kings shape nations—and God blesses or curses nations depending on how they respond to Him. Since a force known as entropy, or just plain human nature, is always pulling us toward disorder and lawlessness, it seldom happens that a people will rise above their leaders in faith and morality. If the leaders are corrupt, the nation will sooner or later be corrupt. Good leaders can lift and inspire people, but seldom, over the long run, will people continuously achieve any lofty standards beyond those set by their leaders.

The writer of Proverbs made this wise comment: "Train up a child in the way he should go, and when he is old he will not depart from it" (Prov. 22:6). It is really very simple. Mothers shape leaders, and leaders shape nations. Without caring mothers there will either be no leaders, or those leaders that do arise will have at the core of their being an uncertainty, an emptiness, and a lack of values.

How can being a forklift operator, an air force pilot, a sales manager, a research director, a physician, or a crusader for causes compare with the privilege of shaping the future of a nation? What irreparable harm will be suffered by future generations if mothers in the United States settle for second best.

We all should recognize that women get the same stimulation from achievement as men do. It is tremendously rewarding psychologically for a woman to achieve a breakthrough in medical technology, or to win a landmark law case, or to close a big sale, or to produce an award-winning television series, or to cover a major news story. But that kind of achievement, and for that matter any significant executive responsibility, makes extraordinary demands not only on time, but on concentration, mental acuity, creativity, and, for want of a better phrase, psychic energy.

It is one thing for a woman to be a shift worker in a factory, or a bookkeeper, or a file clerk with a clearly defined workweek. I dare say there is little extraordinary satisfaction in many of these jobs, and, lacking the financial reward, most mothers holding such jobs would probably want to leave them as soon as possible. But for the higher-level jobs where there is unusual satisfaction and pay, women must be prepared for out-of-town travel, long hours, work at home, and intense pressure.

Leading Two Lives

A mother in such a position has to live two conflicting lives. She has to be a wife, mother, and homemaker. Her children need her—her love, her time, and her undivided attention. Her husband needs her—her love, her concern for his work, her support, and their life together. Her home and social life need her. But then what about her client presentation? What about her work deadlines? What about the vendors that are late or the salesmen who aren't meeting quotas? What about the quarterly budgets? What about success and achievement?

Remember the sultry lady in the television commercial singing, "I can bring home the bacon, fry it up in a pan, and never let you forget you're a man, for I am woman." Well, the supermoms of the eighties are getting burned out supplying the bacon, the housework, and the glamour all in one package.

Some mothers in these positions make a conscious decision. Their work comes first and the family can shift for itself, or the family comes first and her career begins to suffer. But few if any human beings can sustain the unbelievable stress of two separate, competing, emotionally charged, full-time lives.

That is why thoughtful women are making what to many is a hard choice—to some an easy choice. They are giving up the financial rewards and the psychological rewards of competing in the work place and are finding satisfaction in their homes, their children, and their families. The loss of a second income normally means less available money for the family. The decision for one partner in a two-income family to stop work clearly means less conspicuous consumption and a simpler, more value-driven lifestyle. But the emerging trend is clear. Women have proven that they can compete successfully. Now they are beginning to put human relationships above career fulfillment and material possessions—and this is part of the turning tide.

It is clear that former First Lady Barbara Bush was on target when she addressed the graduating class at Wellesley College in June 1990 with these memorable words: "At the end of your life, you will never regret not having passed one more test, [not] winning one more verdict, or not closing one more deal. . . . You will regret time not spent with a husband, a child, a friend, or a parent."

The Cost of Folly

The breakup of the American family and the abandonment of traditional moral values have cost this nation a tremendous amount. Over and over again we hear people saying we must concentrate on the economy. The Democrats made the federal deficit the theme of their election strategy in 1992, and even some Republicans were saying that we must abandon our focus on social and family issues in favor of pure economics. But when we take into account the cost of problems such as alcoholism (which may be as high as $75 billion) and the cost of health problems attributable directly to smoking, drugs, and other high-risk lifestyles, it becomes apparent that lifestyles and family breakup are a major source of financial stress. It is fair to say that with behavior-related problems adding at least $200 billion to the nation's economic burden, coupled with the emotional problems and welfare dependency it engenders, the breakup of the family is the number-one economic and social problem in America today.

In the thirty years since the birth of the welfare system under Presidents Kennedy and Johnson, government social spending has climbed some 400 percent. To date we have poured more than $3 trillion into welfare with no visible result. Poverty still hovers at 20 percent. At the same time, the divorce rate has quadrupled, the number of children born out of wedlock has quadrupled, the number of children living in single-parent homes has tripled, the number of teen suicides has more than doubled, and the scores of high school students on the Scholastic Aptitude Test have dropped an average of 80 points nationwide.

If we take into account the crimes that result from children from broken homes—if we take into account the amount of theft, rape, and drug use that can be traced back to our loss of strong religious-based moral values—if we take into account the enormous economic toll of abandoning our traditional standards for marriage and the family—the total cost would be staggering as it approached hundreds of billions of dollars. But the real cost of this devastation can be measured more appropriately in terms of the millions of broken homes and tens of millions of wasted lives. The problem of the family is not just one of our economic concerns; it is the very heart and soul of a national crisis.

War on the Family

In her sensational article in the *Atlantic* proclaiming that "Dan Quayle Was Right," Barbara Dafoe Whitehead, writer and researcher for the Institute for American Values, marshaled a formidable arsenal of research from sociologists and other scholars that proved beyond question that child welfare in America is at an all-time low and the so-called liberation of women is largely to blame.[4]

At the same time, Senator Daniel Patrick Moynihan wrote in the *American Scholar*, "The amount of deviant behavior in American society has increased beyond the levels the community can 'afford to recognize' and that, accordingly, we have been re-defining deviancy so as to except much conduct previously stigmatized, and also quietly raising the 'normal' level in categories where behavior is now abnormal by any earlier standard."[5] However the analysts look at it, it is becoming increasingly clear for everyone to see that the efforts of liberalism to redefine and restructure the family have had disastrous consequences for the nation. For all their highly touted virtues, the changes of the last half-century have amounted to all-out war on the American family.

Professor Armand Nicholi of Harvard has done extensive studies of young people and the disadvantages brought on by disruptions in the constitution of the home. In addition to problems with behavior and socialization, such studies show that attitudes that develop from family breakup and the loss of traditional family values have contributed to social dependency and the growth of the vast welfare bureaucracy in this country. Through a complex process of government manipulation, the deterioration of family values over the past thirty years has had a huge impact on the mushrooming of our national debt.

More recently we have seen scores of studies conducted with children who were raised without one of their parents, either father or mother, in residence. These children exhibited greater dependency on their peer group, were less willing to achieve or to take the risks required in life, and were more susceptible to drug and alcohol abuse. Children from broken homes are more easily influenced by peer pressure because they have a poorly developed sense of identity and, therefore, lower self-esteem.

When Dr. Judith Wallerstein began preparing her research for the California children of divorce study in 1971, she and her colleagues were expecting a short-term project. As the *Atlantic* article states, at that time, most experts believed that the emotional effects of divorce were "like a bad cold. There was a phase of acute discomfort, and then a short recovery phase."[6] They discovered they were wrong. In her book on the subject, Wallerstein concluded, "Parent-child relationships are permanently altered by divorce in ways that our society has not anticipated." In many cases, children of divorce never fully recover from their emotional scars.[7]

At War with Human Nature

The whole concept of the loss of sexual identity—what has recently been referred to as gender bending—grows out of these situations. We aired a CBN news story on "The 700 Club" in May 1993, in which our reporter discovered that young people all across the country, as young as twelve years of age, admitted that they were engaging in all kinds of sexual experiences, not just promiscuous heterosexual activity but homosexual and lesbian activity, because that is what is being encouraged in the schools, in the popular culture, and even by confused parents.

This perversion of sexual identity is not just childish experimentation, but the result of deliberate exploitative propaganda. Consider, for example, the following pledge of the homosexual movement that was recited, among other places, on the floor of Congress to attest to the self-avowed aims of today's gay and lesbian shock troops:

We shall sodomize your sons, emblems of your feeble masculinity, of your shallow dreams and lies. We shall seduce them in your schools, in your dormitories, in your gymnasiums, in your locker rooms, in your sports arenas, in your seminaries, in your youth groups, in your movie theater bathrooms, in your army bunkhouses, in your truck stops, in your all-male clubs, in your House of Congress, however men are with men together. Your sons shall become our minions and do our bidding. They will be recast in our image.[8]

One of the oldest truisms of historians is the idea that when the women of any culture no longer stand for virtue and moral restraint, that culture is doomed to collapse. That is clearly a risk we face today in this country. The rising crime rate among women, the growing numbers of women in prisons, and the statistics of drug and alcohol abuse among women indicate that profound and disturbing changes have been taking place in the female psyche. Such reports should be shocking, but this is precisely what feminism set out to accomplish: to make men and women equal in all respects, even the most sordid.

The real agenda of "feminism" places unfair and unnatural burdens on both women and men, and it is contrary to the natural inclinations and desires of those it claims to support. Unless enough women and men rise up in protest and cast off the shackles of the feminist ideology, the pressures being heaped on women will only continue to mount, leading to burnout, profound feelings of frustration and failure, and even clinical depression in some cases.

The Kids Suffer

More than half of all first and second marriages today end in divorce. Nearly 60 percent of those involve children under the age of eighteen, and each year more than a million children will see their parents split up. Myron Magnet writes:

> Contrary to the longstanding received opinion that children recover quickly from divorce and flourish in families of almost any

shape, these changes have harrowed and damaged kids. Though of course many single-parent families work very well, lovingly nurturing children fully capable of happiness and success—and though everyone knows intact families that exemplify Franz Kafka's dictum that the middle-class family is the closest thing to hell on earth—in general, children from single-parent families have more trouble than children from two-parent families.[9]

Studies show that children in single-parent families are more likely to be victims of poverty than kids from two-parent families. On average, children in single-parent homes have less than one-third the median per capita income of children from two-parent homes, and half of them fall below the poverty line. But Magnet also reports, "Growing up in a single-parent family puts its mark not just on a child's external economic circumstances but on his or her innermost psyche as well." A nationwide study for the National Center for Health Statistics showed that children from single-parent homes were up to 200 percent more likely than children from two-parent homes to have emotional and behavioral problems. At least 80 percent of all adolescents hospitalized for psychiatric and emotional problems were from single-parent homes.

Many people have argued that these kinds of problems are solved by remarriage, but the evidence shows that children with stepparents fare no better than children from single-parent homes. In fact, in many cases, stepfamilies suffer even greater trauma than single-parent families. Barbara Whitehead reports that the findings of researchers, such as Dr. Nicholas Zill, show that "stepfamilies disrupt established loyalties, create new uncertainties, provoke deep anxieties, and sometimes threaten a child's physical safety as well as emotional security."[10] In short, there is simply no substitute for an intact and properly functional family for the well-being of both adults and children.

Restoring Family Fortunes

The closer people look at what these liberal policies have actually accomplished, the more they come to realize that marriage has to be protected. Common sense is coming back and saying we have to preserve the family, we have to bring in some kind of fault provision in the event of divorce, and we cannot allow husbands to walk away from their homes and abandon their wives and children without penalty. Nor can we allow women to walk out on their husbands with no consequences whatsoever. Suddenly, many groups from the Right and the Left are coming forward and saying that society has a vested interest in supporting the institution of marriage. Take, for example, the words of the editor-in-chief of *U.S. News & World Report*, Mortimer Zuckerman, who writes in a hard-hitting editorial on this subject:

> The impact that family disintegration has on children's lives is a national crisis that has weakened our social fabric and placed unbearable burdens on schools, courts, prisons and the welfare system. The nuclear family must be nurtured. It must be at the center, not the periphery, of social policy. Too many policies and attitudes undermine this central value.[11]

In short, marriage is good for America. The strength of the family is directly related to the strength of the entire nation. To disregard the welfare of families is to risk the futures of millions of women and their children, and it is a dereliction of our responsibilities as citizens. We must fight for a return to common sense, and, Zuckerman concludes, "Above all, we must fight the idea that the family is irrelevant. The time for silence on these issues is behind us."

The dilemma facing us today is that this somber vision of society must either reverse itself because of its obvious failures, or there will be a sudden and devastating collapse. As horrifying as it is to say that, this is the image that confronts American teenagers today. Unless there is a dramatic change right now in the way we care for, teach, and nurture the young people of this country, you can be certain that the future awaiting them will be bleak and hopeless. It is a vision that should be intolerable to everyone.

Fortunately, the collapse of communism signaled the beginning of many hopeful changes in our world. It is as if God has given civilization a second chance to find itself and learn from its mistakes. But before we can begin to appropriate this opportunity and restore common sense to government, we have to recognize where these problems came from. The radicals have not yet attained final victory, nor will they, because suddenly the tide is turning against them. But they haven't given up trying, and serious threats still remain.

Institutionalized Day Care

One of the most destructive threats is institutionalized day care, which is turning millions of children into a generation of zombies. In 1992, Diane Sawyer of ABC's "Primetime Live" did a story on institutionalized day care that was one of the most horrifying things I have ever seen. The poor children featured in that documentary wandered around aimlessly, uncared for, unattended, and with little emotion. They were like zombies, and at one point the hidden camera showed a day-care worker slap the face of one little child. All she wanted him to do was to shut up and not bother her. It is no longer a secret that this kind of thing is happening all across America today. Busy mothers and busy fathers are parking their neglected children in cold and unloving warehouses while they go off to pursue their personal dreams. They have no idea what damage they are wreaking upon their own offspring. No wonder they are out of touch with their children. No wonder they can't understand what's wrong with their kids. No wonder family life has become a nightmare for so many. Men, women, and children have become strangers to each other.

There is no doubt that institutional day care is the most devastating thing that has ever been done to a generation of children. Now the liberals are calling for government-controlled day care. But does anybody believe that the government will perform the task better than private industry? When was the last time you were in contact with a government bureaucracy? Did you feel cared for and loved? Now envision your children or your grandchildren in the hands of this same kind of government workers.

I'm sorry to say that even church day-care centers and church schools are hardly any better. Children do not flourish unless they have personal, individual attention, especially during the critical first three to six years of life. They must feel that to someone (and preferably to their own mother) they are the most important and most precious thing on earth. Instead of making them spoiled or dependent, genuine and unreserved affection gives children a sense of security and helps them to develop independence and to have greater self-respect and emotional balance. When they are loved and cared for in the home with genuine warmth and affection, they begin to flourish, to develop more sophisticated verbal skills, their minds are quicker, their bodies grow stronger, and they are more emotionally mature. All you have to do is look at the pictures of those poor little children in the orphanages of Rumania to see how destructive it can be when children are abandoned, neglected, or put into the hands of government.

This is the behavior the liberals not only condone but subsidize. Within a few weeks or months of a mother's giving birth, she goes back to work and her baby is handed over to some day-care provider. The mother gets back in step with her fellow workers and is forced to minimize the attachment she feels for her child. Suddenly deprived of the personal warmth of the mother, the child goes through a sort of shock and, over time, evidences behavior that is alternately withdrawn, sullen, and then suddenly angry, loud, and apparently irrational under stress. This is a distinctive and easily recognizable childcare syndrome that illustrates the severe shock and imbalance occurring in the mother-child and father-child relationships. Researchers say that in many cases the wall of resentment that grows up in these relationships is irreversible; yet this is the pattern of "normal" existence for as many as half of all American families today.

Most of the time, day-care workers are unskilled women or men who just want a job. They are not prepared to make any sort of emotional commitment to a bunch of demanding kids. Even in the best day-care centers, workers come and go, so the child cannot build a lasting relationship with any adult. Soon the children decide that this is how life is going to be, and they turn off. Why should we be surprised when these children find it impossible to form attachments or bond with another human being?

The Unattached Generation

We have a generation of children growing up "unbonded." This is a relatively new psychological term that describes a newly identified phenomenon of children who have no sense of relationship or responsibility to other people. They have no allegiance to parents, no loyalty to friends, no concept of right or wrong, truth or falsehood, and they become social misfits and ultimately a menace to society. These are the kids who turn to tobacco and alcohol at an early age, then to drugs and heavy metal music. They are easy prey for every exploitation, from pornography to Satanism. It is one of the most shocking results of what happens to children when they are cut off from natural family relationships. What is shocking is that this is not happening in some Third-World jungle but in civilized America.

Unbonded children have no respect for authority. In school they frequently have attention deficit disorder. When teachers speak to them, they don't listen and they don't trust the teacher. Later, when they get married, their marriages almost always fail. We are talking about a significant portion of a whole generation of Americans who are growing up pathological.

What is the common-sense approach to this situation? First of all, we have to return to the traditional family and the traditional relationships in the home. Women must be permitted (not forced) to assume the role that God intended for them as wives, mothers, and nurturers of the young. This is so much more important than making a few more dollars, having a new car in the driveway, or proving that she is the equal of some man. She already has the most important job in the world, caring for the next generation and raising up her children in the way that they should go. There is no higher calling on earth.

Study after study proves that the working wife and mother on average contributes little or nothing to the family financially. The additional income brought in by the working wife is more than offset by the additional taxes, the cost of additional clothes, makeup, hair care, car, transportation, lunch, expenses, day care for the children, and all the other things it takes to keep her working. A 1985 study of working women in America showed that the net take-home pay of the working woman after all these things are taken out averaged about $1,800 per year. That paltry sum is no substitute for all the things she and her family are giving up in order for her to work. If wives could quit work and stay home with their children, think what dividends they and the nation would gain by allowing them to lavish their love and affection and guidance on their children. Instead of trying to pay for ill-conceived welfare, our government should give a direct subsidy to working mothers either in cash or tax credits to enable them to quit work and stay home with their children. Not only would this give us better adjusted children, it would serve to shrink the labor pool, reduce unemployment, and bring about higher wages for workers.

Murphy's Law

The sensation surrounding the out-of-wedlock birth to television's Murphy Brown reveals some of the deep issues involved in this national crisis. For months, fifth-column liberals praised the courage of the producers who decided to use their highly visible platform to raise the profile of single mothers. Dan Quayle said in absolute honesty that the Murphy Brown message was reproachful and destructive. Of course, he was savaged by the media.

But suddenly voices of reason began to emerge, voices like Harry Stein, a columnist for *TV Guide*, who wrote that Murphy Brown's motherhood was "parenthood as designed by people with zero love for children." Again the media flushed with rage. But Stein insisted: "Say what you will about the much-mocked Ozzie and Harriet, in their world the kids came first. In Murphy's, as in ours, they far too often come last."

Little by little, as *Los Angeles Times* writer Lynn Smith observed, Clintonian Democrats began joining sides with Quayle Republicans over the issue, laying the blame for today's troubled youth "on the doorstep of fatherless homes." Even Clinton adviser William Galston wrote in *Mandate for Change* that while millions of American women are struggling to provide homes for their children, "a large body of evidence supports the conclusion that the intact two-parent family is best suited to the task of bringing up children."[12] Pediatrician T. Berry Brazelton helped to clarify the position of the child in such situations when he explained that children of single parents are haunted by two questions: Why would one parent desert me? and Will this one go too?

The popular television doctor then goes on to say, "Unless that single parent is there to give the child a sense of how important he or she is, right from the first, they grow up with a pretty flaky self-image." Most single parents, he adds, can only pull that off by a lot of hard work. Unfortunately, the trendy, wishful thinking of Murphy Brown sends all the wrong messages. It says any bright young woman can have it both ways, just as Murphy does. But the truth is a whole different matter.

Leave It to Nanny

Consider the example that we glimpsed briefly in the spring of 1993 when Zoe Baird made headlines because of her nanny problems. Here is a highly capable woman earning in excess of $500,000 a year as general counsel for a major corporation, desperately looking for some capable person to look after her children. But being the counsel for a large corporation is an all-consuming responsibility. It is almost impossible for a woman to take on such a role and then come home and read to the kids, look after them, love them, and nurture them. She hardly ever gets home before eight or nine o'clock. She frequently works on Saturdays and Sundays, and she must be prepared to work up to twenty-four hours a day when the situation warrants.

Any key executive, male or female, is under incredible stress most of the time. Every decision he or she makes will either beneficially or adversely affect the well-being of the corporation, so an executive can't ever let down. In Zoe Baird's case, she had to worry about finding a nanny to watch after her children. But the government had all these regulations about hiring and Social Security and taxes, and she found it doubly onerous to find the necessary help. Instead of sympathizing with her, she was stigmatized for doing what seemed to be right at the time. But this is not an uncommon problem for women at that level.

Among other things, this situation illustrates the degree to which we are penalized by bureaucratic nonsense. We are crazed by regulations, and we have put regulations above human need. Our little rules and regulations have totally obscured the common-sense way of doing things. But common sense says that the children of America are hurting, and we should do everything in our power to craft laws to make the care and nurture of children easier and less institutionalized.

When we developed the Mother's Touch program at Regent University, we found that any form of institutionalized day care—whether private, corporate, government, or even church—was hurtful to children. The only organized approach that was actually helpful was a home environment where one or two women would look after six or seven children. In the home environment where there were rules, where the setting was consistent and predictable, where the personnel did not change, and where there was individual attention and personal affection, children thrived. In fact, they sometimes cried when they had to leave to go home. It was like a family situation in which the five or six other children were more like brothers and sisters, so it was fun for them.

But we are in a vicious cycle. By its spending policies government has forced the rapid rise of prices and inflation. To keep up with the inflationary spiral, government has raised tax rates, so people lose more and more of their income in taxes. Under the Clinton tax proposals, it will be common in places like New York for people to be paying upward of 50 percent of their incomes in taxes. The tax burden is already terribly onerous and has forced many wives and mothers into the workplace to relieve the financial burden laid on their family. Soon families get locked in a vicious cycle of dependency. The more they come to rely on the money the mother earns, the harder it will be for her to quit and return to her home and family. At the same time, all the new expenses and obligations they might have incurred while she was bringing in additional money have to be reevaluated and, in most cases, dropped. So there is a feeling of loss associated with the decision of doing the right thing—to return to the role of homemaker.

Pernicious Dependency

A similar thing happens with people who get hooked on welfare. They may want to get off the government rolls and get back into the work force, but the minute they do they face heavy taxes and every extra penny seems to go back to Uncle Sam. They take home less money from working forty hours a week than they had when they were on welfare, so they quickly lose any incentive they may have to become self-reliant and responsible for themselves. They say, Why should we work? Why should we improve ourselves? Why should we study? We'll just come out worse off than we are now. If we have babies out of wedlock we'll get even more money.

The common-sense solution is to reduce the tax burden on families, to get government spending under control, and to regain control of the cycle of inflation and deflation. The common-sense solution is to provide people tax benefits that can be saved in IRAs for college, health, and other long-term needs. They can shelter money and let that money work for them. That money, in turn, will go into the private sector, which would allow more goods, more jobs, and more growth in the economy in a noninflationary mode.

Senator Pete Domenici and other conservatives in Congress have been working on a plan to create a universal IRA with favorable tax advantages that would encourage people to save for their own retirement and take the Social Security burden off the people and off the government at the same time. I have been recommending this sort of option for years, especially for younger workers. It would be a compulsory IRA in which they could invest as much as they desire. They and their employers would be putting their own money into the retirement IRAs tax free. Then, at retirement age, they would enjoy a comfortable retirement from their own money and not be dependent on the whims of politicians. The way it is now, nobody knows for certain what lies in store for younger workers when they retire. For these younger workers, Social Security is a huge transfer tax; its "trust fund" is an illusion. By 2015 Social Security will be in deep trouble, which gives workers the added fear that their benefits may not be there when they reach retirement age.

Of Social Bondage

The concept that government owes everybody a living is fallacious. We have to encourage the attitude that people are responsible for their own destiny. The idea that government will take care of you from womb to tomb is ridiculous, but it is one more example of the socialist environment that has pervaded the American government since the heyday of the New Deal. If you go to countries like Sweden, Norway, or Eastern Europe, you will see the tragic legacy of these socialist systems firsthand. Their all-consuming social welfare programs have literally devastated these countries and crippled their middle classes.

Sweden is a perfect example of a country that has been bankrupted by welfare. People can sit at home for years without doing any kind of work and still receive generous payments from the government welfare system. That is socialism run amok. The *Wall Street Journal* has done a number of features showing how a market economy can be destroyed by such systems. Many people still recall the segment on "60 Minutes" that dealt with government support for the arts in Holland. The leftist government had agreed to pay a living wage to virtually anyone who claimed to be an artist. As a result, it has warehouses full of pictures that are absolute junk. It could make better use of most of the "art" it is getting if it used the stuff for fuel, but the Dutch government keeps paying and piling up deficits. The government spends 58 percent of the entire national income on its version of the liberal welfare state.

In all of these welfare nations one gets the feeling that someone has legislated madness as the principal means of administration. Government is so removed from reality, it seems hardly aware of the most basic rules of business. What they have to recognize is that every business has to balance benefits against the cost. That's common sense. There has to be cost analysis with every program. If there is no benefit, then cut the program and cut the cost. The second common-sense rule is restraint.

Government should restrain itself. The courts should restrain themselves. And the people especially need to restrain themselves.

The Welfare Industry

The *Wall Street Journal* reported in May 1993 that welfare spending went up from $53 billion in 1970 to $172 billion in 1991. That includes federal, state, and local spending for public aid, Aid to Families with Dependent Children (AFDC), food stamps, public housing, Social Security, and Medicaid. To date we have spent in excess of $2.3 trillion on welfare for a whole host of expensive and frequently counterproductive entitlement programs.

When the spending started under the Democratic administrations of the mid-1960s, roughly 12.3 percent of the American people were living at or below the poverty level. Today, after an outrageous thirty-year spending spree, the percentage of people at or below the poverty level is between 12.3 and 20 percent, depending on the type of measure used. We have not improved the problem at all, but we have provoked many more dangerous problems and social disasters—from the breakup of the family to ethnic polarization—by convincing the underclass that society is responsible for its problems.

The federal government has scrupulously avoided using anything close to common sense in dealing with these problems. What we have done with welfare is what is called a "paradigm shift." For the first time we have started to pay out money to employed people in the middle class. It was as if there was to be a vast wealth redistribution. But as far as people in the ghetto are concerned, this spending has created a dependency that has taken away their self-reliance and crippled them in the process. So instead of independence, we have created wards of the state.

We have a welfare system that pays benefits if a woman is single with children, but once a man comes into the house the benefits stop. So obviously there is a disincentive for the woman to be married, and this only contributes to the deterioration of normal, healthy socialization and the development of healthy families. Even more troubling, in the case of people who are already married, frequently couples will choose to separate or divorce because of the greater financial rewards for those who are single and disadvantaged. The government-sponsored assault on the family in the name of welfare is truly gigantic.

Of course, there is the incentive to have children. If a girl gives birth, she finds that she is "entitled" to a generous monthly stipend. If she has another child, the stipend is raised—she gets even more. It doesn't take a rocket scientist to deduce that this system promotes illegitimacy, discourages stable families, and promotes dependency.

Multigenerational Dependency

I was shocked by the story I was told during a briefing at the Department of Health and Human Services about a woman who was a welfare grandmother at the age of twenty-eight. She had a child at thirteen and they both went on welfare. Her daughter in turn had a child at thirteen and went on welfare. Now there are three generations growing up on welfare without a father or grandfather in the house. This is not an isolated instance. I fear that this type of thing is rampant throughout our welfare system. Through welfare, the government is not only responsible for keeping people in poverty, but it has created a dependency that is virtually impossible to break. In the process, it has severely undermined the American family.

The flip side is that the tax burden continues to rise on those who are paying for the welfare state, crippling the traditional family. It has forced mothers into the workplace, placing their children in the hands of strangers through the day-care system and robbing mothers, fathers, and children of the sorts of normal and healthy interaction that have always made up the moral and emotional fabric of the nation.

In 1950, only 2 percent of the income of the average family of four went to pay income taxes. Today, that figure is 24 percent. When state, local, and property taxes are included, the typical family of four spends 37 percent of its income on taxes. The key thing we have to keep in mind is that, as far as the liberals and feminists are concerned, a working man with a wife taking care of the children and keeping the home has a decided advantage over a woman who is working and taking care of the household. So the goal was to place a penalty on those who are married. Right now there is a marriage penalty for a couple making more than $53,500 per year and filing a joint return.

It costs more to file jointly than for two wage earners to file separately. The marriage penalty is written in the tax code, and discriminates against people who have worked hard to build and maintain the institution of the traditional family. The standard deduction started out at $600 per dependent several decades ago; it is now $2,300. If the standard deduction had kept pace with inflation since World War II, its value today would be approximately $8,000. No family of four with an annual income of $32,000 or less would pay any federal income tax.

Several proposals to provide tax relief for families have been introduced in Congress, but as yet none have passed. The common-sense approach, which I have proposed over and over again, is that women who are homemakers should be allowed a tax deduction to encourage stability and security in the home. If there is a tax deduction for childcare for working mothers, why shouldn't there be an equal deduction for mothers who stay at home and care for their own children? The whole concept of having children is a good thing for a country, not a bad thing, but only within the confines of strong families. That is the only security for the emotional health of this nation. So the legislation should be to assist families and empower them to make a better life.

The Traditional Model

It is always easy to be simplistic in analyzing a complex situation, but it is clear that among other forces at work the social impetus of liberalism and feminism has played a significant role in diminishing and downgrading the traditional family. Before I discuss the war against the family any further, I believe it would be appropriate to set out the standard of the family according to Christian tradition. The Bible teaches, and Christians believe, that almighty God, the Creator, created "man" in His image, "male and female created He them." Male and female are both parts of the generic "man" or "mankind," and the Bible uses the singular "him" and the plural "them" interchangeably. The verbal foolishness we have inflicted on ourselves in trying to avoid slights to gender could have been easily avoided if we could just realize that man or mankind (the word *anthropos* in Greek means "man," from which we get *anthropology*—the study of the human race) is the generic name for all of us. Instead we have "chairperson," "police person," even "waitperson." (I really saw such an oddity in an advertisement for a restaurant.) Soon we will have personkind, personhood, and a borough of New York named Personhattan.

God said that the male should not be alone, so he created a "help meet" called woman to be a part of the male. God then instituted marriage, saying "shall a man leave his father and mother, and shall cleave unto his wife: and they shall be one flesh." Then God warned of breaking the marriage union saying, "What God had joined together let not man put asunder."

"And God blessed *them*, and God said unto *them*, Be fruitful, and multiply; fill the earth and subdue it, and have dominion." God did not give the power of multiplying, possessing, subduing, of having dominion exclusively to the male or exclusively to the female. Filling the earth and subduing it was to be a joint effort by two people who were made to complement one another, to work in harmony with one another, and to be "one flesh."

The male was given more strength for fighting, for hunting, and for tilling the soil. The woman was given a body that could bear and nurture young and a nature with the ability to be more intuitive and sensitive to the needs of others. The phrase "I feel your pain" is primarily a female response, not a male response. Obviously in a true division of labor, the stronger male would guard over the female while she was unable by the physical weakness of childbearing and child nurturing to hunt and gather and defend herself. The female in turn would care for the young and the home, while the male obtained the family's food. Since there was no birth control, many pregnancies were undoubtedly the norm for women in the early days of our history. It would be relatively obvious that the roles of the two sexes early on became fixed—man the protector and provider, woman the giver and nurturer of life.

But the Victorian concept of what a "lady" could or could not do was hardly derived from Holy Writ, especially when we realize that a "lady," Queen Victoria, ruled the nation. There was nothing particularly sacred about this division of labor; nor do we have any reason to believe that women, if they gave up pregnancy and motherhood, could not develop activities like hunting, gathering, or fighting that were associated with the male or that the male could not keep house or care for children. But as long as biology is what it is and women desire to mother children, the more sensible division of labor would be for the man to "bring home the bacon" and the woman to "fry it up in a pan." But remember, only when they are together, male and female, can they be fruitful, fill the earth, and subdue it.

In New Testament Christianity a model for family living was set forth that is the ideal for maximum satisfaction and stability. A husband is commanded to honor his wife as one who is not only physically weaker, but as a "joint heir with him of the kingdom of God." He is also commanded to love his wife in the same sacrificial, giving way that Jesus Christ loved the church. In fact, he is to love and care for his wife as if she were literally part of his own body.

A husband in a Christian marriage is to make Jesus Christ the head of his life, and in that relationship of submission to Christ, the husband has been made the spiritual leader of the family and the head of the wife. A wife in turn is to join her husband as "one flesh," standing beside him to possess and subdue that part of the earth that has been entrusted to the two of them. In that relation, they are to be as one. Nevertheless, the ultimate spiritual direction for the family is to come from God through the husband. The wife is to recognize her husband's role and submit to his wisdom in matters where there may be disagreement. Needless to say, most women are happy to do so as long as their husbands love them as Christ loved the church.

As one, then, husband and wife are to regard their children as special gifts from God and to join together in bringing up their children in the nurture and admonition of the Lord. Despite the rhetoric of the Left, the Christian view of woman exalts the status of women above anything ever before known in the ancient history of the human race.

Regrettably, God's model has not been followed through the centuries of human history. Men have used their strength and economic power to strip women of their rights. Women have in many cultures been treated as chattels, sold as child brides or concubines, placed in harems, and even physically mutilated to prevent sexual desire. They have been denied rights to property and inheritance, rights to vote, and rights to engage in skilled professions. They have been forced to bear many children and, to repeat the cruel joke, "kept barefoot and pregnant." When jobs have been available, they have been offered to women at wages far below those of men. Although it is not as true today, there has been a "glass ceiling" to keep women executives from the higher levels of many corporations, universities, and professions.

Tearing Down the Patriarchy

However, the fact that God's plan and standard for the elevation of men and women as partners together in this world and heirs together in His kingdom has not been kept by society is no reason to reject what is clearly the optimum arrangement for people in families. During the liberal assault on all things traditional, the Radical Left has taken particular aim at the Christian concept of the family and the traditional family structure as well. What most women do not realize is that the movement for the abolition of slavery, the movement for child labor laws, and the suffragette movement to gain women the vote all sprang from the evangelical churches of America. These abuses needed correcting, and Christians initiated the political action needed for reform.

But the radical women's movement of the 1960s and 1970s has not been geared for reform, but destruction. It has turned fanatical and ugly. These women launched programs that were anti-God, anti-capitalism, anti-family, anti-birth, and anti-heterosexual. Gloria Steinem sounded the war cry, "We don't just want to destroy capitalism, we want to tear down the whole f[———] patriarchy." Men were not husbands, lovers, employers, or friends, they were "PJs"—patriarchal jerks. This movement was not about women's rights, it was about virulent hatred against anything having to do with males.

Since the radical feminists regarded pregnancy as one more form of patriarchal bondage, the shrill cry went up to insist that every woman have legal access and, where necessary, government funding of abortion. Married women were shamed by the feminists at being housewives and mothers and were literally driven to seek "fulfillment" and "freedom" from the alleged patriarchal bondage by moving toward economic independence in the work force.

Feminists considered marriage a legalized form of slavery; Betty Friedan called it "a comfortable concentration camp." Beginning in the 1960s and 1970s they launched an all-out assault on our nation's time-honored laws protecting the marriage union. Within a few years, they and their Radical Left allies succeeded in overturning all fifty of the nation's "fault" divorce statutes and replacing them with what is called no-fault divorce.[13]

In their zeal they also stripped away from women, especially mothers with children, many of the economic and legal protections they had historically enjoyed in this nation. The numbers of women with children falling below the poverty line rose astronomically. As one wag put it, "Any woman voting for no-fault divorce is like a turkey voting for Thanksgiving."

But this was not enough for the Radical Left. In their warped view, women could never be free from the "patriarchy" as long as it was necessary for women to have sexual intercourse with men. So the logical solution to them was sex between women. The president of the National Organization for Women, Patricia Ireland, is bisexual—that is, she has a male husband plus a live-in lesbian lover. In a campaign against her, another candidate for her office alleged that she was not fit for the task because she was only part lesbian. Of course, the next step is childbearing for lesbian women without the necessity of sexual intercourse with males. The course many are taking is either to resort to artificial insemination from a sperm bank or to get lesbian adoptions declared legal. To the feminist, the message of television character Murphy Brown was not just a single mother with a child, but the feminist ideal of a woman bearing a child with minimal reference to a male.

When America was gripped in a battle over what was called the Equal Rights Amendment, I often wondered why the advocates of the amendment did not change the language to read "no discrimination on account of gender" instead of "no discrimination on account of sex." They steadfastly refused to change the language, even if it meant the defeat of ERA. With the hindsight afforded us by three decades of radical feminism, it is clear that the words "on account of sex" could as easily mean the way sex acts are performed as well as male or female gender. Clearly the radical feminists and their homosexual allies were using the Trojan horse of equal rights for women to enshrine protection for homosexuals and lesbians into the very Constitution that governs our entire land.

Of course the ultimate symbol of the patriarchy is a male God—the Father. Feminists at the National Council of Churches pushed through a unisex version of the Bible in which God is "our father and mother in heaven," and Jesus Christ is not the "Son of God," but the "child of God." But that wasn't enough for those seeking to eliminate Christianity, so the Minnesota chapter of NOW published an article advocating the return to "primitive goddess worship" as a replacement for Christianity. Indeed, not only witchcraft, but goddess worship has become a major component of feminist activity all over the country.

When the nation began to understand the legitimate grievances of women in our society, it was relatively easy for an enlightened and tolerant people to make those adjustments within the traditional framework to accommodate them. But the tortured logic of the feminist Radical Left intended to destroy the traditional framework. Their unnatural notions have already caused untold suffering by women whose marriages have been wrecked, who have taken work responsibilities they did not really want, who have been victimized by abortions that have left a permanent legacy of pain, guilt, and shame, and who have been cast adrift in poverty after divorce. Even worse are the millions of children whose lives have been permanently marred in the feminist struggle to tear down the patriarchy.

Every free society has its share of kooks, weirdos, and far-out radicals. Part of freedom for everyone is our ability to accommodate the lunatic fringes of both Right and Left. The danger comes when the Radical Left not only receives a warm and respectful hearing in the major organs of communication in society, but then these people are elected to the Senate and the House. We find their stalwarts not only parading half-naked down Constitution Avenue with dildos strapped around their loins, but performing simulated sex acts on the pavement and enshrined in positions of power where decisions are made that affect the whole of society.[14]

What Men and Women Want

Common sense screams out at us—the insanity of radical, destructive feminism cannot be allowed in government!

Common sense calls out, Return to the way God made you and protect your families as the most basic unit of your society!

Common sense tells us that men and women want the joy and fulfillment that shared love, shared goals, shared intimacies, shared triumphs, shared tragedies, and shared strength can give them. They want stable, secure marriages based on fidelity, trust, and commitment. They want children to love and to leave as a legacy. They want and they will demand a government structure that will facilitate their marriage and provide their children an environment best-suited to their growth and development. The tide is turning in that direction, but it will take a supreme effort by all of us to reverse the damage that the decades of liberalism have done to the families of our nation.

8

Sex, Lies, and
Common Sense

*T*HERE HAS NEVER BEEN a greater need for a return to common sense in the history of this nation. As confirmed by many indicators, we have already sacrificed two generations of young Americans to the destructive forces of social programming, leaving an immense gap in the ranks of the future leaders of our country. Heightened materialism and the loss of religious values, as the late James Burnham concluded in his classic study of American liberalism, has no doubt weakened our national will and made us vulnerable to pernicious social decay. But the damage already done to the nation's social fabric also makes the prospect for recovery much less certain, unless we can engage effectively on several emotional fronts.

As we examine the evidence of the turning tide in subsequent chapters and as we look for signs of a values shift in the popular culture, we can take hope in the words of William J. Bennett, who remarked recently that ultimate responsibility in any democratic society rests with the people. He said, "The good news is that what has been self-inflicted can be self-corrected." If there is to be a renewed commitment to life, liberty, and the pursuit of happiness in America, it will have to rise up from the grass roots, since government long ago lost its sense of perspective and proportion on such matters.

But the question is this, Will enough people with the power to influence change be willing to do whatever it takes? Will they say the things that must be said in order to heal the wounds of this nation? Or have we already grown so partisan and so entrenched on one side of the culture wars that we cannot enter into creative dialog with those who have the capacity to bring about change? As we will see later in this discussion, lasting change will only come when our commitment crosses all boundaries of politics, race, religion, and social involvement. But this is a thorny issue, strewn with risks.

No one can argue with the reality and the seriousness of the crisis of values facing America's young people. Although liberals refuse to consider it a moral issue, it can be nothing else. Statistics compiled by a national research foundation illustrate some of the dangers facing America's youth today and present a sobering view of the moral decline that has been sweeping this country during the past thirty years. According to the study, the following things happen each day in America:

- 2,795 teenage girls get pregnant, a 500 percent increase since 1966
- 1,106 teenage girls have abortions, an 1,100 percent increase since 1966
- 4,219 teenagers contract a sexually transmitted disease, an increase of 335 percent since 1966
- 135,000 children bring a gun or other weapon to school
- 10 children are killed by guns
- 6 teenagers commit suicide, a 300 percent increase since 1966
- 211 children are convicted of drug use

These data are not from a CBN study. Nor are they from Focus on the Family or the DeMoss Foundation. Instead, they are from a secular, liberal organization, the Children's Defense Fund, the national research and advocacy group supported by First Lady Hillary Rodham Clinton. What they show is that, despite our vast wealth, affluence, and international status, this nation is hardly better off than the most deprived Third World countries when it comes to the emotional well-being of our children. But even more, the most serious deprivation is not a matter of food, shelter, or material comforts, but a raging famine in the human heart.

American Enterprise scholar James Q. Wilson, author of such important works as *Crime and Human Nature* and *On Character*, offers strong evidence that the collapse of moral restraints in contemporary society can be directly linked to the shift in popular attitudes over the past three decades. In place of the traditional sources of character-building that have sustained our nation from its foundation until the mid-1960s—the family, the church, the neighborhood, and the school—young people today are more likely to appropriate their values from the media, their peers, or experimental forms of "socialization" being tested on children by educators at all levels.

The result, Wilson says, is that "the powers exercised by the institutions of social control have been constrained, and people, especially young people, have embraced an ethos that values self-expression over self-control." We live in an era of unprecedented "diversity," "individualism," and "free choice." But all too often the choices are all bad.

What Is Truth?

Given the climate of permissiveness and tolerance in today's culture, it should come as no surprise that young people lack judgment and direction. When we see the results of their excesses and failures, we must also see that the revolutionary doctrines foisted upon them have failed. We should also observe the degree to which young people have been cast adrift on a sea of "cultural relativity" and expected to taste and touch and discern for themselves from a complex array of ideas that have meaning.

Separated from the tried and tested moral structures of society, today's young people are more like orphans raised in a box. They are behavioral experiments based on flawed premises, with no contact with the principles and institutions that undergird civilization. Stripped of a vision of something greater than ourselves, which even Norman Lear concedes is vital to society, they become wards of the state and its surrogates, the schools and the media. And we are surprised when they behave like animals?

One survey of high school and college-age young people found that most believe that honesty is no longer the best policy. The 1991–92 study of the opinions and values of a statistical sample of seven thousand youths showed that it is common for young people to lie, cheat, and steal at school. Furthermore, they are just as likely to be dishonest with parents, teachers, employers, and even their friends.

The study found that 33 percent of high school students and 14 percent of college students indicated that in the previous twelve months they had taken at least one item from a store without paying for it. One in six said they have lied on a résumé, job application, or interview. A third of them said that they would lie in the future to get the job they wanted. Among university students, 40 percent said that they had lied to employers, and 30 percent said they had lied to customers at least once in the previous twelve months. In addition, 60 percent of the high schoolers and 30 percent of those in college said that they have lied to their parents.

Michael Josephson, president of the California-based foundation that conducted the study, says, "There is a hole in the moral ozone layer, and it is probably getting bigger." An indication of the degree of the values crisis, Josephson said, is that students ranked getting into college and getting a high-paying job ahead of honesty on their list of priorities. While a majority of students rated their personal ethics as very good or excellent, barely more than half (54 percent) considered honesty and trustworthiness "essential."

How do you interpret such findings? Josephson attributes these findings to the fact that parents and adults have provided poor examples for young people. In addition, American society no longer imposes consequences for words and actions. "Their misbehavior," he says, "is more often the product of survival strategies and coping mechanisms than moral deficiency." An arresting observation, perhaps, but we must demur. Their misbehavior, while it certainly involves coping, is a moral deficiency brought about by stripping America's classrooms, Sunday schools, and family rooms of a knowledge of and reverence for God's truth.

If nothing else, we should hear the words spoken by God through the Old Testament prophet Hosea, when He said, "my people are destroyed from lack of knowledge. Because you have rejected knowledge, I also reject you as my priests; because you have ignored the law of your God, I also will ignore your children" (Hos. 4:6 NIV). This is the heart of America's crisis of values, and our nation will remain at risk until we do come back to our senses.

Practically Speaking

In the first edition of the *Index of Leading Cultural Indicators*, produced by Empower America and the Heritage Foundation, William Bennett points out the disparity between the material and moral achievements of the past thirty years. He says that since 1960, the country's population has increased 41 percent, the gross domestic product has nearly tripled, and total spending by all levels of government (measured in constant 1990 dollars) has risen from $143.73 billion to $787.0 billion—more than a fivefold increase. Inflation-adjusted spending on welfare has increased 630 percent and inflation-adjusted spending on education has increased 225 percent. The United States has the strongest economy in the world, a healthy entrepreneurial spirit, a still-healthy work ethic, and a generous attitude—good signs all.

But during the same thirty-year period there has been a 560 percent increase in violent crime, more than a 400 percent increase in illegitimate births, a quadrupling in divorce rates, a tripling of the percentage of children living in single-parent homes, more than a 200 percent increase in the teenage suicide rate, and a drop of almost 80 points in SAT scores.

The relationship between financial well-being and spiritual decay is not as unrelated as it may appear. The overall boom in the economy since 1960 owes a great deal to the expansion of the work force brought about by the introduction of more and more female workers. Lower salaries on average for women who occupy slots once filled by men boost corporate profits, but the absence of mothers and fathers from the home in growing numbers changes the dynamics of family life in profound and frequently disturbing ways. Of course, there are many associated problems. Day care is one of the most significant. But rising divorce rates, parental exhaustion, the dramatic changes in the "media culture" (which has become the babysitter of choice in many homes), and the effects of institutionalized behaviorism in the schools weigh heavily. Those most threatened by these changes are the children.

Hand-wringing is certainly no solution to these problems, although there is much of that going on in the media as well as in public platforms and pulpits. With their strong conviction that there is yet hope for solving these problems, Bennett and his colleague, Jack Kemp, have articulated ten specific goals they recommend as public policy initiatives. These goals include improvements in the justice system, educational reforms and school choice, removal of marriage penalties for welfare mothers, tax incentives to help break the cycle of poverty, elimination of no-fault divorce statutes for families with children, and other initiatives to restore the role of fathers in the family. In summarizing these issues, Bennett writes:

> The social regression of the last 30 years is due in large part to the enfeebled state of our social institutions and their failure to carry out a critical and time-honored task: the moral education of the young. We desperately need to recover a sense of the fundamental purpose of education, which is to engage in the architecture of souls. When a self-governing society ignores this responsibility, then, as this document demonstrates, it does so at its peril.

That is precisely where we find ourselves today. Already we have compromised essential domestic and cultural values out of ignorance and out of a mistaken faith in the rule of "experts." Unless we can take back possession of our homes and families and pry loose America's soul from the icy grip of government, the turning tide of history may submerge us instead of lift us up to new heights. In short, I am convinced that the social well-being and spiritual renewal of this nation is *the* key issue of the challenge before us. They are not two issues, but one, for what is at risk is the very soul of America.

The Realities of Change

The most poignant symbol of the turning tide has been demonstrated in the Soviet Union, in Eastern Europe, and most recently in France, where socialism has been soundly defeated by the voters. Burdensome regulations, bureaucracy, punitive taxation, and other manipulative programs of those socialist governments had been grinding people down for decades. Thanks to the unique set of circumstances, which I believe to have been orchestrated by God, the people voted it out. Perhaps the most remarkable thing is that the changes that occurred in the East Bloc countries during the winter of 1989 and 1990 have now reached deep into Europe. The oppression was so bad in the east, something had to give. But now those changes have come to France, where the voters expressed their dissatisfaction not only with socialism but with the cultural and moral decay that it brings. And they did it through the democratic process.

What you have to realize is that the goal of the Radical Left is never to build up society but to tear down existing structures and replace them with a massive social bureaucracy. That is not meant to be an inflammatory statement; it is simply a statement of what the Left, by definition, has always determined to do. The dialectic of socialism is that existing orthodoxies are constantly being replaced by new ones. That is what the liberal wing of the Democratic party in this country is dedicated to doing and why key leaders in the party keep speaking of change as if change were necessary for its own sake. They do not want to improve an existing situation or attempt to revitalize the historic institutions of our nation. They are focused on swift and radical changes in the way America works, from the top down.

The only thing they do not want to change is their own access to power. The cultural elites who orchestrate and bring about change are a privileged cadre here, just as they were in the Soviet Union—a small, well-educated core of liberal leaders who are entitled to have the fantastic dreams, while the rest of us do as we are told. That elite cadre, or politburo, was one of the principal instruments of Marxism, expressed in the principle of "the dictatorship of the proletariat." It is hardly different from the inner circle of the president's cabinet in Washington today.

If you read the writings of the thought leaders on the Left, you will discover that theirs is not a haphazard agenda but a deliberate, long-range, and methodical program to reshape the framework and the foundations of this nation. When Bill Clinton came to the White House, we suddenly had a child of the sixties who was a radical, anti-American demonstrator while at Oxford. From his first steps into the political arena, he drank deeply of radical philosophies. When you see the high priestess of political correctness, Donna Shalala, installed in the Department of Health and Human Services, the department that has the largest budget in government, you see where these radical beliefs inevitably lead.

All through the halls of this new administration you can see the same sort of agenda. We now have a militant lesbian, Roberta Achtenberg, as assistant secretary of the Department of Housing and Urban Development (HUD). The administration came within a hair's breadth of installing as assistant attorney general Lani Guinier, a militant activist who wants to go back to the philosophy of John C. Calhoun, who urged a minority veto over the actions of the majority. According to Guinier's proposals, which were published in a number of journals, if the minorities don't agree with anything that's done by the majority, they would have the right to nullify the majority decision by fiat.

Such choices are polarizing America, forcing both sides in this ideological debate to retreat to their respective corners. The pro-family conservative Christians will never acknowledge or support the values of Achtenberg, but Bill Clinton knew that when he named her to public office. What this says is that the administration is not concerned with the interests or values of the pro-family or any other conservative element that would make personal morality an issue. Despite the best efforts of liberals to convince the Republican party that these conservatives are a minor disturbance and a nuisance, they are finding it is harder and harder to argue with the eighty million Americans on the Right who have suddenly found their voices.

Diversity and Intolerance

Another form of attack on traditional values is the whole issue of homosexuals in the military. From the outset, this was an agenda perpetrated by the extreme Left that set out to weaken the military, to cut defense appropriations back drastically, and insinuate people into the midst of America's fighting forces who would destroy morale and cause critical divisions of authority. The whole thrust of this program has not been, as the media claim, a sign of tolerance and a respect for diversity. Instead, it is a fundamental tenet of socialist beliefs—ideas held by what some commentators are now calling the *Fundamentalist* Left—to undermine authority and to bring down the structures that contribute to the cohesiveness of our society.

At the top of their hit list are such things as family values, social ethics, sexual morality, judicial probity, and governmental restraint. Sadly, we have already come a long way down their list of priorities, thanks in part to the rhetoric of tolerance and diversity that has paved the way for liberal permissiveness. But someone has to say that silence in the face of a moral disaster is not tolerance; it is insanity. Worse, it is criminal. Abraham Lincoln said, "To sin by silence when they should protest, makes cowards out of men." That is an unacceptable risk.

Until now, almost no one has pointed out just how dangerous these doctrines of the Left really are to the future of American society. They are inimical to every foundational principle of this nation. They are contrary to the very institutions and aspirations of our founding fathers, and they are guaranteed to bring us face to face with chaos and collapse. The focus on change in the 1992 elections should have been a tip-off. What these people want to change is everything we have stood for during the past three hundred years, from the leadership of respected elected officials to the moral foundations of liberty. They never speak of retaining America's greatness; they want to remake it after their own image.

The way the fifth-column liberals have gained power has been subtle. They have done it by infiltrating the press, the government, and the educational institutions. They have gone on the attack against anyone who dared speak against them. Remember how liberal students and faculty at Harvard railed against General Colin Powell, the distinguished chairman of the Joint Chiefs of Staff who guided our military policy during the Persian Gulf War, simply because he had spoken out against the wisdom of allowing gays to serve in the military. They excoriated him in the vilest language because he was not "politically correct," to their way of thinking.

I was attacked viciously by the Left and by homosexuals because of one line in my speech at the 1992 Republican Convention in Houston, in which I said that if Bill Clinton was elected he would put homosexuals in the military. The media and the liberal politicians said I gave an anti-homosexual speech. Well, in fact, I was reporting precisely what Clinton said he would do, and that is precisely what he has tried to do. But I was castigated in the media and at demonstrations all across this country and characterized as a reactionary right-winger and a "homophobe." Yet more and more thinking people are beginning to understand this vicious criticism used to assail anyone who goes against this destructive agenda—and especially those who try to defend the traditional values and Christian beliefs of this nation.

Dr. Kinsey's Fraud

Of course, the liberals and homosexuals have gained some allies in the general population, fellow travelers, if you will, but to build their coalition they have had to misuse statistics and to rely upon false information, such as that fabricated by the Kinsey reports of the forties and fifties that portrayed America as a sexually profligate nation. Now widely reported, incontrovertible evidence shows that everything Albert Kinsey reported, in both of his so-called classic studies, was a deliberate fraud. He surveyed men and women in prison, many of whom were sex offenders, and on the basis of that evidence he projected the moral condition of America.

The evidence is overwhelming that Kinsey falsified his findings, rejected scientific sampling methods in order to obtain the predetermined results he wanted, and used seriously flawed methods in reporting his data. The academic community and everyone associated with scientific sampling methods should be outraged, especially considering how flagrant Kinsey's data really were and the travesty of perversion they helped to unleash upon this nation during the so-called sexual revolution. Every respectable newsmagazine and journal in this country should be screaming foul—but the issue has been ignored.

Seward Hiltner's book, published in 1953, reported on the travesty of Kinsey's findings. A year later, Elam Daniels wrote *I Accuse Kinsey*, showing how bizarre and how tortured Kinsey's interpretations really were. More recently, Dr. Judith Reisman and Edward W. Eichel, Dr. J. Gordon Muir, and Dr. John H. Court provided an exhaustive analysis and discussion of the Kinsey studies and proved, incontrovertibly, that Kinsey lied. Their book, *Kinsey, Sex and Fraud: The Indoctrination of a People*, demonstrates how Kinsey perpetrated an act that has left a deadly legacy for more than half a century. Fraudulent reports have been presented as truth by many otherwise intelligent people all these years. Although no major organization has yet spoken against them, the truth about Kinsey's lies will prove to be one more pivotal point in the turning tide.

It was Kinsey who originated the statement that homosexuals made up 10 percent of the population. At one point, based on his statistics, it was estimated that the homosexual population of New York City was half a million strong. Ironically, it was the AIDS epidemic that forced researchers to determine the precise number of homosexuals. They discovered that the total was less than one hundred thousand—one-fifth the original estimate. We have reliable and widely reported evidence that fewer than 2 percent of the population are homosexual and fewer than 1 percent are lesbians. America is waking up to the lie of homosexual power, but Hollywood, the media, and the educational establishment are still pushing to make homosexuality a protected right, as if it were a major factor in American life.

America's Holocaust

We have seen the shocking escalation of the number of abortions in this country. Even conservative reports indicate that more than twenty-eight million children have been aborted in the twenty years since *Roe v. Wade*. Promiscuity leads to pregnancy, but rather than face the legitimate consequences of their actions, the people who want to promote unrestrained sexual license have made abortion on demand a universal right, and history will record—if anyone survives to write it— that the holocaust of abortion has far surpassed the Holocaust of Nazi Germany in the sheer number of innocent victims.

Instead of working to restore respect for human life and stability to the family, Bill Clinton pledged to make abortion "safe and legal— but rare." There is no doubt time and attention is being focused on keeping the contraceptive uses of abortion safe and legal, but keeping it rare will be much more difficult, since whatever government subsidizes invariably grows, and the Clinton administration has every intent of subsidizing abortions for women.

In an editorial in *U.S. News & World Report* written prior to his appointment as communications adviser to the president, Republican David Gergen wrote that the Clinton administration appeared to be committed to riding "roughshod over the sensibilities of most Americans" on the divisive issue of abortion. He says that many polls during the last few years have suggested that most Americans have come to a point of intellectual compromise with their consciences. While they don't like the idea of abortion, they have agreed not to resist. George Gallup reported that approximately three-fourths of Americans disapprove of abortion and a third believe it is murder. Nevertheless, more than half believe it should be legal. Gergen writes:

> Where most Americans draw the line is on paying for other
> people's abortions, especially abortions on demand. In an ABC-

Washington Post survey [in 1992], 69 percent of those polled said
the federal government should not pay "for an abortion for any
woman who wants it and cannot afford to pay." Strikingly, a 1992
survey from *Reader's Digest* by Richard Wirthlin found that poorer
Americans are the most opposed to federal funding. Among those
earning less than $15,000 a year, opposition ran 63 to 32 percent
against funding, while those making over $60,000 favored it by 57
to 41 percent!

Then a columnist, now a presidential adviser, Gergen asks, "Is
Clinton listening to the people he wants to help?" Obviously not. The
Alan Guttmacher Institute reported that one year before *Roe v. Wade*,
only 12.5 of all pregnancies ended in abortion. By 1976 the number had
almost doubled to 23.1 percent. Today, despite the Hyde Amendment
which prevents federal funding of most abortions, one in four pregnancies ends in abortion. Liberals claim that limitations on federal funding penalize the poor. However, as Gergen reports, the Guttmacher
study shows that poor women are three times more likely than others
to have an abortion. In 1991, 61 percent of all pregnancies among
black women ended in abortion.

Recently one report stated that the most dangerous place to be in
America today is in a mother's womb. The place that God made as a
haven and a refuge, as a sacred and mysterious laboratory for the development of life, as His greatest promise of renewal for the human race,
has become a slaughterhouse. Abortionists murder up to 1.6 million children each year in their mothers' wombs. Is anybody listening to these
cries of the heart? Where are those who want to save the baby seals, the
dolphins, the red squirrels? Don't they want to save the children?

After the Boom

This is the kind of damage that is already being done to the next generation, and now we are seeing what is called the generation of "baby
busters" growing up with no hope, no goals, no moral convictions, no
sexual identity, no feelings of patriotism, no identification with

society, and no peace or even a capacity for happiness. It is one of the most pathetic groups of people that has ever come up in the history of the world. These are the people who are going to become our future leaders. On average, they have no religious faith to speak of, and they have no realistic concept of God. They are syncretistic about spiritual matters—they will take a little of this and a little of that. If they like the Christian view of heaven, they'll take that, and if they like the Hindu concept of Karma, they'll take that. Then they'll throw in a little spiritism, astrology, and nature worship and believe they know about God.

If it sometimes seems that this is what the radicals set out to achieve, you're absolutely right. If you want to see what it looks like after a few years, when the trends are all well-established, take a look at Amsterdam, Holland, where the hippies took control of the city and legalized sex, drugs, and every kind of aberrant behavior imaginable. Short of a miracle, this is a vision of America's future.

As many as seventy-five to eighty thousand young people come pouring in to Amsterdam every weekend looking for cheap and accessible drugs and every conceivable sensual experience. There are homosexual hotels, a red-light district that would be an abomination to Sodom and Gomorrah, and sex shops where women are displayed in the windows like pieces of meat. Somebody, man or woman, will come along and pick one out of the window, and then another girl will step up to take her place. There is nothing more demeaning and degrading. But this is the gift of liberation, the legacy of postwar nihilism, the full expression of the existential philosophy of Jean-Paul Sartre, and the final pathetic and withered flowering of the God-Is-Dead movement. This is the glorious dream the advance guard of American liberals want to bring to this country.

The common-sense response to this vision of life in the abyss, which no one in government seems to understand, is that you have to have discipline with children. You have to set standards of behavior and see that they adhere to them, whatever it takes. A few years ago, U.S. cigarette manufacturers put $3 million into an ad campaign saying, "Let youth decide." Obviously they knew that under the humanistic system of child choice, by which kids make decisions on impulse rather than on the basis of knowledge or reason, children were more likely to smoke cigarettes at an early age if they were given that choice.

Of course they are right. Children are also more likely to abuse alcohol, experiment with drugs, indulge in promiscuous sex, and dabble in every other self-destructive behavior if there is no moral guidance and no restriction on what they can or cannot do. So the level of morality in the cigarette companies becomes quite clear when they weigh in with a $3 million brainwashing campaign to put this deadly and life-threatening decision—whether or not to smoke cigarettes—into the hands of children. All the evidence demonstrates conclusively that smoking cigarettes, or even breathing secondhand smoke, can produce fatal lung cancer if continued for a period of time. So the tobacco industry reasoned, using the educational mantra, "Let youth decide," to strip away the guidelines that responsible adults should provide for impressionable youth.

The AIDS Revolution

Along with this, of course, we have the AIDS crisis, now supported by an entire movement that has taken a disease that could have been controlled by normal health standards and, by politicizing it, made it into a killer epidemic. AIDS is the first disease in history to be endowed with civil rights by the government. It is absolutely contrary to common sense to say that a virus has civil rights, but that's what the government has done. So we are treating a deadly disease differently from any other pandemic in history and denying the magnitude of the contagion involved for fear of offending the delicate sensibilities of those who suffer from it. Instead of following medically approved practices for limiting exposure and warning others of potential risks, we are allowing it to spread throughout the population.

Today there may be as many as sixty million HIV-infected carriers in the world, with an infection growth rate of 100 percent per year. In 1991, the *Journal of the American Medical Association* (JAMA) reported on the incidence of AIDS since its symptoms were first reported in 1981.

At that time a total of 189 cases had been reported to the Centers for Disease Control (CDC) from fifteen states and the District of Columbia, with the majority from New York and California. Of those, 97 percent were men, 79 percent of whom were homosexual/bisexual men.

But by 1990, there were forty-three thousand cases from all fifty states, the District of Columbia, and the U.S. territories. Two-thirds of those cases were from outside New York and California. Researchers found that 11 percent of the reported cases were among women, and there were approximately eight hundred cases among children under the age of thirteen.

Since the disease was first recognized in 1981, the U.S. Public Health Service has gathered information on more than 179,000 persons with the AIDS virus. Approximately 63 percent of those have since died. Subsequently, the World Health Organization (WHO) predicted that the total number of AIDS cases by the year 2000 could exceed twenty million.

Without doubt, AIDS is the most deadly epidemic of our time and may yet be the most fearful killer of all time. Adding to existing concerns is the WHO statement that as many as 90 percent of the actual occurrences of the disease may never have been reported. By some calculations the actual total may be as high as ten million cases. Dr. Dorothy Blake, deputy director of the Global AIDS Program, estimates the total number of cases by 2010 could surpass forty million men, women, and children.

Whenever anyone recites these figures, particularly Evangelicals, activists immediately cry that we are prejudiced. But the greatest threat and the most inhumane response would be to keep silent—and, as Lincoln said, it would also be a sin. But we should not speak of the AIDS epidemic without noting also the alarming rise in sexually transmitted diseases (STDs), especially among the young. Research suggests that as many as 63 percent of all STD infections in this country are among young people twenty-five years old and younger. Each year there are a million new cases of pelvic inflammatory disease, 1.3 million cases of gonorrhea (some strains of which have become resistant to treatment), 134,000 cases of syphilis (a disease that had virtually disappeared just ten years ago), and a half-million cases of herpes. In addition, there are twenty-four million cases of human papilloma virus (HPV) among American women, and four million new cases of chlamydia each year. It is reported that three million American teenagers are affected by STDs.

The Problem with Truth

The great tragedy of our day is that truth is no longer very popular. It is not politically correct. Sex within marriage, sexual restraint, and delayed gratification are concepts that have lost their appeal for many people in our society. Aided and abetted by the philosophies of Hugh Hefner and the *Playboy* generation, sensual self-indulgence has become a national pastime. Even the people who are most deeply addicted to it, however, understand that this is a practice whose outcome is self-destructive. The pandemic of venereal disease sweeping our nation is just one more proof of this fact.

But denying the truth in order to rationalize sinful behavior is nothing new. In his study of the lives and legacies of some of the best-known sexual libertarians of our time, author E. Michael Jones examines the philosophy that puts passion above reason and desire above truth. "There are ultimately only two alternatives in the intellectual life," he says. "Either one conforms desire to truth or one conforms truth to desire." But truth shines forth from history, art, literature, and human experience. And above all, truth radiates from the Scriptures and the historic teachings of the church. But for many modern intellectuals and thought leaders, the universe does not derive from history or the arts, or especially the Bible. It derives from "their own minds," which means that they must find some way of rethinking and restructuring the sources of authority. Jones writes:

> The intellectual life, then, is a peculiarly modern invention, whose rise is predicated upon the demise of the Church as a guide to life. It is then no coincidence that the rise of the intellectual should coincide with something like the French Revolution. The

two things were, in effect, causally related. The demise of the Church created the moral and intellectual vacuum in which the intellectual needed to flourish. Just what the flourishing entails is depressingly common and documented *ad nauseam* in Johnson's book [*Intellectuals*, 1988]. The modern intellectual is, for the most part, a lecher and a fool. His theories are propounded for everyone but himself.

At the outset of the modern intellectual tradition, Jones adds, came men like Jean Jacques Rousseau, the eighteenth-century philosopher and author of *Emile*, "the first modern book on child rearing," who sent all five of his own illegitimate children to orphanages at birth. Considering the harshness of the conditions in the orphanages in those times this was, in fact, a death sentence.

But the legacy of intellectual hypocrisy doesn't end there. The list of philosophers and scientists with comparable skeletons in their closets is long and shocking. Karl Marx fathered an illegitimate child by his maid and sent the child off to live with a working-class family. He refused to see the child for fear it might hurt his reputation as a revolutionary. There is convincing evidence that Sigmund Freud carried on a long affair with his sister-in-law and had a morbid fascination with incest. Margaret Mead, the American anthropologist whose work on sexuality in Samoa became such a rage among intellectuals, was involved in many kinds of promiscuous behavior, including an adulterous affair, and it is clear now that her theories of "cultural relativism" were "a clever rationalization for her own adultery."

Michael Jones observes:

> Lust is a common enough vice, especially in this age. The crucial intellectual event occurs, however, when vices are transmuted into theories, when the "intellectual" sets up shop in rebellion against the moral law and, therefore, in rebellion against the truth. All the modern "isms" follow as a direct result of this rebellion. All of them entail rationalization. All of them can be best understood in light of the moral disorder of their founders, proponents, and adherents.

He concludes his study with the observation that, "The mind is like a window. It is transparent only when it is clean. If it, through strenuous effort, catches some glimpse of truth, then it is the truth that shines forth in that system and not the personality of the thinker." He then goes on to say:

A mind clouded by passion is like a window covered with dirt. It is not transparent; it is aware only of itself. Virtually all the artistic breakthroughs of the modern age . . . are a function of the mind turned away from truth and focused on its own desires instead. The turning away from the truth at the behest of disordered passions does not mean that the mind will stop functioning; it only means that that mind will not perceive the truth. And after a period of laboring in the dark, the mind can choose disorder over order and create for itself idols that it will serve instead of the truth placed in the universe by the Creator who is synonymous with truth.

When we turn from truth, we turn from God, and when we turn from God, disaster always comes. That is the burning lesson of the Scriptures. God spoke through Ezekiel: "Because you have forgotten me and turned your backs upon me, therefore you must bear the consequence of all your sin" (Ezek. 23:35 TLB). "AIDS is a fitting epitaph for our century," writes Jones. "What started out in rebellion ended in death. The rebellion against the moral succeeded and we overthrew ourselves."

A Revival of Hope

With such a dark assessment of the accomplishments of our age, can we still hold out hope for survival? Now that we have achieved at least a temporary reprieve from the threat of nuclear holocaust, is the enigma of AIDS to be the newest menace to sweep the world? Or is the collapse of society to come about through a continued deconstruction of rational inquiry and moral restraint?

Oddly enough, one of the voices of hope comes from *Playboy* magazine, which published an article by Joe Conason entitled "God As Their Co-Pilot," which claims that the Religious Right is on the move, recommitted after the defeat of George Bush to take back America. "The defeat of George Bush," Conason writes, "may mark only the true takeoff point for the increasingly powerful religious right, a movement far more ominous than any represented by Bush or Ronald Reagan." What makes us a threat in the eyes of *Playboy* is that grass-roots America is rising in unprecedented numbers and winning elections from New York to Los Angeles. With more than 450,000 members nationwide, the Christian Coalition now has 860 chapters in all 50 states, and thanks to highly professional training courses and publications like the full-color newspaper, *The Christian American*, millions of Evangelicals, pro-family Roman Catholics, and observant Jews are flooding into leadership roles throughout America.

If we sometimes feel weak and despondent, maybe we should recognize that our enemies are terrified that we may take this nation back to its moral foundations and cast off the shackles of corruption and national dissipation. The pornographers should shudder! *Playboy* says the new Religious Right is "the wealthiest, fastest-growing, most powerful, and best-organized grass-roots political movement" in America. What they also need to know is that it has not happened by accident. What is happening today is an answer to generations of fervent prayers by God's people, and now a genuine revival of hope is just ahead.

When evangelist Mario Murillo came on our program in July 1993, he said that God had given him a powerful new vision that this generation of young people, which we have come to think of as the new "lost generation," are actually going to be the spark of revival in our nation. Today their souls are empty; they have no moral vision, no history, and no sense of identity. They have been stripped of moral foundations, and thanks to the work of atheists like Madalyn Murray O'Hair and the ACLU, they have no concept of God. But God is going to turn things around, and where there was once barrenness there will be richness. Where there was slumber there is going to be a great awakening. Mario believes these young people are going to light up the world, and instead of burning up and destroying themselves as so many have feared, he told my co-host Ben Kinchlow that these young people are going to be the kindling for a nationwide, perhaps even a worldwide, return to faith in God.

Beyond Victimism

In his landmark book, A Nation of Victims, Charles J. Sykes identified another very important element of the modern dilemma: The reduction of sin to a psychological disorder that demands, not religion, but therapy. This belief in "victimism" has become so common we find ourselves today living in a therapeutic culture. It is the world of pop psychology and victim's rights, sensitivity training and political correctness. Citing Thomas Szasz's 1988 work, The Myth of Psychotherapy, Sykes says:

> The triumph of the therapeutic can perhaps best be understood as the ascendancy of a substitute faith. Filling the vacuum created by the decline of institutional faith and the collapse of the moral order it has provoked, psychoanalysis has assumed many of the functions traditionally performed by religion, and has done so by translating many of the theological and existential issues of human life into therapeutic terms. What had once been the "cure of souls" by the church has now become the treatment of psychological illness by medical science.

Today, America is overrun by armies of therapists. Not just M.D.'s in white lab coats, but government workers, politicians, educators, experts on criminal justice and the law, local bureaucrats, and quacks of a thousand different varieties. The media are overrun by them, graduates of politically correct journalism and broadcast schools telling us that society is to blame for our problems. Murder, robbery, rape, and abuse are not decried as reprehensible acts that need to be punished; they are symptoms of "dysfunction" that demand "rehabilitation." Instead of "sin" we find "poor socialization." Instead of "redemption," society's victim needs "remediation."

Such examples of absurd logic have become commonplace today, defying common sense. The growing cult of victimization routinely confuses the violator with the victim, and by tossing out the concept of "blame" for wrongdoing, it substitutes empathy and understanding. It is not difficult to see the fruits of such false logic. We find ourselves living today in a society based on victimism that grants opportunities to the oppressed of every description, not because they are deserving, but because they are "disadvantaged." The courts return criminals to the streets because they have been convinced by shrewd defense attorneys (and their expert witnesses) that the criminal was only crying out for help.

But sooner or later, common sense has to prevail. Charles Sykes suggests, "Ultimately, common sense is the stumbling block that victimism may not be able to overcome. At some level of our being, we all know that something is required of us, however much we may try to shake it off. Instinctively and rationally, we know our responsibilities; we know that we are not sick when we are merely weak; we know that others are not to blame when we have erred; we know that the world does not exist to make us happy."

Jesus said, "You shall know the truth, and the truth shall make you free." As we have seen, the journey to common sense must lead us to the essential truths that have sustained civilization for centuries: that we are children of God, designed to seek truth and wisdom and enabled to live in peace with man and God. As we shall see in the next chapter, the fabric of society will never be restored until we come to know the authentic source of truth.

9

What Every Child Should Know

*I*N MY LIBRARY IS A 1970 edition of *Webster's Collegiate Dictionary*. Under the word *educate* is this definition: "To develop mentally and morally, especially by instruction." The classic meaning of education was to train the *minds* and *morals* of students. Education by common definition existed to impart to the young the moral and intellectual heritage of a nation, a culture, or a civilization.

In the famed Northwest Ordinance, finally approved in 1789, which is considered, along with the Declaration of Independence and the Constitution, one of the three founding documents of the United States of America, are these words: "Religion, morality, and knowledge, being necessary to good government and the happiness of mankind, schools and the means of education shall forever be encouraged."

Nothing in the classic definition of education included the arsenal of today's liberal educators—brainwashing, psychological manipulation, destruction of religious faith, accommodation to bizarre sexuality, or subversion of the norms of society.

The goals of classic education were to train young minds to think and to impart to them both a set of facts and skills plus the moral standards necessary to place these in perspective. In today's education scarcely any facts are being imparted and absolutely no morality. Children do not learn multiplication tables or precise mathematics. They do not learn the facts of history, geography, or science. Imagine my shock to learn that 25 percent of the students surveyed in a Dallas, Texas, high school could not name the country that borders Texas. An equal number in a Florida high school could not locate their state on a map. A sizable number of Boston students could not name the New England states that bordered Massachusetts.

In New York City, some 43 percent of students drop out of school before finishing high school. In a suburban Philadelphia high school, 85 percent of the graduates were functionally illiterate. An Alabama employer had to interview a hundred students from an adjoining Georgia town before he could find two with sufficient skills to do the simplest math problems.

America has roughly twenty-eight million functional illiterates and somewhere around eighty-three million people who are in some way learning impaired. Some 60 percent of all the inmates in our prisons are functionally illiterate. In Mississippi, I was told by the superintendent of corrections that the percentage of functionally illiterate inmates in that state was 70 percent.

Clearly the basic skill for any education is reading. Unless a person can read and write, he or she cannot function successfully in modern society. Unfortunately the current system of education defies all the common-sense speech patterns of young human beings. All people in all cultures learn to talk by pronouncing syllables—da-da, ma-ma, wa-wa, etc. Lacking a genius IQ, no child starts to talk in full words and full sentences.

Yet modern educators have forced children into an illogical exercise called "look-say." Instead of teaching children to work phonetically and build words through the consonants, vowels, and letter groupings that they have learned to sound out, the look-say method forces them to memorize words. The result is disastrous. A good phonics program can produce the ability to read an adult vocabulary of more than twenty thousand words. The look-say memory technique at best yields facility with about fifteen hundred words; at worst it yields illiteracy. I have seen estimates that as many as 90 percent of the students in the New York City public schools read at or below the third-grade level. This says that most of the course material in grades four through twelve is essentially gibberish to these students. Is there any wonder they are bored, rowdy, and inclined to delinquency?

Instead of admitting the utter failure of an attempt to teach reading by memorizing words and returning to the phonics system that clearly works, professional educators plunged deeper into the abyss. They embraced a system called "whole-sentence reading." Learning to read by memorizing individual words was extraordinarily difficult; now they are giving students the impossible task of learning to read by memorizing entire sentences.

The Moral Vacuum

Moral instruction is even weaker. I will never forget the television interview I conducted with a high school teacher from Alabama. He described the teacher's manual that had been given him for a class in behavior modification. The manual proceeded as follows: "What do you tell a student who asks you if shoplifting is wrong?" Answer, "You answer that you cannot tell him if shoplifting is wrong. He must decide that question for himself."

Imagine such situational nonsense! If the child shoplifts and gets caught, he will be convicted of a possible felony and sent to jail. He then would carry a police record the rest of his life. If caught at a job, he could be fired. Furthermore stealing is wrong. It breaks not only the Ten Commandments, but every moral code of all known civilizations. In the Muslim world under the *Sharia* or Islamic code, a shoplifter would not merely be jailed, he could have his hand amputated.

How then could any sane curriculum development committee expose an impressionable youth of fifteen or sixteen to a possible prison term, loss of a job, loss of reputation, family disgrace, or worse? The answer is simple. No sane person would do such a thing, but the leaders of public education in America today are not sane. They are a group of ideological extremists who are so fixated with their illogical educational theories that they have lost touch with reality.

As is the case with every other theory not anchored to the objective reality of theistic truth, idealistic theory, as was the case in both the French and the Russian revolutions, can lead to extremism that can lead to fanaticism that can lead to cruelty, insanity, and atavistic self-destruction.

Whether this nation wants to admit it or not, and despite the numbers of dedicated, conscientious public school administrators and teachers, the truth is that public education in America today is firmly in the grip of fanatical ideologues whose crackpot theories are fast destroying not only the public school system but an entire generation of our young.

As a consequence, American education is now the worst of any developed nation. In a recent math test, American students scored behind students from all developed nations and were slightly ahead of the students from the African nation of Swaziland.

Return to Local Control

Our spending for education has skyrocketed because the professional education union and its left-wing allies have succeeded in intimidating state legislatures and the Congress. We have been sold a bill of goods that public education in America is the key to democratic survival. In actual fact, public education in America—certainly in its major cities—is destroying democracy in America. In the age of privatization of publicly owned monopolies, the public school system in America has become an inefficient anachronism that resembles the state-owned factories of the former Soviet Union, the state-owned telephone monopoly of Juan Peron's Argentina, and the state-owned railroads and steel mills of Great Britain under the socialist government of Clement Attlee.

It is extremely difficult, even in the face of overwhelming evidence, for the American people to admit that the school system in their town is no good. Maybe the nation's schools are inadequate, but not theirs. Maybe the national teachers union is corrupt in other towns, but not in their town.

The worldwide tide is running against state-owned monopolies. Everywhere one hears the cry for privatization, free enterprise, and competition. Consumers demand more choice, lower prices, new technologies, and increased efficiency. Whether it is five-hundred-channel digital television, interactive home shopping via television, or worldwide direct-dial satellite telephone service, consumers are expecting old monopolies to give way to radical improvement as we move into the twenty-first century.

Public education is no exception. Its day of reckoning is coming, and the vehicle for creative competition and accountability is the simple free-market concept of giving the consumer—in this case the parents of school-age children—a choice of schools for their children among private schools, parochial schools, or newly designed public magnet schools that feature a drug-free, crime-free learning environment with strict discipline, a dress code, enriched learning, and clear-cut standards of excellence. Once the market can decide, those schools that don't measure up, as is the case with all second-rate businesses, will be forced either to change or close down.

The Struggle in Jersey

Mayor Bret Schundler has his hands full, but he is adamant and he will not give up the fight. The National Education Association (NEA) and the American Federation of Teachers (AFT) have declared his town, Jersey City, New Jersey, as one of ten target cities for all-out war. The problem is that 70 percent of the people in Jersey City, in both political parties, favor school choice, allowing parents to choose where and how their children should be educated. The teachers' unions are irate and have promised to bring the full weight of their influence down upon Schundler and Jersey City until the mayor and the city get back in line with their liberal policies.

NEA President Keith Geiger is calling for a strike force to defeat the residents of Jersey City, including a deduction from the paychecks of teachers throughout the state to fund an "anti-choice" political campaign. But Mayor Schundler says he is only thinking about the betterment of his community. "I want to save inner-city public schools by forcing them to improve," he told the *Wall Street Journal*. "They may have a monopoly now, but no one enjoys working in them. They are an urban tragedy."

What is the radical idea behind Schundler's plan? Just the principle that has made American business great: it's called "competition." By giving parents back $3,000 to $6,000 of the aid money now going to the schools, and by allowing parents to use that money to pay tuition at the school they believe to be best suited to their child's needs, the entire educational process will gain an unaccustomed shot of reality. "My message to the suburbs is this," says Schundler, "Stop giving cities what you don't want to give us, namely money. Instead, give cities what we do want, namely choice."

Already this New York City suburb is spending an astonishing $9,240 per student and $300,000 per classroom for substandard education. For all that money, just 40 percent of Jersey City students graduate from high school, and many of those are functionally illiterate. Schools being run by NEA standards are so poor that the state had to seize control of them in 1989, but to date virtually no improvements have been made.

The Will of the People

Where choice has been tried it has worked. When parents and children decide what is best, without being stiff-armed by bureaucrats into a "status quo" educational system, test scores go up and attitudes improve. As the *Wall Street Journal* pointed out, "The status quo stultifies the efforts of great teachers, but it also provides protected employment for all union members. In much of the Northeast, even marginal teachers can earn $75,000 or more a year plus benefits for 180 days of work a year. The cost of all this is just mind-boggling."

This, the *Journal*'s editorial writer adds, explains why the national NEA wants to crush school choice in Jersey City. As Mayor Schundler says, "The teachers unions aren't afraid we'll fail. They're afraid we'll succeed and show that empowering parents instead of bureaucrats is the key to improving schools and weeding out poor teachers."

In its battle against the citizens of Jersey City, the NEA plans to bus teachers from all over the state. They plan to do the same all over America, in other targeted cities, to batter the resistance to their union monopoly. But can they trample the will of the people? Will the NEA's war defeat the citizens of New Jersey? Mayor Schundler says he dared anyone in the New Jersey legislature to bet against the people of Jersey City, but no one would take the bet. Neither should the NEA.

But New Jersey is not the only skirmish line in the education war. In an article in *National Review*, Charles J. Sykes reports that the same thing is happening in Wisconsin, where liberal groups supporting the public school cartel have launched an assault against private citizens and small school programs where gifted teachers are attempting to improve the chances for students in Milwaukee's inner city. Wisconsin public schools have failed so miserably, Sykes says, they have become "educational Bhopals" in which only 32 percent of their black students ever graduate. The failures are so pronounced, in fact, that politicians were forced to give school choice a try, and it is working.

The school choice program in Milwaukee organized by a black Democrat, Polly Williams, is one conspicuous example, but everywhere choice programs have been implemented, they have succeeded beautifully, far surpassing the results of the public schools. Liberals, however, are not interested in giving power to the people; they want power for themselves. So now the NEA, the NAACP, and the Wisconsin Association of School Administrators have joined forces to carry out a vicious smear campaign against these choice programs, solely to protect the public school monopoly and to keep their tight-fisted grip on inner-city power.

In unison with the *Wall Street Journal's* assessment of the real motives behind the NEA's attack on Jersey City, Sykes writes:

> It is no longer beefy white racists who are standing in the schoolhouse door; today it is beefy white liberals, who care so deeply about the poor that they cannot imagine giving them the

power to make decisions over their own lives. They know that empowering parents can be a contagious idea. The educrats are not afraid that choice will fail; they are terrified it will succeed.

Against the Grain

But betting against the will of the people goes against the grain in this country. The Boston Tea Party was a good example of how Americans feel about the abuse of power, but the provocation for citizen action has never been greater than it is today. Although the liberals in government refuse to be dissuaded from their social agenda by mere public opinion, they and the liberal leadership of the NEA have decided to target anyone who stands in their way. And their most hated enemy is the Religious Right.

Everywhere you look today, there are signs that the secular establishment has targeted Evangelicals and other religious groups for political attack. "Alarms are being raised," writes *Forbes* columnist Thomas Sowell, "that conservative or religious indoctrination will be imposed in the public schools." But in truth, he says, any real or perceived dangers from the Right don't even come close to the dangers represented by the awesome education bureaucracy already in place in this country, which has been conducting a systematic brainwashing of America's children. He writes:

> The techniques of brainwashing developed in totalitarian countries are routinely used in psychological conditioning programs imposed on American school children. These include emotional shock and desensitization, psychological isolation from sources of support, stripping away defenses, manipulative cross-examination of the individual's underlying moral values, and inducing acceptance of alternative values by psychological rather than rational means.

The columnist, an economist and senior fellow at the Hoover Institute at Stanford University, says such practices are employed throughout the educational system today, not only dealing with personal and relational issues, but even in such subjects as history and social studies. They are especially prevalent in courses dealing with social issues, such as sex education, death education, drug prevention, nuclear education, and multiculturalism. Sowell writes:

> Shock and desensitization procedures range from taking children to morgues and funeral homes to see and touch dead bodies to pairing boys and girls to have conversations with each other about sex, showing ghastly movies of war, or raw movies showing sexual activity or close-ups of childbirth.
>
> Verbal examples include classroom discussions of lifeboat dilemmas, where the limited capacity of the boat forces decisions as to who should be left to drown. Sometimes children are asked to decide whom they would sacrifice among members of their own family.

In 1990, CBN received a letter from a sixteen-year-old junior in a high school in Gorham, Maine. She told us that she was forced to fill out the following worksheet and pass it in for a grade in her Social Issues in Science class. This questionnaire was written from a patently homosexual point of view and clearly intended to cast doubt on the heterosexual lifestyle. Ask yourself how you would feel about a teacher (homosexual or heterosexual) asking such intimate questions of your daughter, your granddaughter, or your sister. What conceivable part of education encompasses this type of outrageous invasion of privacy? Here is the questionnaire for a sixteen-year-old girl:

1. Define heterosexuality.

2. How can you tell if someone is heterosexual (straight)?

3. What causes heterosexuality?

4. Is it possible that heterosexuality stems from a neurotic fear of others of the same sex?

5. The media seem to portray straights as preoccupied with (genital) sex. Do you think this is so?

6. Do you think straights flaunt their sexuality? If so, why?

7. In a straight couple, who takes the dominant role and who takes the passive role?

8. 40 percent of married couples get divorced. Why is it so difficult for straights to stay in long-term relationships?

9. Considering the consequences of overpopulation, could the human race survive if everyone were heterosexual?

10. 99 percent of reported rapists are heterosexual. Why are straights so sexually aggressive?

11. The majority of child molesters are heterosexuals. Do you consider it safe to expose children to heterosexual teachers, scout leaders, coaches, etc.?

12. Are you offended when a straight person of the other sex "comes on" to you?

13. When did you choose your sexual orientation?

14. How easy would it be for you if you wanted to change your sexual orientation starting right now?

15. What have been your reactions to answering these questions? What feelings have you experienced? Why?

It would be convenient to believe that such examples are only isolated cases, or the actions of a few bizarre people, but that is not the case. As Sowell stresses, it is a nationwide trend supported by educational psychologists and program materials being distributed to educators, school boards, and curriculum administrators nationwide. Included in these packages are detailed guidelines and instructions on how to deal with parents and others who object. Along with this, the NEA has produced an instructional video, booklets, and a militant action guide for defeating the Religious Right and like-minded conservatives.

"Mobilizing schoolchildren for the political crusades of the Left has also been going on for years," writes Sowell. At one time the Oval Office was routinely flooded with "anti-nuclear" letters from schoolchildren, orchestrated and initiated by liberal teachers and their educational curriculum. More recently we have seen multiculturalism being force-fed to children through politically correct textbooks and teaching methods.

How do the schools deal with complaints? Teacher handbooks offer specific guidelines. When parents complain to the schools, they are to be told, "None of the other parents has objected!" or "You're the only one who has complained." Such tactics are designed to isolate and humiliate those who are rightly shocked by what their children are seeing and doing in school. When parents come together in groups to resist the indoctrination of their children, the cry of censorship goes up loud and clear, and the liberal media are quickly put on the trail, to accuse and vilify the troublemakers in the eyes of the community. Unfortunately, the troublemakers are decent people like you. They are not outlaws; they're your friends and neighbors.

But, says Sykes, the NEA liberals and other school board administrators have it backward. The battle over school choice, he says, points out just how differently the "educrats" and the parents feel about the education of their children. He writes:

> Given the dangers young blacks face in the nation's inner cities—illiteracy, drugs, gang violence—few black parents lose much sleep worrying that their children will be exposed to *prayer*. The educrats, however, worry about it *for* them. (Repeat after me: A crucifix submerged in urine is art; a crucifix in a classroom is a threat to our constitutional freedom.)

The National Education War

One of the major publications of the NEA's assault on conservative values is called *Combating the New Right,* and it describes the pro-family movement in America as the "barefoot and pregnant coalition." Another publication, *What's Left after the Right,* written by Portland professor Janet Jones, is a resource tool for educators distributed by the NEA. This handbook includes the following sections: "The Typical Censorship Scenario," "Profile of a Censor," "How the Religious Right Views the New Age and the Force," and "Friends of Public Education."

Throughout this literature, parents who resist on moral grounds are labeled as censors and extremists, while left-wing activists and social reformers are called friends and supporters.

A self-test is also included in the handbook, entitled, "Your Radical Right IQ." The quiz is designed to help reinforce the indoctrination and lock certain names of friends and enemies in the teacher's mind. It begins by saying, "Administrators in this district know several state and national organizations that will supply resources and supportive assistance to this district in the event of a censorship controversy." Then the teachers are supposed to list and categorize the groups they have been reviewing.

Under "destructive," the teachers are expected to write such names as "The 700 Club," Focus on the Family, Citizens for Excellence in Education, Eagle Forum, and Concerned Women for America; under "supportive" they are to list the NEA, the ACLU, and People for the American Way. For an example of their objectivity, consider the remarks of People for the American Way's Michael Hudson at an Institute for Development of Education Activities (IDEA) Workshop, in which he told his audience that Focus on the Family, as one of those on the enemies list, is a "nationwide force that has a very anti-education agenda" and is "a significant threat to American democracy and to public education."

All across the country, liberal educators and school boards are using such literature to support their war against historic American values and authentic content-based education. In many places, revolutionary experimental programs based on the politically correct theories of "experts" are being implemented without either parental consent or community approval. One such example is the state of Pennsylvania, where educators have installed an outcomes-based education under the name, "Required Student Learning Outcomes" (SLO).

According to Kathy Robinson of the Pennsylvania Coalition for Academic Excellence, these new reforms attempt to scrap traditional content-based education in favor of the SLO program that requires students to demonstrate their understanding and acceptance of several politically correct social concepts before they can be promoted to the next level. Predictably, these values include environmentalism, global citizenship, multiculturalism, and acceptance of homosexuality.

Nancy Stabile of Citizens for Excellence in Education told a reporter for the *Christian American*, "Over 50 percent of the goals do not deal with academics (learning how to think). Most of the value outcomes are politically and socially in opposition to traditional Judeo-Christian values." In one textbook currently in use, the chapter on environmentalism talks about the "carrying capacity" of the Earth and then gives very positive information on the importance of birth control and abortion to the future of the planet.

Over the protests of concerned parents and educators, the government of Pennsylvania has authorized the outcomes-based education curriculum for a three-year trial period. But the attorney for the Pennsylvania House Local Government Committee, William Sloane, predicts that all they will learn is that outcomes-based education is an experiment that pushes values at the expense of learning. "You don't have to be a Fundamentalist to see that it's a concern," he says.

Intimidation and Extortion

A ten-page feature on the NEA in the June 7, 1993, issue of *Forbes* magazine shows the alarming results of the NEA's domination of public education for the past thirty years. Statistics show that unionization, government spending per pupil, and teacher salaries have skyrocketed while SAT scores and every other measure of student achievement have plummeted. It is not coincidental that these changes began at the same time that the NEA began taking control. *Forbes* says, "The NEA's rise is directly linked with the thirty-year decline of American education that occurred simultaneously—not just in terms of quality, but especially in terms of quantity: education's crushing, and incessantly cumulating, cost."[1]

With 2.1 million members, the NEA is larger than the Teamsters Union. The *Forbes* writers say it has become "the worm in the American education apple." Next to the U.S. Postal Service, the NEA is the most unionized organization in the country, and it is the most formidable liberal lobby in Congress. Former Education Secretary Lamar Alexander said he was constantly battling the NEA over his plans to improve the system. Another former secretary, William J. Bennett, said that the NEA is "the absolute heart and center of the Democratic party."

The *Forbes* article also reports that the practices of the NEA are often flagrant and possibly even illegal. When the citizens of Alpena, Michigan, voted against raising property tax contributions to public education, NEA President Keith Geiger shut down the public schools of Alpena and threatened to do the same to other communities until the voters could be forced to compromise and pay up. In another community, a similar shutdown forced the citizens of Kalkaska, Michigan, where the median income is just $22,000, to give teachers mandatory annual pay increases, so that the average teacher salary is now $32,000. Teacher compensation now makes up 65 percent of all school budgets in the area.

The NEA stranglehold on public education is dangerous, pernicious, and a continuing threat to America's hopes for its young people. As an aggressive liberal trade union, the NEA is not interested in education, but in power and money. *Forbes* shows in detail how the organization and its lobbyists and supporters (including Bill Clinton, who pledged to make the NEA his "partner" once he reached the White House) manipulate finances, pension funds, and health benefits to leverage their liberal political adventures. But, as the *Forbes* article points out, the Achilles heel of the NEA is school choice, the use of tax-supported vouchers to give parents the freedom to choose how and where their children will be educated. All over America that battle is growing stronger by the day.

After successfully undermining the first attempt at a choice initiative in California in 1992, the issue is slated to reappear on the ballot in 1994. Other campaigns are now under way in Wisconsin, Vermont, Minnesota, Iowa, Florida, Idaho, Illinois, Georgia, New Mexico, Pennsylvania, Oregon, Arizona, Massachusetts, Colorado, New Jersey, South Dakota, Connecticut, and Texas. The people of America have seen the miserable failures of the NEA's way of doing things, and they are responding with common-sense proposals to restore order.

In each of these battles over public education, headlines will be made in the days ahead. The government and the liberal media have already shown where they will put their support—not behind the people but behind the NEA. But common sense is on the march, and we are predicting that school choice will become one of the most important revolutions of the 1990s. Be assured, if this fight has not yet come to your community, it will. The question is, How will you respond? Will you accept the liberal agenda of sex education and outcomes-based education? Whatever happens, the choice will be yours.

Is Public Education Necessary?

When I was a child, my teachers were never afraid to speak of what was right and wrong. In college I was taught noblesse oblige. Because of the privilege of a college education, I had responsibilities. The concept was clear: There are no rights without responsibilities. But today we hear all about rights and little or nothing about responsibility. They don't seem to belong in the same sentence in our country anymore. Rights is an issue by itself: "I've got my rights!" This attitude may grow out of the fact that we have become such a litigious society, where it seems everyone is suing someone else to get his or her rights. All of society suffers as a consequence.

However you look at it, individual responsibility and self-control are the irreducible minimum requirements of any individual in society. But there is no true self-control without an underlying religious belief. Such self-control will not come any other way. It certainly will not come in a society where everything is relative and where there is no such thing as right and wrong.

In 1981, noted author Samuel Blumenfeld wrote the classic, *Is Public Education Necessary?* which traced the history of public education in America and then how it was seized early in the nineteenth century as a vehicle for socialism and anti-religious cleansing. According to Blumenfeld, who lives in Massachusetts, the earliest public education in the country, in Massachusetts, was essentially twofold: to promote general learning and especially religious study. Laws from that state in 1642, 1647, and 1648 prove this.

The first public schools were common schools, created in the early days of the Commonwealth in Massachusetts to ensure the transmission of Calvinistic Puritanism from one generation to the next. The Reformation had replaced papal authority with biblical authority, and that required a high degree of literacy. One goal of the common schools was to develop students for higher studies at Harvard, which had been founded in 1636 as a seminary to educate the commonwealth's future leaders.

But in 1805, one of the most important events in American intellectual history occurred when the Unitarians took control of Harvard after a long struggle with the Calvinists. The Unitarians could not accept the concept of the innate depravity of man. As Blumenfeld puts it, this was in part because they had been brought up in a Puritan society of high moral standards, which didn't permit them to express their sinful nature as they would in other surroundings.

Harvard became the citadel of Unitarianism. The Unitarians believed that evil was caused by social and environmental factors, hence education was the way to eliminate the ignorance that caused evil. Moral progress seemed as attainable as material progress. The Unitarians chose the public schools as the vehicle for secular anti-religious education since they were essentially the easiest to control.

Socialism American-Style

Over time, Robert Owen, the founder of modern socialism, emerged as one of the leading figures in this movement. Owen had tried the first true experiment in communism anywhere in the world in Indiana in 1825. It was called New Harmony, and for obvious reasons it failed within little more than a year. Owen decided that man was too corrupted by society to succeed in creating the new society he wanted, so man had to be educated in his youth to eliminate the vices of society and let his perfectible nature shine through.

Owen and his followers, including his son, worked hard at their task. One follower, Orestes Brownson, gave up and wrote in his autobiography that the Owenites had, as quoted by Blumenfeld, gone "underground in 1829 and organized their activities nationwide in the form of a secret society in order to attain their goal of universal public education."

Brownson goes on to say, "The great object was to get rid of Christianity, and to convert our churches into halls of science. The plan was not to make open attacks on religion, although we might belabor the clergy and bring them into contempt where we could; but to establish a system of state schools, from which all religion was to be excluded, in which nothing was to be taught but such knowledge as is verifiable by the senses, and to which all parents were to be compelled by law to send their children."[2] Brownson said these people worked hard in New York, but he did not know if the secret societies extended into other states or how long they lasted.

Nonetheless, Owen, who in 1817 denounced religion as the source of all mankind's woes, despite his failures, persevered, setting forth essentially the program for progressive education that John Dewey promulgated a century later. Thus, one of the fathers of modern compulsory state education was also the first modern socialist, and education in his eyes was the means to accomplish his program.

The ideas of the various public education proponents, such as Horace Mann, were controversial and often exceedingly unpopular, especially as people got to know more about them. Nonetheless, they stuck with their agenda over the decades, whereas eventually the Christians and "typical Americans" retreated. Keep in mind that education was the main way for the true leftist believers to accomplish their goals. As Blumenfeld concluded, "*the most potent and significant expression of statism is a state educational system. Without it, statism is impossible. With it, the state can and has become everything*" (emphasis added).

We cannot begin to understand the full complexity of the problems in the schools unless we understand the theories and the legacy of John Dewey, who followed the pattern of the earlier radical educators. Dewey was an ardent believer in what the nineteenth-century philosopher William James called "pragmatism," which holds that the best choice is always the most practical choice. In modern business, the pragmatic approach says, "Do whatever it takes, regardless." We see the results of this type of thinking all the time in the headlines. Ivan Boesky and Michael Milken were two of its proponents.

Dewey applied this concept to education by teaching that learning comes through doing. This is the perspective that values physical and emotional experience over reason and discernment. It is this kind of learning that leads to a repudiation of the importance of history and tradition. It denies existing cultural values in favor of change and other radical new agendas. I dealt with Dewey's influence on education in greater depth in my book, *The New Millennium*, but it is hard to overemphasize the damage that has come from these ideas. The impact on higher education brought about by Dewey's long tenure at the Columbia Graduate School of Education is being seen today throughout our nation's universities.

The newest application of Dewey's model is outcomes-based education (OBE), which holds that it doesn't matter whether or not children know any specific facts so long as they feel good about themselves and develop "tolerance for cultural diversity." If students can get a basic job and make a basic living, some educators feel that is enough. This form of behaviorism has wreaked havoc with every level of achievement of American public school students.

This issue brings to mind Allan Bloom's classic comment in his bestseller, *The Closing of the American Mind*, when he said that American high school graduates are among the most sensitive illiterates in the world. In all the standardized achievement tests comparing the educational attainments of U.S. students with young people of the same age from other countries, American students had by far the highest levels of self-esteem, but they consistently placed near the bottom in every academic category. They are incredibly sensitive and pathetically ignorant.

Education in Denial

In the final analysis, the theories of modern education can be summed up as a basic denial of the value of Western tradition and a repudiation of the role of religion in the welfare of the community. Modern educators are moved not only by a denial of the existence of God, but militant hostility to any form of Judeo-Christian theism. Professional educators say that Creationism cannot be taught because it requires a belief in God, morality cannot be taught because it requires a reverence for the Word of God, and history cannot be taught without major revisions because our entire history speaks of the importance of God and religious values throughout the entire record of human affairs.

A lead article in the journal of the School Boards Association of America prefers to substitute, in the place of God or organized religion, role-playing games such as Dungeons and Dragons, which teach children about sinister plots, intrigues, murders, and occult powers. While attacking the influence of leading Christians and libeling many other conservative organizations, the article defends the practice of witchcraft and New Age religion, outcomes-based education, values clarification (which has long been identified with the left-wing agenda for the psychological manipulation of our children), and even whole-sentence reading.

Such beliefs and practices are horrifying to most Americans. They defy common sense. Parents don't want their children to be manipulated, and we can see how they have responded to these teachings in our larger cities. It is not just racially motivated "white flight"; there is a massive flight away from liberal ideology and all the incumbent dangers associated with the loss of a moral foundation. It has gotten to the point in many cities where families who can afford to send their children to private schools where they will get a wholesome, quality education are doing so, even if it means having to cut out things such as new cars, vacations, or luxuries of one type or another. It is flight all right: flight from the outrage of the doctrinaire public schools that are trying to bend the minds of America's youth and to force upon them the extremist mind-set of John Dewey and psychologist B. F. Skinner.

A Tortured View

As we saw in chapter 5, the liberal social engineers decades ago determined that their tortured view of the brave new world would never be accepted by the American people or their elected representatives. Their only hope to impose their so-called progressive concepts on this nation would be in the courts against weak and ill-prepared opponents.

Here is how the battle was waged. Leftist professors in law schools across the land began propounding radical views of Constitutional law in the scholarly journals. Then lawyers on the Left, primarily those from the ACLU, began probing the court system to find a judge or judges to buy their arguments. Once they won a victory, they would use the language of that case to expand the so-called right they had just won. Then would come a Supreme Court victory and a dramatic escalation of the battle.

The battleground, of course, was the neighborhood school. There were two objectives. First, under a fanatical view of the First Amendment to the Constitution, the Left had all Christian standards, symbols, and moral instruction removed from the schools. Second, under the pretense of achieving racial balance and equal opportunity through forced busing, they broke up the cohesiveness and pride of neighborhoods and left children and their parents defenseless against the subsequent liberal brainwashing.

The landmark case handed down on June 25, 1962, was *Engel v. Vitale*, in which the Supreme Court ruled, despite overwhelming historical evidence to the contrary, that it was unconstitutional for a simple prayer written by the Regents of the New York State Educational System to be read in school before the start of classes. One year later, on June 17, 1963, in *Murray v. Curlett*, the court stripped public schools of their right to read the Holy Bible to students.

My father, an eminent Constitutional authority, appeared before the Senate Judiciary Committee chaired by his colleague, Senator Sam Ervin of North Carolina, in 1962 to protest the *Engel v. Vitale* decision. To paraphrase his words, "James Madison was the author of the First Amendment. He entered the Congress directly from the Constitutional Convention. Madison's first task as a congressman was to chair the committee charged with the task of selecting a chaplain to lead the House of Representatives in prayer before each session. *Are we to presume today that James Madison did not know what was constitutional?*"

David Barton, in his book entitled, *America, To Pray or Not To Pray*, has performed a magnificent service in compiling the indexes of national life in our country during the thirty years since the highest court in our land decided to ignore almost two hundred years of the clearly enunciated history and customs of this nation and kick almighty God out of our public schools. One or two isolated trends could be dismissed as arising from other causes, but there is no way to explain all of these extraordinary happenings originating in a single year except as a sign of the lifting of God's blessing from our land.[3] Consider these incredible statistics:

1. SAT scores have plunged from 980 in 1963 to 900 in 1990, an extreme drop in this logarithmically derived scale.

2. Birthrates of unwed girls age fifteen to nineteen have soared from 15 per 1,000 to 35 per 1,000.

3. Total pregnancies for unwed girls age fifteen to nineteen have soared from 100,000 in 1963 to 650,000 in 1987.

4. Sexually transmitted diseases among teenagers have soared from 350 cases per 100,000 to 1,200 cases.

5. Premarital sex among teenage girls has jumped from 23 percent to 70 percent.

6. The divorce rate has skyrocketed from 2.2 per 1,000 in 1962 to 4.7 in 1990.

7. Single-parent households have risen from 4.6 million to 10.9 million.

8. Incidence of violent crime leapt from 250,000 in 1962 to 1.7 million in 1990.

In short the court-mandated removal of religious restraint from our schools has been the major contributing cause of the moral breakup in our society. To me the destruction of a generation of our youth is every bit as heinous as the destruction of millions of lives through abortion.

Violence Stalks Our Children

Time magazine calls it a "deadly love affair," while *Newsweek* said it was a "virtual epidemic" sweeping our nation. They are talking about young people and guns, and this is one of the deadliest trends in America today. The most recent Department of Justice report says that the number of both criminals and victims among juveniles has increased dramatically. Between 1987 and 1991, the number of teenagers arrested for murder jumped by 85 percent. In just one year, twenty-two hundred kids under the age of eighteen were murdered. Tragically, not only are our youth being killed, they are becoming murderers themselves. No doubt almost every reader of this book has heard stories of random drive-by shootings. One of our own CBN employees, living just two miles from the CBN complex, recently moved out of her condominium because someone shot into her bedroom at 1:00 A.M.

Gun violence has spread nationwide. At Weber University in Utah, one student opened fire during a grievance hearing. When a campus police officer tried to stop him, the boy shot the officer in the face, killing him instantly. One victim of this horrifying trend of teenage violence was James Jordan, the father of basketball superstar Michael Jordan. Authorities arrested two eighteen-year-olds in the case, saying that when Jordan pulled off to the side of a well-traveled road to rest, they shot him so they could rob him. Although authorities captured suspects in the case, one has to realize that had their victim not been the relative of a national celebrity, no major investigation would have been undertaken. No suspects would have been captured, and the killers would be like so many others: free to do it again.

Why is this? Analysts say one reason is because the criminal justice system itself encourages violent behavior, because juveniles know that they can literally get away with murder. In a recent CBN News story on the subject of teens and guns, a juvenile court judge in Virginia told our reporter, "You could murder or rape somebody or whatever, and about the worst we could do is put you in detention for a year, maybe in some cases a little big longer than that. There's no real deterrent for juveniles."

One group that is most afraid of this trend is the teenagers themselves. A recent Harris poll suggested that those who are not using guns are afraid of the ones who are. In that survey of twenty-five hundred students, 35 percent said that they did not think they would survive to old age because their lives would be "wiped out" by guns. Some teenagers told one of our reporters that the reason more young people carry guns is to protect themselves from others in their age group. One high school freshman said he wanted safety from "gangs fighting gangs," while another sixteen-year-old said that the young people carry guns for "protection—you never know who's gonna smoke you."

Analysts have offered various explanations for the gun plague. Many point to the violence on television and in the movies. Others say that the spread of drugs is responsible. Without question, such links exist, as the rise in crime is often directly tied to the rise in drug use. Still others say that the root cause is the break-up of the family. The juvenile judge mentioned earlier also told our reporter, "I think it's all a result probably from a breakdown in the family unit. It seems that, not always, but in most cases, there's no real close-knit family unit. Then there's no real incentive for the young person to abide by the law."

While these factors are unquestionably important, we shouldn't forget that the modern school system has worked hard to remove prayer, the Ten Commandments, and biblical values and principles from our public education.

An Education in Hypocrisy

But it shouldn't escape anyone's attention that the people who are conceiving and carrying out the radical school agenda aren't sending their children or grandchildren to the public schools. They send their children to exclusive private schools where they can be protected and educated to become the liberal elite of the next generation. Jesse Jackson doesn't send his children to the public schools in Washington, D.C. Al Gore doesn't send his children there either. None of those in power would do that. The self-styled cultural elite refuse to put their own children into the politically correct ghettos they have helped create. Perhaps even more shocking was a news story indicating that as many as 40 percent of all the teachers in the Chicago public schools were sending their own children to private schools.

Syndicated columnist Cal Thomas wondered in a March 1993 column how the president explains his own hypocrisy in the school choice matter. He has been a staunch defender of public education, a friend of the NEA, and an enemy of parental choice. Yet rather than send his daughter, Chelsea, to a public school to indicate the strength of his convictions, he has chosen to send her to the exclusive Sidwell Friends School, populated by the children of the rich and famous.

Thomas asks, "Why is it that liberals favor federal funding and freedom of choice when it comes to abortion, but oppose tax dollars going to private or religious schools to educate children fortunate enough to have been born?" The logic of the situation suggests that the poor must be given an equal right to abort their children but not to educate them once they're born. But Thomas says,

> It is because public education is the training ground, the hothouse, the farm team for the next generation of liberals. How else to inculcate multiculturalism, political correctness and historical revisionism into children? How else to drum into them the view that they evolved from slime, that sex is an intramural sport and that the liberal agenda is best? Children might not be expected to encounter these "truths" on their own and are less likely to learn them in private schools, especially private, religious schools where a real education, a moral conscience and wisdom can still be found.

The columnist correctly surmises that public education is no longer about education, it is about indoctrination. It is about controlling the minds and hearts of the young; about a plan to train "sufficient numbers of left-thinking drones to replace them when they're gone." While Chelsea gets a good education at Sidwell Friends, the rest of us can make do with an education in hypocrisy.

Radical Engineering

To bring about the massive social changes they have in mind, liberal organizers know that they will have to destroy neighborhood cohesion and stamp out pride and caring and family values wherever they find them. It used to be that neighbors knew and looked after each other's children. People got to know one another, and they developed attachments and friendships. But the social engineers undermined all this, first, by an incredible, massive busing system that no one but the most radical programmers liked. Black Americans didn't like it; white Americans didn't like it. Nobody liked it except the social engineers. It violated common sense.

Then the "experts" brought into the curriculum new forms of study that didn't work. They tried new math. It didn't work. They tried the look-say method of reading. Even now it is producing a generation of illiterates. They are no longer teaching students the facts of history. Textbooks are imprecise and misinformed, and publishers and school boards allow textbooks to go out with glaring errors relating to historical truth. They no longer demand excellence and accuracy in scholarship, and then they wonder why at the end of twelve years they're turning out people who are incapable of functioning in society.

Now they want to extend the school year to twelve months instead of nine and to add another year to the curriculum—from the current twelve to thirteen. But this is folly. William J. Bennett spoke about the plans being put forth to increase public education to thirteen years. He said, "It's like this. I ask my wife what's for dinner and she says, 'Tuna casserole.' So I say, 'That's too bad. I don't like that.' So she says, 'Okay, then I'll make more of it.' That's what this proposal for thirteen years really amounts to. More of a bad thing doesn't make it better, and if they can't educate children in twelve years—which is a long time by any standard—then how can they even imagine they will do better with one more year?"

Outcomes-based education simply magnifies the illiteracy and irrelevancy of public education. Students will have no coherent knowledge about subjects they will need to compete in society, and they will have no fund of knowledge to draw upon, but the educators say it is the outcome that counts. As long as they can struggle along and survive in society, meaning a basic job and subsistence survival, then that's enough. I don't know about you, but that is not what education means to me.

Boys and girls growing up on the prairies a hundred years ago in poorly heated one-room schoolhouses with eleven grades packed in one room received a better education than kids are getting today with the latest in technology. It is not a matter of computers or higher pay for teachers or racial balance. Quality education means setting basic standards of intellectual attainment and teaching people not only to survive but how to compete successfully in a highly complex world. It means knowing with reasonable precision the landmarks and important fundamentals of history, literature, language, science, mathematics, and the arts. Those are the hallmarks of what has always been known as a "liberal" education. But young people have no way of knowing what they are missing. Such things are rarely if ever covered in their history books anymore.

Vouchers for Choice

One of the most hopeful trends in public education today is the move toward a school voucher program. By returning to parents the right to choose the appropriate type of education for their children, this approach would restore autonomy to the family and reduce the government's ability to keep its stranglehold on our children.

We have to understand that the NEA and the liberal teachers' unions hate the idea, of course, and they will continue to fight it with all their might. The idea of parental choice flies in the face of the education establishment's desire to manipulate and control children. But the idea is gaining adherents, and support is growing all across the land. Choice is the natural and common-sense answer to inferior schools. When a large state such as California holds a referendum on the proposal to institute a voucher system, you know the idea is gaining momentum. When any large state experiments with this process, be assured it is just a matter of time until the idea of choice sweeps the nation.

Competition is the best way in the world to get better products at lower prices. If the minds of our children are the product we're concerned with, then shouldn't we support any system that would guarantee a better product for a better price? Yet that is precisely why the NEA and their cronies are against the idea: because it would work so well it would take the prerogative of social engineering away from them and prove how destructive their policies have been the last forty years.

They say vouchers would spell the end of public schools in America. To which we say, So what? For all we've been getting for our tax dollars out of the public schools, they should have disappeared years ago. So long as we have standards that ensure that our goals of quality education are achieved, then the very idea of maintaining an antiquated and ineffective public education system is absurd.

I should say that among the frequently overlooked victims of the current system are the thousands of honest, moral, and well-meaning teachers who are captives of the public school system. Many of them do not like the NEA or the liberal policies it endorses any more than we do, but in order to keep their jobs they frequently have to go along with policies and procedures they find galling and objectionable. I have known teachers to weep over the things they have to do and say in the classroom in the name of multiculturalism and diversity and all the other liberal claptrap.

A Change for the Better

The NEA has been very strong up to this point, but it cannot maintain its hold much longer in light of its intolerable record of failure over the last three decades. The results of Polly Williams's program in Milwaukee show conclusively that the idea of school choice is working extremely well. The only thing keeping it from becoming a nationwide program is the iron-claw grip of the liberal educational bureaucracy and its socialist friends and supporters. Here in the inner city of the Wisconsin capital, children are being empowered with real knowledge through educational choice. It is working beautifully, and the children who have this choice won't have to be satisfied for a life of welfare in the ghetto.

For generations the Catholic schools of this country have flourished in the inner city. The students in these schools are the same types of people, the same ethnic makeup, the same socioeconomic brackets as the children in the local public schools. While the public schools are largely out of control and turning out nothing but illiterates year after year, the Catholic schoolchildren are well disciplined and doing their homework. Their minds are being stretched. Going to those schools is considered a privilege. If any student gets to the point where he doesn't want to behave or he is unwilling to do the work, then he is no longer welcome in the school. Consequently, these children take their work seriously and, in most cases, they get a first-class education.

There are so many examples in this country of schools where common-sense principles are working. "60 Minutes" featured an extraordinary oil man, Patrick Taylor, in Louisiana who has totally changed the odds for children from troubled backgrounds. He told the CBS reporter that no worthwhile young graduate from any high school should be denied the privilege of going to college, so under the Taylor Plan he offers scholarships to any student who maintains a B average through high school. It is amazing how that promise motivates the students. Suddenly there is the hope that if they work hard and do their best, despite the problems they may have to overcome, they will get a scholarship and be able to go on to college. He told me that these students not only do better in school, they are much less likely to abuse drugs or begin delinquency.

I participated in an enrichment program in Richmond, Virginia, put together by Governor Douglas Wilder and the late Arthur Ashe. It was called Virginia Heroes, and the purpose was to bring together a wide variety of people who had attained some degree of prominence in their field—in the military, government, business, the media, etc.—and have them spend a day teaching a group of about six hundred sixth-grade students. The organizers divided the students into groups of ten, and each of the speakers had the chance to speak to about fifty children in five different sessions. We would teach one group and then move on to the next. The object was to motivate these children to excel, to have a dream to pursue, and to stay in school.

It was a very interesting experience. But the last group I taught opened my eyes to the seriousness of the problems we are facing. I asked them, "What would you like to see in your school?" One little boy raised his hand and said, "I would like to have guards and metal detectors at all the doors of our school."

When I asked why, he said, "To keep people from bringing guns and knives."

So I asked, "You mean, in Richmond, Virginia, that sixth graders are bringing guns and knives to school?" He said yes. I asked, "Do you have gangs in this school?" Again he said yes, "And they beat me up."

Then someone else said, "The kids in the gangs don't care anything about school. They don't want to study or learn anything. They just want to beat people up and make trouble for everybody else." Maybe I am naive, but I was shocked to see how real and how dangerous these problems are for these children. Yet this was not an isolated incident. The Justice Department has issued reports showing that each day more than a hundred thousand children come to school with guns and knives. The latest figures I have seen show that there are more than three million crimes committed in the public schools every year. That amounts to more than seventeen thousand crimes every single day. There are two thousand cases each month where teachers are assaulted or raped. The violence in our schools is beyond belief, and there are some two hundred thousand children who refuse to go to school because they are afraid of being shot, beaten up, or violated in some way.

Common-Sense Education

You simply cannot allow young people to do what they want to do without discipline and moral guidance. There is no ancient wisdom within the minds of children as the New Agers would have us believe that makes them wise and perceptive beyond their years. Rousseau propagated the idea of the "noble savage" during the French Enlightenment, which suggested that, stripped of the superficial mores of society and what he considered the terrible and false superstitions of religion, man is essentially a noble and wise animal. He said that, in nature, the savage holds the keys to truth and pristine beauty when he is in harmony with his environment.

That may be the idea of poets and philosophers, but in the real world such an idea is preposterous. Stripped of social values and moral understanding, man is a savage who will plunder and destroy and live in chaos. You don't have to look far for the proof of that. You can go to virtually any inner-city school in America and see what it is like when traditional moral values have been stripped away. This is the end product of a century of socialist reprogramming. No school system and no nation can long survive in such an environment.

Common sense says there are guidelines to behavior, and if we do not follow them we will be punished. Children understand that, and they know this is how it is supposed to be. Rules are not there to punish us; they are there to help maintain order and respect for everyone. Rules and regulations in the public schools keep children on the right track; they protect the weak and limit the strong, just as rules have always done. They also help establish logical, orderly, common-sense boundaries that children and their parents should appreciate, and without which serious study and learning is virtually impossible.

Why can't we get back to the common-sense schools? First of all, we now have the NEA and an entire generation of Skinnerian psychologists blocking the way under the delusion that "behavior modification" will keep children in line. But, second, we also have the ACLU standing outside the door ready to bring a lawsuit against any teacher who attempts to discipline students.

One of the heroes of this country is Joe Clark, the New Jersey principal who was fired because the liberals said that he was too brutal. Well, he said there were rules that were designed to be obeyed, and he insisted that his students abide by those rules. As a result, he had a crime-free environment. Children were learning, and they were excelling. As the young people learned to behave they also began to perform at a higher level. But the liberal, do-your-own-thing, let-youth-decide, don't-oppress-the-downtrodden-types refused to support Clark's initiatives, and he was fired.

So what do we get for all this benevolence? Now they are back to bringing knives and guns to school, they rage in gangs, they terrorize the other students, and they terrorize the teachers.

Perhaps the most difficult aspect of where we are right now is that we are in-between the realization that things cannot be allowed to continue as they are and the ability to do something about changing it. At one moment we can become very optimistic, thinking, "Yes, the people of America see the problem, and they're going to demand that order be restored!" But in the very next moment we think, "But it just keeps getting worse, and the education establishment will not release its hammerlock around the throat of public education."

Creative Alternatives

Our discussion has focused primarily on the problems with a system of public education in America that has been stripped of religious and moral values, has been a vast social science laboratory, and is overrun by crime, violence, drugs, alcohol, and sexual permissiveness.

Most parents are locked in this morass until they band together against the propaganda barrage of the Left to vote in meaningful school choice. But they have been taking creative alternatives for years. Estimates of church-related schools have grown from one thousand in 1965 to as high as twenty-five to thirty thousand in 1987. Although the growth of these schools has tapered off a bit from the 1980s, estimates then projected the establishment of three new church schools every day.

The second major trend is toward home schooling. Having overcome numerous legal challenges and other roadblocks, America's home-schooling parents now have between five hundred thousand and one million children being schooled at home, and that number is growing. Interestingly, the academic performance of children schooled at home easily meets or exceeds the best that the public schools can offer.

However, important as these alternatives are, only 4,758,190 students are currently enrolled outside of the public school system, while 47,286,093 are enrolled within it. Something has to give, but no one should think that help will come from the public schools. If we are to have real and meaningful change in education, it will have to come from parents themselves. It won't be a system based on the theories of experts; it will be a return to logical and common-sense values based on respect for the dignity and worth of the individual and a commitment to quality education. There will be a time once again when children can pray in the public schools of America, when we are no longer denied the right to teach our children the moral values based on the Bible, and this nation once again can be justifiably proud of the quality of its education.

10

A Portrait of America

UNLESS WE CAN GET a firm grip on the ethical moorings of this country and stop its slide down the slippery slope of moral relativity and social decay, our entire culture will soon find itself on a high-speed ride to chaos and anarchy. We find ourselves caught between two views of reality and thrown into a battle over ideologies.

On one side of today's cultural divide are those who cling to traditional values and historic, republican virtues. On the other side are those fighting for some grand, opaque vision of a collectivist future with no absolutes. "The rules of morality," Scottish philosopher David Hume observed, "are not the conclusions of our reason." Rather, they are natural and eternal principles, the kind that make possible the vision of one nation, under God, with liberty and justice for all. A vision that could give a secure moral foundation for those men and women who desire a better world for themselves and their children is found in Robert Kennedy's much-quoted statement, "Some men see things as they are and ask, 'Why?' But I dream things that never were and I ask, 'Why not?'"[1]

This clash over cultural ideals has raged for more than thirty years. There is no one today who is not engaged in one way or another in this monumental conflict.

Two Views of America

One side of this struggle is made up largely of everyday American workers and their families who want a simple, wholesome life, a better standard of living, and freedom from regulations and social distress. Pulling with them are the vast majority of small businesses, store owners and managers, and even a majority of large corporation leaders who perceive the benefits of a prosperous and unstressed society. The majority of clergy and established religious institutions are here as well, joined by conservative politicians and the leadership of the Republican party.

It is also noteworthy that most new Americans, including large numbers of Hispanic and Asian immigrants, are pulling for this side. For them the American dream means personal safety and the opportunity to compete in a free and open society. With it comes the promise of protection from the dangers of anarchy, social engineering, and immorality. It means limited government, lower taxes, and a healthy respect for individual rights *and* responsibilities. By and large, everyone on this side of the debate is pulling for a conservative and morally responsible society in an environment of mutual support and common sense. For twelve years this team also included the presidents of the United States, but now that has changed.

The opposite side of this debate fills its ranks with those who want to bring about massive changes in the form and focus of American culture. They would call themselves progressives. They want greater and greater liberties for smaller and smaller groups of people and sanctions that would restrict others from infringing upon their "social welfare." They do not want competition, equal access, or freedom of speech for all people. They want special status based on race, physical, mental, or social disabilities, and personal and sexual preferences.

This group is not nearly as large as the other, but it has enormous strength due to the support it receives from those in positions of power and influence in the world. There are some ordinary citizens among them, but the majority of these people are experts, bureaucrats, union leaders, journalists and publishers, media professionals, university professors, public school educators, and members of fringe industries that trade on permissiveness, self-indulgence, and vice. This group also includes the leadership of the Democratic party and all three branches of government—executive, legislative, and judicial—with few exceptions. This side has a large number of lawyers, those who profit from disturbances in society, along with large numbers of lawless people who thrive on anarchy and corruption.

Sexual liberation and all it entails is one of this side's loudest battle cries; public responsibility for personal choices is its creed. Liberals, socialists, and many libertarians are fully engaged on this side, while a number of socially active religious groups fill out the group. These spiritually and socially sensitive individuals are politically weak and contribute little, but they feed off the commotion and frenzy, and they do their best to offer aid and comfort to those actively involved in the struggle.

Two Views of Tolerance

One of the most challenging differences between these two groups is to be seen in their very different reactions to their adversaries. The first group is intolerant of crime and mischief, and they have little patience with those who habitually break the rules. But contrary to the claims of their enemies, they are remarkably tolerant of the natural philosophical differences between people. They believe in law and order, and consequently they expect the maximum sentence for offenders against the law, but they do not wish to punish people who disagree with them because of what they may think, say, or believe.

The other group, however, considers crime and public disorder to be political and philosophical issues, not moral concerns. Criminals, for example, need understanding and therapy. The only group these people wish to punish are their ideological opponents, and they punish them harshly and openly through public censure, ridicule, and imprisonment whenever possible. They are generally opposed to the death penalty for criminals, regardless of the crime, but they would no doubt harbor mixed feelings on this matter if the political and philosophical beliefs of their philosophical opponents could be included.

No doubt this illustration is overly simplistic, but I believe it illustrates the essential differences in the world-views of the principal opponents in today's culture war. Michael Jones, whom I cited in chapter 8, has said that there is an essential pattern of thought that underlies all of civilization; that is, either we shape our desires to truth or we attempt to shape truth to our desires. That seems to be the key difference here.

The traditionalists have no argument with truth. Most accept a historic view of truth based on Judeo-Christian values, and they hold the belief that there are absolute standards of right and wrong in the world. These standards establish for them the terms of all debate and the priorities of individual behavior in all situations. In Jones's terms, they have recognized the need to bring their desires into submission to the standards of truth.

The liberals, however, generally see rules and standards as euphemisms for imposing the will of one group upon the other groups. All laws are discriminatory, they hold, and traditional values are merely a codification of the prejudice and bigotry of a bygone era. Organized religions, many also claim, provide a pretext for enforcing the bias of the few upon the many. The only truth is the truth of the individual. Whatever works for one person is all the truth there is; there are no absolutes, no ultimate right and wrong, and no laws of importance except those the people voluntarily choose to obey for the good of the community. Truth must be shaped to accommodate one's personal desires.[2]

Two Views of Morality

In his book *Why Johnny Can't Tell Right from Wrong*, William Kirk Kilpatrick describes the first view, which transforms desire to truth, as the "moral imagination." It is a world-view that seeks to interpret life on the basis of visible and perceived restraints. He describes the other view as the "idyllic imagination." It is a view that looks beyond reality to the ideal. It admits no restraints. "The moral imagination holds up an ideal that is attainable," writes Kilpatrick, "although only through hard work." But he adds:

The idyllic imagination wants to escape from the harsh realities of ordinary life, either to a dream world, or to nature, or to a more primitive life. It follows mood rather than conscience, and rejects conventional morality in favor of a natural morality that will, it believes, emerge spontaneously in the absence of cultural restraints. When the idyllic imagination takes a spiritual turn, as it often does, it prefers a spirituality without morality or dogma.[3]

The author goes on to say that the moral imagination understands the practical, the pedestrian, and the tragic elements of life. It accepts the view that much of life is ordinary, "daily," and sometimes desperate. But the idyllic imagination—especially that which blossomed in the 1960s and still makes up the core of modern liberalism—is idealistic and lacks a tragic sense.

Such people hold idealistic fantasies about the meaning of life; they have an existentialist view of reality that demands "engagement." They visualize popular movements, causes, and demonstrations on behalf of the oppressed peoples of the world, and they seek out relief efforts to save any endangered species of whatever variety happens to seize their imagination. It is not, after all, the species that fascinates them, but the idea of fighting tyranny. They are in love with rebellion, and they are, as Kilpatrick suggests, modern Romantics who share their beliefs not only with the hippies of Haight-Ashbury, but with the poets and dreamers of literature.

This idyllic, or Romantic, temperament makes them all the more easily defeated by harsh realities and real tragedies. They have difficulty dealing with life as it is actually lived. "Last year's Romantic idealist," writes Kilpatrick, "turns out to be this year's suicide. And because the Romantic is essentially naive about evil, he is less resistant to it."[4] Writers such as T. S. Eliot and Russell Kirk have suggested that unless the idyllic imagination is tempered by morality, it can easily devolve into the "diabolical imagination." If you look at the Left's fascination with promiscuous sexuality, free speech, abortion rights, and legal protections for pornographers, it is not difficult to assume that this conversion has already taken place in our culture.

Look, for example, at Hugh Hefner, founder of the so-called *Playboy* Empire, who has funneled millions of dollars into the Playboy Foundation. Hefner's money also goes to support feminist political action groups, such as Emily's List, and pro-abortion candidates for public office. According to a study by Cliff Kincaid, available from the Capital Research Center in Washington, D.C., *Playboy* donations are not only used to support free-speech litigation for pornographers but many other liberal causes. Regular recipients include the ACLU, the National Gay and Lesbian Task Force, People for the American Way, the National Abortion Rights Action League, and the National Women's Political Caucus. Individual candidates supported by *Playboy*'s PAC money include Senators Carol Moseley Braun, Barbara Boxer, Diane Feinstein, and Alan Cranston, and Jesse Jackson, Gary Hart, Jerry Brown, Michael Dukakis, and Bill Clinton.

Two Views of the Future

It is important to recognize that the war being waged by these alleged progressives is not silent, and it is not merely intellectual or literary. It is potent, all-encompassing, and to date it has been enormously successful, to the point that every aspect of American life is now fully involved in the predictable combustion of ideologies. Bringing unrestrained license into our homes, schools, workplaces, recreations, and even the churches has had a crippling impact on culture. Redefining crime as pathology has loosed unprecedented numbers of sadists and psychopaths onto our streets. Devaluing the moral currency of public welfare in favor of the merely monetary has helped to create a godless, greedy, and acquisitive underclass that feeds on bureaucratic generosity and public indifference.

Too often today the man on the street feels helpless, unable to enunciate his hopes and fears, and unable to believe that his voice will even be heard. He dreads the future and distrusts the past. The world around him appears to be changing so rapidly he can hardly make sense of it. But he wonders if he can trust others to take care of things. Or must he, by force of will, become engaged in some way? And if so, how?

It is true that larger and larger numbers of people are beginning to enter the fray, but they are often unsure of themselves and the terms of the debate.

While most Americans hold on to some part of their religious convictions, they can see that these ideas are being assaulted by a highly articulate "cultural elite," supported by scientists and educators. Although statisticians report that 90 percent of Americans are affiliated with some religious group, most are leery about expressing their beliefs openly. So how do they face the future? Apparently, not very well. In his book *Facing Tomorrow*, journalist Thomas Hine writes:

> Having a sense of the future has always required an act of faith. But while the unseen was once the province of religion, it is now the territory of science, and an arena for human actions as well. We intervene in the chemistry of the atmosphere, the mechanics of heredity, the structure of matter, and we struggle to glimpse the paradoxical world of subatomic particles. Yet we still lack a convincing theory, or even a widely accepted hypothesis, that links such quantum phenomena to the world of everyday reality. We can therefore declare that our lives are based entirely in delusion, which is arguable and possibly even true, but it does not help us make it through the day.[5]

The Search for Transcendence

The fundamental impact of the crisis of values in America today is that a large number of men, women, and children have lost their handle on reality and meaning in life. For many, and perhaps most, there is no longer a transcendent vision, a big picture, from which they can take comfort.

Paul Weyrich, president of the Free Congress Foundation, says that most people tend to think of the evangelical political movement of the past ten to fifteen years as an *offensive* movement designed to seize power. But in fact, he says, it has been a *defensive* movement from the start—a movement that came into being only when government began to meddle in the affairs of the church, and particularly in the affairs of Christian schools. Now that it has become politically mobilized, there is a sense of moral imperative. Evangelicals, pro-family Roman Catholics, and others with whom they are politically aligned suddenly realize that "there are no enclaves in this society, that the government is going to come in and dictate how even churches behave," and this has triggered an "enormous burst of energy and activity" on the Right.[6]

This burst of energy is problematical, however, when we realize that many Americans have come to distrust politics and political involvement. The hostility of the warfare between the Right and the Left has only increased the public's anxiety and resistance to involvement. But, as E. J. Dionne concludes in his best-selling book, *Why Americans Hate Politics*, we simply cannot afford to withdraw from the conflict; the stakes are now too high. The tide of democracy that is racing around the globe is patterned on a political ideal that was born in this country.

It was not the American military that won the Cold War, but American enterprise and American democratic values. What the nations of Eastern and Central Europe are attempting to formulate now are governments based on republican values and individual liberties. Dionne stresses that "we would do well to revive what made us a special nation long before we became the world's leading military and economic power—our republican tradition that nurtured free citizens who eagerly embraced the responsibilities and pleasures of self-government." He adds:

> With democracy on the march outside our borders, our first responsibility is to ensure that the United States again becomes a model for what self-government should be and not an example of what happens to free nations when they lose interest in public life. A nation which hates politics will not long thrive as a democracy.[7]

But despite the public's tendency to let someone else do it, and its former faith that somehow the right side will win in the end, thousands of new faces are entering the political arena. New voices are rising, new images are being offered, and there is a growing sense of urgency among conservatives that we have endured too much and suffered too long. The tide is truly turning.

Politically Incorrect

As we have seen in these chapters, there is good news from the culture wars. The death of the Religious Right has been greatly exaggerated, and common sense is making a dramatic comeback. The rule of experts is being challenged in all quarters, in part because the Democrats who control the White House, the Senate, the House of Representatives, and the bureaucracy have shown that they are not the moderates they claimed to be. They are firmly committed to leftist politics and the growth of big government. While they are stacking the cabinet, the courts, and the halls of state with the most radical women and men they can find, the public has lost patience with them and is beginning to lay out the hardware for a new attack.

What's more, government liberals and their cohorts in the media and the universities are coming under intense fire as well. The big news from the university campuses is that "PC" is no longer politically correct! Better yet, politically "incorrect" is in, and on more and more campuses the language of multicultural diversity is on its way out. A lead story in the lifestyle section of USA Today reported on the nationwide backlash against the PC movement, saying that "being perfectly PC may be passé. To the point that the scales are tipping backward."[8] Early indicators of the change come from media personalities as diverse as radio talk show host Rush Limbaugh and liberal cartoonist Gary Trudeau. The latter's cartoon strip, "Doonesbury," has portrayed the vicissitudes of PC on the university campus and the bubbleheaded rhetoric of left-wing academics.

The problem is that each year more than 13 million students enroll in American colleges and universities. Of those, just under 20 percent, or about 2.5 million, are ethnic minorities. Most of these people begin the life-changing transition into the world of higher education with a combination of anxiety and hope. They undertake the changes with the understanding that they will be developing new friendships, new relationships, and taking a giant step toward adult independence and responsibility. Most of them will also be moving away from home and discovering a new world of ideas and new ways of dealing with the issues of daily life. But there are some surprises ahead.

Unfortunately, what they actually discover on many campuses today is not what they had expected. Instead of encouragement, enlightenment, and intellectual stimulation, they receive massive doses of indoctrination and a dark and somber vision of the future. Author Dinesh D'Souza says:

> By percent and example, universities have taught them that "all rules are unjust" and "all preferences are principled"; that justice is simply the will of the stronger party; that standards and values are arbitrary, and the ideal of the educated person is largely a figment of bourgeois white male ideology, which should be cast aside; . . . that all knowledge can be reduced to politics and should be pursued not for its own sake but for the political end of power; . . . that double standards are acceptable as long as they are enforced to the benefit of minority victims.

In other words, the reality of political correctness is no joke for students. Distorted though it is, it becomes a way of life and often the key to academic survival.

Breaking the Academic Monopoly

The best-selling English author and historian Paul Johnson offers another apt assessment of the current state of affairs in British and American universities today. Writing in the London *Spectator*, he says:

> Universities are the most overrated institutions of our age. Of all the calamities which have befallen the 20th century, apart from the two world wars, the expansion of higher education in the 1950s and 1960s was the most enduring. It is a myth that universities are nurseries of reason. They are hothouses for every kind of extremism, irrationality, intolerance, and prejudice,

where intellectual and social snobbery is almost purposefully instilled and where [faculty members] attempt to pass on to their students their own sins of pride. The wonder is that so many people emerge from these dens still employable, though a significant minority, as we have learned to our cost, go forth well equipped for a lifetime of public mischief-making.

In commenting on Johnson's analysis of the situation, Richard John Neuhaus, editor of the journal *First Things*, also cites the comments of the Heritage Foundation's Midge Decter, who has offered a brilliant formula for bringing university administrators back to their senses. She suggests, "If five or six major corporations would announce that they are no longer going to require a college degree, that they are going to train their own people, and that they will make provision for workers to learn Shakespeare and other good things in night school (which is more than they are learning in university now), the current system of higher education would collapse overnight."[9] In plain business terms, they propose to break the monopoly of the universities. Make them compete for students like any other business and, miraculously, they will be forced to return to the real world for a change. Even if the universities should collapse, Neuhaus suggests, the truly gifted teachers would have no shortage of students. That is, after all, how the universities began some thousands of years ago.

Like the disaster of the public schools in this country—which also came about entirely as a result of empowering a state-run monopoly of public educators—the universities have transformed their mission of educating future leaders into a mandate for philosophical brainwashing. The perpetrators of PC on both British and American campuses—otherwise known as the academic "thought police"—are the same tenured radicals described in Roger Kimball's important 1991 book on the subject, entitled *Tenured Radicals*. They are, by and large, middle-aged hippies who have brought the idealism and anarchy of the sixties into the classroom, and they refuse to perceive the tortured logic of their position even when it is undeniable and distasteful to everyone else.

The situation is much the same wherever PC has broken out. Science, history, and precedent mean nothing to campus leftists or the legions of slavish bureaucrats who accede to and implement their bizarre policies.

Unfortunately, the universities are not the only place where PC reigns. Many of Bill Clinton's appointments, as we've noted earlier, demonstrate how political correctness has infiltrated the Oval Office. If Donna Shalala, Roberta Achtenberg, Joycelyn Elders, and Ruth Bader Ginsburg are the people the president has picked for the highest offices in the federal government, one has to wonder what he really had in mind during his campaign when he said he wanted to give us "a government that looks more like America." On the surface, a government that is representative of the real America is a terrific idea. In fact, it was the idea that led our forefathers to install the principles of representative democracy into the framework of American government. But, somehow, one gets the impression that the Clintons may have something quite different in mind.

Nevertheless, if we take the comment at face value, it should be quite easy to draw a demographic portrait of America from various studies and government census records that are conveniently available in libraries, bookstores, and other places. So, to help determine how "a government that looks like America" might be constructed, I propose a demographic tour of our nation. First, a fairly broad-brush approach based on generally available U.S. Census data, and then a more precise and interpretive look.

A Demographic Tour

At the outset, the most notable trend of the past fifty years has been the influence of the large group of men and women, ranging from their mid-twenties to their late forties, who have been at center stage for most of the past three decades. In the eighteen years from 1946 to 1964 some seventy-five million children were born in this country. They were born into an era of national pride, post-World War II exhilaration, and unprecedented affluence, and they became known as the baby boom generation. Demographers today call them "Boomers." Prior to World War II, the highest average birthrate was about twenty births per thousand women, but during the boom years the birthrate topped twenty-four per thousand, for a population growth rate of about 1.6 percent.[10]

Dramatic changes in lifestyles today, however, confirm that the boomer generation has now past, and for a number of reasons. Fears of population explosion, compounded by a higher infant mortality rate, legalized abortion, and other lifestyle issues, have led to a decline in the rate of population growth. Today it is about .71 percent per year. If the trend continues, census analysts expect the birthrate to drop to about .53 percent per year during the first decade of the coming century.

The vigor and enthusiasm of the baby boom generation is being replaced by a very different mood. The children of the Boomers have been dubbed the "baby busters," and they are coming of age. The prospects for these young people seem much less hopeful than what their parents experienced. The ascendancy of the Boomers had a profound effect on American culture. It was a generation some scholars referred to as "the pig in the python," and it has been working its way through society, often distorting things to fit its own shape and redefining the way things are done.

In the 1950s, the suburbs began to blossom. Schools and new forms of recreation were booming. Television came of age, and from "Davy Crockett" and "Ozzie and Harriet" to Elvis Presley and the Beatles, the popular media and the popular culture have seemed synonymous. The baby boomers are still the predominant consumer force. No doubt influenced by the age of advertising, the Boomers have had an unprecedented appetite for accumulating "stuff." Although they are now approaching middle age and opting for less conspicuous consumption, they are still the dominant sociological force in this country with a disproportionate influence over popular tastes.

With the turn of the century, however, the boomer generation will be heading for retirement. The problem, as we saw earlier, is that their numbers are so vast that there may be more people eligible for retirement assistance than there will be workers to pay into the system.

So unless something comes along to change the formula, there will be no government assistance for these people. Our demographic portrait must consider the interests of this large group of people, and it must recognize their political interests.

The Trend to Urbanization

Since the 1920s, more than half the U.S. population has been located in urban centers. During the decade of the 1980s, the number of people residing in cities increased from 167 million to 187 million—a 12 percent rise. Currently California has the largest number of citizens living in urban centers, with 93 percent of its residents living in cities and towns, while Vermont has the highest number living in rural areas— 68 percent.

The direction of population growth for the past three decades has been toward the West and the South. As one indicator of this redistribution of population, California gained seven congressional seats during the past decade, Florida gained four, Texas gained three, and Arizona, Georgia, North Carolina, Virginia, and Washington, D.C., each gained one new seat in Congress. At the same time, New York lost three; Illinois, Michigan, Ohio, and Pennsylvania each lost two congressional seats; and eight other states (principally across the Midwest) lost one.

The number of whites increased by 6 percent during the 1980s. The number of blacks increased by 13 percent, and the Hispanic population increased by 53 percent (a factor of both population growth and large-scale immigration). But the fastest growing ethnic group during the past decade has been Asians and Pacific Islanders, with an increase of 108 percent. The number of this latter group has doubled in the past ten years from 1.5 percent in 1980 to 3 percent today—with a total population of about 7.3 million.

Most Americans are affiliated with some sort of household. Of the 251 million individuals in the 1990 Census, 248.5 million are members of one of the 94.3 million households in this country. Of those, 211 million are identified as family groups. The average household has 2.63

members. Statistically, this is a significant change from earlier Census reports that indicated fewer households and more members per household unit. In 1960, for example, there were 52.8 million households with an average of 3.33 members per household.

Analysts conclude that the major reasons for the change in size of American households are the rising divorce rate and the growing number of young singles who have opted out of marriage. In 1991, more than 23.5 million Americans were living alone, and 2.9 million couples were living together but not married. The number of cohabiting couples increased 120 percent during the 1970s and another 80 percent during the 1980s. These are significant and potentially troubling changes.

Changing Structures

Along with the changing relationships within households, demographers have remarked on the growing number of changes in family structures as well. The visibility of single-parent homes on television, in women's magazines, and as a social issue of both the Right and the Left is a reflection of the growing numbers of single-parent homes. The 1990 Census reported more than 9.7 million families made up of at least one child and no more than one parent. Some 8.8 million of these included children under the age of eighteen. Approximately 7 million of the total number of single-parent homes were headed by a female, and according to race, 58 percent were black, 33 percent were white, and the remaining 9 percent were of other races. Compare this to the general population that is 85 percent white, 12 percent black, and 3 percent other races.

The data also reveal that approximately 7 percent of single-parent homes were caused by the death of a spouse, 46 percent by divorce, and 21 percent by separation. While the number of single-parent homes is just 9 percent of all U.S. households, they make up 26 percent of all households with children. What these numbers reflect is the fact that 16 million American children are being raised without the influence of one or the other parent on a full-time basis. That is twice as many as reported by the 1970 census. The analysts suggest that 61 percent of all young people in this country can expect to spend a portion of their growing-up years in a single-parent home.

Another discouraging implication of the data, however, is the increased likelihood that these children will also be living at or below the poverty level. While just 8 percent of married couples with children have incomes below the poverty level, 45 percent of all female-headed households and 19 percent of single-male-headed households fall below the poverty level.[11]

There are two other types of living arrangement that reflect the social and sexual changes taking place. First is the number of adult children living with parents; second is the number of children being raised by grandparents. The Census data show that in 1991, 31 percent of all unmarried persons between the ages of twenty-five and twenty-nine were living with parents, and 16 percent of unmarried persons between the ages of thirty-five and thirty-nine were living with parents. This is a remarkable phenomenon that clearly involves a wide range of factors. Normally, young people prefer to be on their own. For comparison, approximately 88 percent of the five million married persons between the ages of twenty and twenty-four had already established independent households. So when single individuals remain at home with their parents into their late twenties and thirties, there are factors involved that imply disturbances in the normal patterns of socialization. Finally, 5.1 percent, or 3.3 million, of the nation's 65.1 million children under the age of eighteen are currently being raised in a grandparent's home. In some cases, one or both parents are also present, but in 28 percent there is no parent present.

Beyond the Kinsey Report

In light of the changing relationships between individuals and the changing structure of the home, some analysis of sexual trends is no doubt warranted. Analyzing this trend is more difficult, however, because of the varying reactions of individuals to these kinds of questions and the difficulty of quantifying survey results. The most reliable data concerning the sexual habits of American women come from the National Survey of Family Growth (NSFG) conducted by the National Center for Health Statistics, which give the responses from a nationwide sample of women aged fifteen to forty-four. Among the major findings of the 1990 study are that 75 percent of women in that age range have had nonmarital intercourse. Approximately 68 percent of never-married women have engaged in sexual activity, and 75 percent of married women in this sample said that they had sex prior to marriage.

Most unsettling by traditional moral standards and most trumpeted by the media at the time were the NSFG findings that 40 percent of women had their first sexual experience prior to age eighteen. By the age of twenty, 60 percent had engaged in sexual activity. Trend analysis also shows that the median age for a woman's first sexual experience is getting lower each year. Women in the twenty-to-thirty age bracket, for example, had their first sexual experience earlier than those in the thirty-to-forty group.

Education is apparently a factor in the probability of sexual experience. Women who attended college tended to have their first sexual experience later than those who either did not attend college or who were high school dropouts. Further, women from single-parent homes began having sexual intercourse at an earlier age than women from two-parent families, and they also tended to marry sooner.

A survey by the National Opinion Research Center (NORC) at the University of Chicago reported in 1991 that most adults are either monogamous or abstain from sex. In that study of 1,481 men and women nationwide, researchers found that 22 percent of men between the ages of eighteen and twenty-nine claimed no sexual partners. Again, this suggests related sociological changes since a similar study in 1988 reported that just 9.7 percent of men claimed abstinence. The threat of AIDS and STDs is apparently a factor in reduced sexual activity. The study also reported that 70 percent of men and women claimed only one sexual partner, 18 percent of men and women combined claimed no sexual partners, and approximately 8 percent claimed two or more sexual partners.

The 1988 NORC survey showed that 98.5 percent of sexually active adults were exclusively heterosexual, with only 1.5 percent homosexual or lesbian. This, as the analysts pointed out, is far below Alfred Kinsey's 10 percent figure. The Chicago report suggests that 2 percent would be a more realistic estimate. They also reported that 80 percent of Americans "strongly disapprove" of homosexuality, which was an increase of 8 percent from a similar study conducted in 1978.

How do Americans feel about abortion? According to the National Opinion Research Center data, a large majority support the use of abortion in cases of rape, when the mother's life is at risk, and if there is a significant risk of birth defects. However, less than half of those surveyed support the use of abortion as a contraceptive or to prevent the birth of a child for financial or emotional reasons. A recent Gallup poll reports that 53 percent of Americans believe abortion should be legal in certain circumstances, 14 percent feel abortion should not be legal under any circumstance, and 31 percent feel it should be legal under all circumstances.

Making Sense of It

Commenting on these various surveys and reports of the past few years, most analysts agree that profound changes are taking place in society, and the implications for the health and well-being of the family are particularly disturbing. The Family Research Council (FRC) report, *Free to Be Family*, comments on both the darker and the brighter sides of the story. The authors observe:

> The family in America today is undeniably weaker than at any point in our nation's history. One child in four today is born out of wedlock. One child in two spends at least part of his childhood in a single-parent household. One child in five lives in a family receiving some form of public assistance.

Still, some experts argue that these trends suggest that the family is not declining per se, only changing. This view ignores the devastating social consequences—such as higher crime and suicide rates and lower educational achievement—associated with family breakdown. Moreover, it turns a deaf ear to the growing number of people (particularly children) who have been the victims of more than a quarter-century of domestic upheaval.[12]

Along with the changes brought about by divorce, out-of-wedlock births, and a more promiscuous lifestyle among many adults and young people, the central crisis of the family, the report concludes, is the lack of cohesion and interaction between parents and their children. Parents today spend 40 percent less time with their children than parents did a generation ago. From about thirty hours per week in the mid-1960s, the amount of parent-child interaction dropped to just seventeen hours in the mid-1980s. Nowhere on earth do parents spend less time with their children than here in the United States.

Obviously children in single-parent homes are bound to be deprived of parental attention, but a University of Virginia study cited by the FRC report shows that employed mothers of preschool children spend less than half as much time with their children as nonemployed mothers. Thanks to the hectic pace of life in two-wage-earner families, children in these homes are often regulated, scheduled, picked up, and dropped off like clockwork, and as a result they too are deprived of the simple joys of the leisurely pace of life that once characterized childhood. There is no time, the writers add, for long walks, kicking rocks, or watching the clouds drift by. Instead, children are forced into the regimen and routines of adults, and they are often deprived of their innocence.

If parents want to defend the welfare of their children, they must begin to react to the negative trends affecting all children today. As the FRC study asserts, *crime begins when childhood ends too soon*. To deprive children of their innocence and their growing-up years not only robs them of a very important part of the learning process, but it transforms many of them into criminals bent on revenge. Children who do not receive love and guidance become targets of opportunity for gangs, for molesters, and for their own unfulfilled emotional needs and longings. Somewhere this cycle has to stop.

Industry Standards

In his important book on the need to return to the values of home and community, Amitai Etzioni writes that if Americans ran their businesses like they run their families, the entire nation would soon grind to a halt. He says:

> Consider for a moment parenting as an industry. As farming declined, most fathers left to work away from home generations ago. Over the past 20 years, millions of American mothers have sharply curtailed their work in the "parenting industry" by moving to their work outside the home. By 1991 two-thirds (66.7 percent) of all mothers with children under 18 were in the labor force, and more than half (55.4 percent) of women with children under the age of 3 were. At the same time, a much smaller number of child-care personnel moved into the parenting industry.[13]

In place of loving homes and friendly neighborhoods, parents have relegated their offspring to "kennels for kids," and the effects are predictably devastating to children and to our entire civilization. "Children require attention and a commitment of time, energy, and above all self," says Etzioni. He adds:

> The notion of "quality time" is a lame excuse for parental absence; it presupposes that bonding and education can take place in brief time bursts, on the run. Quality time occurs within quantity time. As you spend time with children—fishing, gardening, camping, or "just" eating a meal—there are unpredictable moments when an opening occurs, and education takes hold. As family expert Barbara Dafoe Whitehead puts it: "Maybe there is indeed such a thing as a one-minute manager, but there is no such thing as a one-minute parent."[14]

In the words of child psychologist Edward Zigler, "We are cannibalizing children. Children are dying in the system, never mind achieving optimum development."

But what else can we conclude about this nation from the statistics? According to the newest Census updates, there are currently 253.5 million people in the United States, with an average population density of 67 people per square mile. As mentioned above, slightly less than 85 percent of the population are white, largely descended from European immigrants of the eighteenth and nineteenth centuries. Just over 12 percent are black, the large majority descended from slave laborers imported from Africa at approximately the same time. The remaining 2 to 3 percent are of other races, principally Asian. Life expectancy for the average U.S. citizen is eighty years for females and seventy-three years for males. Literacy is at 97 percent.

Just over 90 percent of Americans claim some religious affiliation. Protestants make up 56 percent of the population, Roman Catholics 28 percent, and Jews about 2 percent. Another 5 to 7 percent have either no religious affiliation or identify with a variety of Eastern or other new religions.

Among all people over the age of twenty-five, the average educational attainment of whites in 1970 was 12.1 years. By 1991 the level had climbed to an average 12.7 years. Among blacks, the average was 9.8 years in 1970, and it skyrocketed to 12.4 years by 1991. Among Hispanics, the 1970 average educational attainment was 9.1 years; by 1991 the level had climbed to 12.0 years.

It would be nice to say that all these various trends confirm a number of long-range improvements in the lives of Americans, an increase in health and welfare, and they show that twelve years of Republican government helped to make the world a better place. Unfortunately, except in a few areas such as the last one showing a rise in the level of educational attainment, too much of the news is still very bad. Things did not get much better for the soul of America under the past two administrations. We are still in crisis.

The Big Picture

Recently I have been reading a book by Gerald L. Schroeder called *Genesis and the Big Bang*, and it gives a fascinating description of the enormity of our universe. According to this author, the solar system started fifteen billion years ago, and the galaxies around us are hurtling away from one another at a speed approaching the speed of light. In our one galaxy, the Milky Way, he says, there are probably a hundred million stars equal to our sun, and in the universe there are at least a hundred million galaxies equal to ours, some a great deal bigger. The earth is like a tiny flyspeck in the middle of all this enormous expanse, and in light of Creation, our existence on earth is, to quote the psalmist, "a handbreadth."

What this says to me is, first of all, how great God must be, and how insignificant we are in the vast continuum of time and space. Yet as big as it all is, the vastness of the universe is made up of empty space, hot gas, and cold rocks. As big as they may be, gas and rocks have very little value or significance. But the Bible tells us that God chose to prepare this vast and mind-boggling universe as a setting for our little planet and people made in His own image. The Bible links three things together: the creation of heaven, the creation of the earth, and the creation of God's chosen race. That is what the whole story of creation is about.[15]

When I read in Deuteronomy where Moses said, "You are a particular treasure among all the nations of the earth," I realized how awesome God's work has been. This gives me tremendous hope for the human race. The Bible says that "the portion of the Lord is His people." From out of all this enormous universe, and out of all the creation, fifteen billion years distilled down to a moment of time, it still comes down to those people on the earth who are the chosen people of God. What an incredible thought!

If we are indeed God's people and we are the most important things in the universe, then He has endowed us with enormous potential that we haven't even begun to develop. That is why Jesus said, "If you have faith as much as a grain of mustard seed, you can say to this tree, be uprooted and go cast yourself in the sea, and *nothing would be impossible for you.*" Carried to its end, Jesus' mandate says people of faith can literally control planets, because after all, people—not stars and planets—are the stuff of eternity.

An Eternal Scale of Values

Every human being has enormous potential to God, because all of this creation was meant for us. Now in light of this great truth, common sense would say that it is only natural for people to embrace the Judeo-Christian view of the dignity of men and women. According to the Bible, man is a little lower than the angels, destined to rule and reign with Christ. But the nihilists and the politically correct prefer to say that there is no God, there is no Jesus, there is no salvation, and there is no hope. That, very simply, is why their philosophy goes against the inner yearnings of all mankind and *why in a very short time liberalism is doomed to fall in America.*

Throughout history, the liberals have tried to reduce humanity to its lowest form and to identify humanity with the slime and the ooze of the earth, rather than identifying humanity as children of the living God and fellow heirs of the kingdom of heaven. The greatness of mankind is found in the dignity we achieve with God. When we see the accomplishments of Christian civilization, we have to recognize that those achievements have been nothing short of awesome.

But the incredible thing is that despite the attempts of the nihilists and the leftists, the tide is turning and we are seeing a movement of freedom. We are seeing a worldwide movement toward faith in God and its accompanying liberties—free enterprise and representative government all around the globe. From the darkest corners of the Third World to the mansions of Beverly Hills an awakening is taking place in the human heart that before long will sweep the land. There will be plenty of fierce challenges to overcome, but destiny is ours.

As we continue the discussion of these important cultural issues and the prospects for our future, I would like to focus now on the outline of those issues that concern the heart and soul of the nation: specifically the importance of ethical standards and the rightful role of religion.

11

The Cornerstone of Democracy

After recent democratic reforms in Russia, religion is coming out of the closet and into the pew. God is making a comeback. The reports of his death were greatly exaggerated.

Syndicated Columnist Mike Nichols, 20 June 1993

An ACLU attorney said: "We stopped prayer at the Round Rock High School graduation." A fellow liberal replied: "Thank God!"

Syndicated Columnist Molly Ivins, 8 June 1993

THE IRONY OF THE SITUATION is undeniable. After seventy years of life under atheism, Russia and Eastern Europe are coming back to their historic Christian heritage. The leaders of fifteen former communist states are begging American Christians to bring Bibles, to teach them how to pray, and to show them the principles of Christian democracy. While all this is going on, America's ruling elites are working feverishly to eradicate all traces of religion in this country and to fortify their makeshift wall of separation between church and state.

When the French statesman Alexis de Tocqueville came to America in the 1830s, he was profoundly impressed by the vigor and passion of American democracy. But what most impressed him was the degree to which religious values helped give shape and focus to American politics. In France, most felt that the church had compromised its values in order to gain privileges from the monarchy, and consequently it had become identified more with oppression than justice. In America, Tocqueville said, religious principles provided the essential framework of law. The American people's faith in divine Providence helped ensure consensus and cooperation with government. He wrote:

> Freedom sees religion as the companion of its struggles and triumphs, the cradle of its infancy, and the divine source of its rights. Religion is considered as the guardian of mores, and mores are regarded as the guarantee of the laws and pledge for the maintenance of freedom itself.[1]

It is certainly true that the precepts of faith are interwoven throughout the founding documents of this nation. The forms of our constitutional government—as implemented by Jefferson, Madison, Franklin, Washington, Adams, and others—were carefully designed to acknowledge the authority of the Scriptures and our dependence upon the Creator.

Civil Obedience

In 1785, James Madison wrote, "Before any man can be considered as a member of civil society, he must be considered as a subject of the governor of the universe."[2] He understood that the secular state holds temporal authority in trust and in deference to God's eternal authority. After all, Madison reasoned, how can we expect men and women who will not bow to their Creator to be obedient to the laws of the state? How can men be expected to rule wisely without an allegiance to the source of wisdom and judgment?

During one particularly difficult moment during the Constitutional Convention of 1787, Benjamin Franklin admonished those present to stop their bickering and to turn to God for a resolution to their debate. He said:

I have lived, Sir, a long time, and the longer I live the more convincing proofs I see of this truth: "that God governs in the affairs of man." And if a sparrow cannot fall to the ground without His notice, is it probable that an empire can rise without His aid?

We have been assured, Sir, in the Sacred Writings that except the Lord build the house, they labor in vain that build it. I firmly believe this. I also believe that without His concurring aid, we shall succeed in the political building no better than the builders of Babel.

The great orator then went on to implore the distinguished leaders present:

I therefore beg leave to move that, henceforth, prayers imploring the assistance of Heaven and its blessing on our deliberation be held in this assembly every morning before we proceed to business.[3]

The dignity and merit of the documents they eventually produced is testament enough to the merit of Franklin's suggestion. It would eventually become a tradition that continues to this day.

One of the most influential figures in law, education, and science in the first half of the nineteenth century, Noah Webster, was even more specific about the value of faith in a democratic society. As an educator he understood that Christian principles were essential to encouraging excellence in young men and women, to giving them a sense of purpose, and to maintaining discipline. As a statesman and jurist he could also attest that a society without a strong code of faith and morality would degenerate into anarchy. He wrote:

The moral principles and precepts contained in the scriptures ought to form the basis of all our constitution and laws. . . . All the miseries and evils which men suffer from vice, crime, ambition, injustice, oppression, slavery, and war, proceed from their despising or neglecting the precepts contained in the Bible.[4]

But today, in an era far removed from these momentous events, it seems we are in danger of losing that clear vision. I maintain that the evidence we have already seen of the turning tide is sufficient proof that the forces of reason will prevail and that we will see an imminent return to common sense. But the threats to morality and the rightful role of religion in American society are nevertheless real and should be clearly understood. So at this point I would like to take a closer look at some of the signs of change and the hurdles yet to be overcome.

Two Views of Authority

To gain a perspective on these issues, perhaps it will help to recognize that from the very beginning there was a subtle warfare under the surface of the American experiment between those who believed that this was a nation ordained by God and those who leaned more toward the views of the French Enlightenment, which put religion and politics at odds. In the South and the West, Anglicans, Presbyterians, Baptists, Methodists, and Roman Catholics maintained a strong grip on their historic creeds, while New England Congregationalists and Unitarians were more "inner directed" and tended to praise individual enterprise and human ingenuity rather than belief in divine intervention in human affairs. The roots of religious controversies were visible even in those early days, but it was not until the mid-twentieth century that the deeper disagreements surfaced.

Looking back from the 1990s, we can now see how great the seismic shift in public attitudes and common morality has been. The 1980s were a time of relative quiet, a time of normalization after the panic-stricken sixties and seventies. For conservatives, the 1980s were an attempt to restore the values of self-discipline and individual initiative. The ship of state had tilted so far to the left it was in danger of capsizing, and the Reagan revolution helped bring it upright again. But for all its achievements, the Republican administration did not go far enough. It walked the middle path so intently that the reforms the country actually needed were never accomplished. Reagan and Bush behaved diplomatically toward their adversaries while the liberals persistently plotted their downfalls.

The Republican administration gave the country twelve years of relative calm, but they were nevertheless years of intense irritation to the generation coming up who were still attached to the fun-loving, free-love, freedom-seeking, anti-American lifestyle of the sixties. Today we can see that the debate between the open lifestyle of the sixties and the Republican values of the eighties was actually just another expression of the battle that has continued since the eighteenth century between pro-church and anti-church forces. In both cases, the arguments reflected two very different views of reality and a deep-seated disagreement about the sources of moral authority.

A Moral Tug-of-War

In the newsletter, *The American Character*, Robert Royal calls this battle of ideologies a "tug-of-war between the legacy of the sixties and the revival [in the eighties] of more traditional beliefs in reaction against it." This battle never actually disappeared, he says, though the relative calm of the eighties may have masked the extent to which the spirit of the sixties still influences public mores and social values in this country.[5]

The fallout of these skirmishes of the culture war is visible throughout our culture today. Moral authority is being undermined, religion is under attack, and moral relativism is not only condoned but encouraged by government. Most dangerous, those who claim to hold religious beliefs have often accepted their relegation to a sort of second-class status. To add insult to injury, people who rate religion as "very important" in their lives are ignorant of many of the essential tenets of their faith.

According to a survey by the Barna Group, 67 percent of Americans no longer believe in absolute truth. Only 32 percent of believers believe the Bible to be infallible. A report prepared by the Gallup Organization and published by the Princeton Religion Research Center says, "Although eight in 10 Americans profess a Christian faith, many cannot name one, let alone all four of the Gospels. They may remember that

Jesus was born in Bethlehem, but many have trouble identifying him as the person who delivered the Sermon on the Mount."[6]

In the 1960s, two-thirds (or 67 percent) of all Americans believed the Bible to be the actual Word of God, word for word. In the seventies and eighties the number dropped to 37 percent. In the most recent survey, the number had gone back up slightly, to 40 percent.[7] A 1988 Gallup survey showed that 45 percent of young people between the ages of thirteen and seventeen regard the Bible as the literal Word of God, while approximately 11 percent of all Americans, young and old, believe the Bible is nothing more than a book of fairy tales and fables. Oddly enough, a 1979 Gallup survey of clergy showed that just 69 percent of clergy believed the Bible to be infallible, 24 percent believed it contains errors, and 3 percent believed it is nothing but tales and fables.

To understand how far we have come in just the past three decades, we can look back to the words of the U.S. Supreme Court in 1892 when, after an extensive review of the definitive documents of government, the justices declared, "These references . . . add a volume of unofficial declarations to the mass of organic utterances that this is a religious people . . . a Christian nation." Later, in a ruling handed down in 1931, Justice George Sutherland affirmed that we are a "Christian people." Justice William O. Douglas, in a 1952 ruling, stated that "we are a religious people and our institutions presuppose a Supreme Being." Yet despite this tremendous legacy, on June 25, 1962, the Supreme Court ruled in *Engel v. Vitale* that Bible reading was no longer legal in the public schools of this nation. One year later, on June 17, 1963, in *Murray v. Curlett*, the Court stripped students in the public schools of their right to pray.

Preparing for Battle

For the near term, we can now see that we are in for a long-drawn-out and increasingly hostile debate with those who would like to displace or redefine our moral heritage. But over the long term we have to see that the choices we are making today will have either very hopeful or very grave implications for our future well-being. In his book,

The American Hour, Os Guinness has described the current clash over moral values as a "crisis of cultural authority." It is a battle that is being waged with words and ideas, he says, but the consequences are very serious for the future of American society. Guinness writes:

> When morality is strong, laws need not be. So if the scope of freedom is to widen, that of law should not. There is therefore great folly in the current notion that, because morality is a private affair, anything is right in public "so long as it does not break the law." Under the guise of this maxim, liberals seasoned in crusades against environmental irresponsibility have presided carelessly over a massive moral erosion of their own. Moral principles have been hacked down, special proprieties bulldozed to the ground. All that is not legally prohibited is socially allowed. Someday these radical rule-breakers will wake up to a world without rules. Then they will lament either the moral dustbowl they have created or the dense underbrush of laws they have had to grow hastily in its place.[8]

This is certainly a prophetic moment in history, and there are great battles yet to be won. But the good news is that people are beginning to see the challenges and to rise to the occasion as never before. Evangelicals have prayed long and hard for an awakening, and now we can see that it is beginning to happen. In America and around the world we are seeing a great revival of faith and a movement back to biblical authority and truth. Those individuals and denominations that hold to the traditional faith of their fathers—whether they are Baptists, charismatics, conservative Evangelicals, or pro-family Roman Catholics—are seeing an incredible resurgence of vigor and growth.

The Bible says, "Let us hold fast the profession of our faith without wavering" (Heb. 10:23 KJV). Those who are willing to tackle these tough issues, who are not ashamed to proclaim their faith, are seeing the power of God poured out in their midst. But those who are wishy-washy and half-hearted are experiencing failure and disappointments. Those who are denying the truth, who are temporizing about the supernatural aspects of the faith, are clearly losing ground. They are being reduced to a footnote in history while the tide of change and the hand of God are lifting the faithful to unprecedented new heights.

The Tide Against Atheism

We reported recently on "The 700 Club" that Madalyn Murray O'Hair, the outspoken atheist who won the case in 1963 to have Bible reading and prayer tossed out of the public schools, has finally conceded defeat. After thirty years of waging war against God and country, O'Hair says her war is over and the atheists have lost. "I think that the window of opportunity for atheism has closed," she told a reporter for her home-town newspaper, the *Austin American-Statesman*. "Our '63 case will be overturned. It's just a matter of the right case coming before the Court. By the end of the decade, I think you'll have full-fledged religious ceremonies return to public schools."[9]

The signs of the turning tide sweeping this nation are so apparent that even the spiritually blind can see them. Even O'Hair can see. But how could she miss it? Her oldest son, William, the child she used to convince the Supreme Court that school prayer and Bible reading are harmful, now has a dynamic ministry as a Christian evangelist. Speaking to large audiences all across America, Bill Murray is helping to turn the tide against the moral disease and distress that atheism has brought upon the nation.

While the American Atheists couldn't even get three hundred people to show up for their national conference, Austin's "Walk for Jesus" march, right at O'Hair's back door, mustered more than twenty thousand Christians. She rightly interpreted this as a sign of defeat.

But even more telling, the atheist who has been battling Christians most of her life says that now she is also battling bad health, and the prognosis apparently isn't very good. "My health is rotten," she said, "absolutely rotten. I'm in trouble more frequently than not." In the July 1993 interview, O'Hair spoke openly about her life as an anti-Christian activist. As she moaned about the failures of atheism to win the hearts and minds of the American people, she also spoke morbidly of her expected death and cremation. "I'd like my tombstone to say,

'Woman, atheist, anarchist . . .' except," she laughed, "there will be no tombstone."

There is no doubt the life she has led has ravaged her body and soul. But that is one of the outcomes of the war against God. The other side of that coin is that a life of faith leads to a longer, healthier life. That is a biblical concept that can be found in the Ten Commandments: "Walk in all the way that the LORD your God has commanded you, so that you may live and prosper and prolong your days in the land that you will possess" (Deut. 5:33 NIV). We have been saying for a long time that religion is good for people, but there is conclusive scientific proof that it is beneficial not just for your soul but for body and mind as well.

Religion and Good Health

In a two-year study of elderly men and women, Yale University researchers found that those for whom religion is important live longer than others for whom religion is not important. The study showed that people for whom religion is not very important have twice the mortality rate of those who consider it very important.

According to David Larson, "The religiously committed, the church attenders, live longer than the non-committed." In studies he has either conducted or reviewed for the National Institute of Mental Health (NIMH), Larson found irrefutable evidence that regular church attendance and spiritual commitment have an undeniably positive effect on physical and emotional well-being. He says:

> I had set out to show that religion wasn't harmful or neutral to mental health. What I found was that for nearly 90 percent of worshipers, religion was a powerful help. In fact, the people who were the most faithful and attended services once a week or more were the ones who suffered the least psychological turmoil, even when dealt the hard blows of life.[10]

Early in his studies, Larson had been told by his advisers that religion was harmful to psychiatric patients, and they tried to persuade him to study some other branch of medicine. But he was not convinced. He tracked down a noted professor at Duke University who not only encouraged his interest in psychiatry, but offered him a fellowship and shared his belief that faith could be a positive and healing influence for patients with both mental and physical disorders. The young man went on to complete his medical degree and eventually joined the NIMH and moved his family to the Maryland suburbs of Washington, D.C.

Since that time the evidence has continued to mount, proving that religion and medicine do indeed mix. People who are religious have a lower risk of experiencing mental illness, drug abuse, or depression. In virtually every category, the connections between mental health and religion were very impressive, and when Larson reviewed his research, he found that religious commitment was beneficial to physical health in more than 80 percent of those cases as well. In thirteen of fourteen studies, religious commitment was a significant factor in preventing alcoholism, and in thirteen out of sixteen studies, the risk of suicide was much lower for people who were religious.

A study at Wayne State University found an inverse relationship between suicide rates and church attendance. As church attendance increases, risk of suicide decreases. A separate study published in the *Journal of Chronic Disease* showed that those who do not attend church are four times more likely to commit suicide than those who do. A University of Akron study reported that the emotional and physical well-being of those they surveyed increased as the amount of time reportedly spent in prayer increased.[11]

In more than a dozen separate studies cited in a June 21, 1993, article in *Citizen* magazine, there is a clear connection between spiritual maturity and physical and mental health. A study at Northwestern University, for example, showed that elderly women with strong religious commitment heal faster, have more stamina, and exhibit better emotional health than others undergoing the same type of recovery.

Other studies show that hypertension is lower among religious people. Among smokers, those who did not consider religion important were seven times more likely to have abnormal blood pressure than those who consider it important. In fact, Larson pointed out, in general, smokers who attend church have the same blood pressure rate as nonsmokers who do not attend church.

Back to Basics

When even science confirms that religion is a positive and beneficial force in society, it is very important that the church stand by its values and principles and proclaim the life-saving benefits of faith in God. It is much too easy for the church to compromise its authority and give way to the social pressures to conform to the world around us. The heart of every Christian in America must have been stirred by the stand of Pope John Paul II during his 1993 visit to Denver, Colorado. Imagine the courage of the great man who, in the presence of a pro-abortion American president and later a pro-abortion vice-president, called on the American people to respect life. Pope John Paul II stands like a rock against all opposition in his clear enunciation of the foundational principles of the Christian faith. Then he urged American Catholics to reach out in fellowship to their Baptist brothers and sisters in faith.

His call was welcomed by many Southern Baptists who had just experienced a revolution that culminated in 1992 and is proving to be a major step in a return to the foundations of Christianity. The turning of Southern Baptists is clear evidence of the turning tide against liberalism in the church. Southern Baptists are the largest denomination in America, yet their seminaries were being overrun by liberals who were doing and saying things absolutely contrary to the Bible and contrary to the historic truths of the Christian faith. As a consequence, thousands of young men and women who had come to seminary to have their faith nurtured and to learn how to teach the Bible were, instead, having their faith shattered by lies and intellectual absurdities. These are the oldest heresies in the world, yet here they were being proclaimed as the "new theology," the "higher criticism," and the enlightened approach to Christian faith. Those teachings had infiltrated virtually every seminary, and it was coming into the churches in a concerted movement.

It took ten years, but under the guidance of the very bold and wise Texas judge, Paul Pressler, who was joined in the struggle by a number of fine Baptist pastors and leaders, there was a sweeping victory for historic conservatism after a bitter struggle for spiritual authority in the church. I suspect that struggle may well be a prelude to what will be happening in other denominations and throughout our entire society.

This is *the* largest Protestant denomination and it is totally in the hands of conservatives now who, again, are exercising common sense. They're going back to the Bible. They are teaching people the Scriptures and how to find God. They are teaching them about Jesus, about discipleship, and about the reality of a practical, day-by-day, living faith, and they are winning many people to the Lord. They are succeeding. I recently talked with the newly installed conservative president of one of the formerly ultraliberal Southern Baptist seminaries, and he told me that under his administration the school's debt has been paid and its enrollment doubled.

Reclaiming the Land

The doomsayers were saying, as we have heard recently in the Republican party, If these guys get control, they're going to split the church down the middle. Southern Baptists will no longer have any strength, and they will lose the majority of their members. The denomination will be reduced to minority status. But they were absolutely wrong, and instead of decreasing, the denomination is growing as never before. It is more unified, with more cohesion and with a clearer message and vision. The people coming out of Southern Baptist seminaries today have a radiant faith and a mature understanding of Christianity.

But Southern Baptists are not the only ones going through changes. A few years ago the Church of England (which is the Episcopal Church in this country) appointed as archbishop of Canterbury a man who did not believe in the virgin birth, the resurrection, or many of the essential tenets of Christianity. I remember the reaction of an editorial writer for the *London Economist*, who said, in essence, "Well, if he wants to believe those things that's his business, but if he wants to be a leader of the Christian church then he needs to believe in Christianity."

That is common sense. If a pastor is going to hold himself up as a leader of the Christian faith, then he needs to subscribe to the tenets of the Christian faith. If he doesn't, then he should leave. It is dangerous, deceitful, and deceptive for teachers in a Christian seminary to teach doctrines contrary to the faith of the people who support them. Common sense says that those who teach at any Christian school should hold to the teachings and the historic confessions of the Christian faith. If they don't wish to do that, then let them go somewhere else. That is not discriminatory, it's just common sense.

It is common sense to believe that anybody who speaks in God's name should know Him. They should obey His commandments and teach other people how to do so. Anyone who rules a nation and claims to be a follower of God and yet does and professes things that are absolutely contrary to the Word of God is a heretic and a deceiver. Nobody forces anyone to be a Methodist or a Catholic or a Presbyterian. But if someone claims to be a member, then such a member has an obligation to believe and practice what he claims to believe.

Faith in Action

With all of the negative changes impacting our society, it is increasingly important for Christians to be involved in all the things that affect our communities. They need to be involved not only in the church, but in government, education, civic activities, and every other area of life. Unfortunately, secular involvement has not been something that Christians have been very good at or very eager to do until now. Many are well educated and successful, but they have kept silent up to now.

Conservatives are by nature people who like order. They like things to work and prefer to ignore things that don't work. But to bring about the kinds of changes that will be needed in a system that has grown increasingly corrupt and is controlled by vocal and well-armed liberals, we are going to have to create some disorder. This is distasteful to them, but now they are beginning to enter the fray despite the cost.

One of the signs that people are ready to get involved is the fact that we are receiving record numbers of applications for admission to Regent University Law School. They're coming in substantial numbers—dramatically higher than we have ever seen before. One reason for this, I believe, is that people are being driven by the excesses of the Clinton administration to seek an education at a Christian law school because they want to be trained now for jobs in government service. Until now they have not had the impetus, but suddenly Christians are realizing that their faith is on the line and the future of our nation is on the line. When they see the incredible blunders of government, they know that they have to be prepared to get involved.

That is why there has been a great surge in support for conservative organizations. It is not just in the organizations I previously mentioned. We are also seeing a surge of growth in Christian ministries, conservative economic and social organizations, and political action committees across the spectrum.

Government Scare Tactics

Christians have been loath to get involved in the political arena, but since my campaign for the Republican nomination of 1988, I have seen significant changes. I believe now that the initial shock of that campaign drove some people away. They decided that politics was very painful and distasteful, and the press made it very unpleasant for them to be involved in this process. At the same time, the IRS certainly did everything in its power to frighten Evangelicals and to keep Christians from getting involved in political movements, despite their constitutional protections. This is a very dicey area of the law anyway, and since tax exemption is such an important consideration for Christian organizations, many of them tended to back away from political engagement.

But it is a very different story today. Now that the provocation is so much greater, they have come to realize that they must either move together or perish. The 1993 school board elections in New York City were a landmark event. It was something that I had dreamed about for years, that evangelical Christians and pro-family Roman Catholics would join together in political unity, and that is precisely what happened. The archdiocese of New York authorized the distribution of Christian Coalition voters guides in all of the parishes and churches in the archdiocese, and there were some fabulous victories because of the strength of the coalition that developed.

I hope and pray that this is just the beginning of mutually satisfactory cooperation. This did not in any way influence Catholics to subscribe to Protestant doctrine any more than it made Evangelicals subscribe to the teachings of the Roman Catholic Church. We said that all of us loved God, believed in Jesus, believed in the Bible, and were united in a core set of values under attack by radicals. We needed to stand together.

A Common-Sense Coalition

One of the foundational principles of coalition building is that we must cooperate with those groups with whom we agree on cardinal issues in order to achieve our mutual political goals. We agree not to attempt to coerce or unduly influence others to subscribe to our beliefs that do not directly impinge upon the issues at stake. In other words, Protestants, Catholics, Mormons, Seventh-Day Adventists, and Orthodox Jews, for example, may disagree on some important theological issues. Yet on certain important political issues they see eye-to-eye; therefore, where they agree they must unite so that together they can achieve their mutual goals with greater unanimity, force, and effectiveness.

One of my dear friends, Orrin Hatch, is an outstanding senator from the state of Utah. He is a Mormon, and while we disagree on many issues of doctrine and biblical understanding, we are very much in unison in our dedication to family values, on creating a healthy moral climate in America, and on protecting and preserving our rights as believers to practice our faith without restriction. When he was appointed chairman of the Senate Labor Committee, I wrote him a letter and said, "Thank God you're there!" I really meant it.

I think people have to hear this. We may differ on some important spiritual issues, and we do, but that does not in any way keep me from making an alliance with Senator Hatch on the major political issues confronting our nation. A political party is not a church. It does not need to maintain a rigid orthodoxy and a statement of faith. Christians who are novices in politics have been concerned about party platforms as statements of faith because that's the way they operate as Christians. But in politics, legislative action flows from holding office, and those who hold office are able to make decisions concerning the lives of the people. It is ridiculous to spend a lot of time arguing over the arcane points of a platform only to see positions of great power won by the proponents of the philosophy we are opposing.

Professional politicians say, Give on principle, but hold on offices. They understand that the principles are at the heart of everything, but the specific wording of any resolution is not legislation; legislation has to be hammered out through debate and compromise. There has to be give-and-take in legislation. The Christian or anybody else who gets into politics has to understand that the name of the game is to win offices and from that position it is possible to pass laws and appoint others to positions of authority. Only after these victories is there any chance that basic philosophies can be transformed into legislative and administrative action. Regrettably, during the past thirty years, the liberals have used this truth all too well to the detriment of us all.

Strength of Conviction

I have seen articles and editorials in various publications suggesting that after the Clinton victory, the Republican party was looking to disenfranchise religious conservatives. Even if that were the case, I am not so sure that in the next few years it is going to have that option. The religious people in the Republican party will be such a powerful force the party could not change even if it wanted to. They will be the party.

The Republican party is becoming more and more the party of Christian social thinkers, and in state after state these people are coming to the fore as the workers and as the leaders of the party. Consequently when 40 to 50 percent of the key membership of the party shares a particular philosophy, it is impossible to shun them and silence their point of view.

The surveys we have seen, however, indicate that in the event the Republican party were to abandon its pro-family positions, as many as 57 percent of the Evangelicals would walk out. They would either form a new party or possibly join with Ross Perot, but they will not sit on their hands nor will they be denied a voice. In the process, the Republican party would be so damaged it would never hold the White House again. It would be political suicide.

In the late 1970s the Democratic party chose candidates and legislative initiatives that alienated evangelical Christians deeply, and as a result more than six million Democrats switched parties—especially Southern Baptists in the South. That was perhaps the first wave of the turning tide. They walked out of the Democratic party, and the Democrats lost the Senate and the presidency. Now we know that these people will provide the margin of victory for countless senators and congressmen in 1994, as well as the race for the White House in 1996.

But there is one more thing that needs to be said. There are many people who are conservatives, with a respect for the traditional values of this country, who may be somewhat religious—at least they believe that there is a God who cares about us—but they would never characterize themselves as Evangelicals or, much less, part of the "Religious Right." Christians in politics need to assure these people that they are not the problem; they are the solution. The only threat Christians represent is to those who hold liberal and socialist views that are contrary to the general welfare and the historical greatness of this nation.

Fighting Fire with Fire

Unfortunately, the elites have so denigrated the image of religious people that when religious people call their senators and congressmen, they are often ignored. But if members of the Left call their senators and congressmen, they are listened to. After an epic vote on school prayer some years ago, Republican Senator Bob Packwood made the statement that he wouldn't have to worry about the Christian voters because Christians have the shortest memory of any group in America.

If that were ever true, it is changing. Thanks to the Christian Coalition, they now have a champion. They have computers. They have money and mailing lists, and they have the power to call politicians to account for their votes. The Coalition is keeping score on every member of the Congress, in both houses of government, and when they go on record for or against any important issue, the Coalition is there reporting those votes back to the electorate. They are going to have to answer for their records and either receive the thanks of their constituents or pay the price at the polls.

This has never happened before in America. Christian people have never had as sophisticated an organization as they have now. Thanks to inceasing technology, the ability to store and communicate data is constantly being enhanced. Conservatives can communicate with people all over America, receiving new input and downloading the findings to other organizations. They are using voice mail, faxes, computer bulletin boards, and every conceivable means of getting the word out.

At CBN we not only have a superb television news department, we have Standard News, a topnotch wire service with thirteen professional reporters in Washington alone. They are watching what is happening and then going behind the scenes to dig up information and bring out the truth. We often cover stories from a common-sense perspective that the rest of the media are ignoring. In the past the media have skipped important stories that reflect the true feelings and values of Americans, but now they cannot do that with impunity. Now the audience has an alternate source of information.

It used to be that the gatekeepers—the three networks, the wire services, and the major newspaper publishers—had a lock on the news. That is no longer the case. Now there are so many different avenues bringing information into people's homes that the traditional gate-keepers have lost a huge amount of their power. In the past, the mainstream media have actually been able to influence and control voter behavior on the basis of their stories and their editorials. But that power is diminishing dramatically. That does not mean that the media didn't play a role in the Clinton victory. They did. But most people now realize what was being done to them, and they're angry about it. The tide is turning.

Youth on the Move

In the May 26, 1993, *New York Times,* I read the story: "Students Challenge Ban on Prayer at Graduation." One of the most refreshing signs of the turning tide is that students are beginning to make prayer a civil rights issue. Interestingly enough, this struggle is pitting students who want free speech against the liberals who want to use the power of the state to keep them from speaking freely.

Who would have thought that with all the bad news we have seen concerning the younger generation, we would now be seeing headlines stating that young people all over America are protesting for the right to pray in school? Suddenly it is clear that the ACLU is the oppressor, trying to stop them from praying and expressing their views openly. One student in that *New York Times* article said, in effect, "if you won't let me pray, I will sue the school." The article said they had been emboldened by Pat Robertson's American Center for Law and Justice!

What a marvelous irony. I believe this may be one of the most important trends of this decade—Christian young people with deep convictions taking a stand against persecution. When the liberals were teaching kids that they had rights, they were thinking of the right to rebel, not to pray, but to be uncivilized and outrageous. But the kids are demanding the right to pray, to be more civilized, and the radicals don't know what to do about it!

What is developing among students may become the most crucial issue before us. Suddenly the students of America are fighting against the ACLU and the liberal establishment for their rights. It is a beautiful sight. If this becomes the big civil rights cry—if the students of the 1990s say that to preserve their rights as Americans they must be allowed to pray—we're looking at something that could mobilize the world.

As a matter of fact, for the "See You at the Flagpole" ceremonies at the start of school in 1992, 1.2 million students turned out to pray for their schools, their teachers, and their communities. In 1993, the number of students gathering to pray is projected to swell to 2 million.

In 1992, at certain locations—such as the city of Metropolis, Illinois—students praying in front of the school were arrested by school administrators and police. One honor student was actually handcuffed like a criminal and forced into a squad car. The American Center for Law and Justice (ACLJ) influenced the Metropolis School Board to back down, but the police would not back down. So the ACLJ attorneys took the police to court, and the students were recently awarded damages. It is highly unlikely, in light of the ACLJ's victories, that any school board would dare to stop the students from praying in the future.

Unacceptable Options

America in the mid-1990s has changed unbelievably from the image presented by Alexis de Tocqueville in the nineteenth century. Many assaults have been made upon the moral and religious values of this nation, but precedent-setting victories have been won in cases all over the country and before the U.S. Supreme Court that have upheld the free-speech rights of religious people. America is returning to its roots.

The American Center for Law and Justice has won important victories in Idaho and Pennsylvania. In the Pennsylvania case, an eleven-year-old boy named Jason Bishop was told that he could not bring his Bible to school because it was an "illegal book." But Jason said that he had learned about his rights by "watching Pat Robertson on television," and he insisted that his father call the ACLJ. His father didn't want to do that at first, but Jason kept saying, "Let's sue them, Dad." That is just what they did and they won and the teacher was forced to apologize to Jason in front of the whole school.

In the end it matters a great deal what you believe. One of the lies put forward by the liberals is that it doesn't matter what you believe and that religion doesn't matter at all, except in a broad, New Age sense that tolerates all religious views however bizarre they may be. That is simply unacceptable.

If we trust in the ultimate authority of God, then we understand that the universe we live in is ordered by God. We recognize that we have authority in the home, in the workplace, and in government only by the grace of God. Common sense tells us that the universe has order. Physics demands that there be an order. If you don't have order, you don't have physics, you don't have astronomy, you don't have predictability. Every tenet of science depends upon natural order, and every one of them ultimately says there is a God. Without that order, life would be meaningless. But because there is meaning, there is hope.

There is also an undeniable sense of urgency and destiny in the wind at this moment. When we see Russia, Eastern Europe, Africa, Asia, and places in the Middle East coming back to the source of freedom through faith in God, we can be certain that the tide of history has turned. The future looms large before us, but what will the future bring? Will it be good or bad? What will our destiny be? What are the options? That will be the subject of the next chapter.

12

Two Destinies

THE AMERICAN INVENTOR CHARLES KETTERING said, "We should all be concerned about the future because we will have to spend the rest of our lives there." What does the future hold? If we knew the answer to that question, much of the drama and variety of our lives would no doubt be lost. As we glance back across the journey that we have taken in these pages, perhaps we are sensing how the past, present, and future are interwoven in the moment of destiny where we find ourselves today. It is clear that there is a tide of change in the world and a vision of great promise looming before us, but there are also many uncertainties about the state of the world today.

The Challenge of the Future

As I come to the conclusion of this work, I cannot help but think of the images in the Book of Deuteronomy—the ancient book of the law in the Old Testament—wherein God laid out for the people of Israel two contrasting images of the future: one promising great hope, the other threatening grave consequences. Because I believe we stand at a similar moment in history with the opportunity to choose between two opposite views of reality, I would like to reflect briefly upon these images and consider some of the undeniable consequences that speak forth from those ancient times to our own.

I am an evangelical Christian and that is my perspective in understanding these things—especially the necessity of upholding the institutions and values that have shaped and preserved this nation for more than two centuries. Indiscriminate changes to those values and any activities that render aid and comfort to the radical agenda of the Left put our national heritage at risk. Disregarding the moral consequences of personal actions will lead inevitably to self-destruction, and by the same token disregarding the moral consequences of public, political, and social behavior will weaken the foundations of society and lead to anarchy and chaos. Those are options no responsible person can afford to entertain.

From this moment in history we can catch a glimpse of our destiny, but while the tide is turning the outcome is not yet a foregone conclusion. The way we respond to the challenges before us will make all the difference. If we choose to ignore the rush of events around us and to hide from the dangers, then we will certainly be lost in the tide and swept away into a sea of change. But if we respond with courage and conviction, then I believe we will see a better world for everyone.

So I invite you to stand with me for a moment upon this promontory of history to look out across an ancient frontier where the destiny of the entire world took a dramatic change of direction. I would like to explore the relationship between this moment of biblical history and the events taking place in our world today, for we stand at a historic crossroads.

The Destiny of the Blessed

"See, I have set before you today life and good, death and evil."

Deuteronomy 30:15

In 1350 B.C., the great lawgiver Moses gave his people one final instruction before his own death and their entry into the Promised Land. He told them that after they had crossed the Jordan River they should set six of their tribes on a hill in Samaria known as Mount Ebal and they should set six other tribes on the hill known as Mount Gerazim, which faced Mount Ebal. Those on Mount Gerazim would offer blessings upon the people; those on Mount Ebal would pronounce curses upon the people. The meaning of the ceremony was clear. No nation can ever rest on its past accomplishments or the good deeds of its ancestors. The nation, depending on its choices, always had before it two destinies.

Wonderful blessings were specified to the nation if it would diligently "obey the voice of the Lord your God, to keep His commandments."

Here in capsule form is what God promised:

- The Lord will set you high above all the nations of the earth.
- You will be blessed in the city and in the country.
- The fruit of your body, the produce of the ground, and the increase of your livestock will be blessed.
- The Lord will cause your enemies who rise up against you to be defeated before your face.
- The Lord will command the blessing on you in your storehouses and in all to which you set your hand.
- The Lord will grant you plenty of goods.
- You shall lend to many nations but shall not have to borrow.
- All the peoples of the earth shall see that you are called by the name of the Lord and shall be afraid of you.

As we review the history of the United States, it is clear that every one of those promises made to ancient Israel has come true here as well. There has never been in the history of the world any nation more powerful, more free, or more generously endowed with physical possessions. The song "America, the Beautiful" sums it up:

> O beautiful for spacious skies,
> For amber waves of grain;
> For purple mountains majesties

Above the fruited plain!
America! America!
God shed His grace on thee,
And crown thy good with brotherhood
From sea to shining sea!

We have had more wealth than the richest of all empires. We have had more military might than any colossus. We have risen above all the nations of the earth. We have had the riches to win the two greatest wars in history and then from our bounty to pour out billions in aid to restore prostrate nations whether in Europe or in other parts of the earth.

America has led the world in science, in medicine, in technology, in agriculture, in telecommunications, in industrial production, in banking, in trade, and in overall gross national product. We have been able to establish a system of law and government that has been the envy of the world. Our individual freedoms are legendary, and our democratic processes have set the standard for nations throughout the world that are struggling to throw off the shackles of slavery and move into ordered liberty.

But these things did not happen by accident, nor did they happen somehow because the citizens of America are smarter or more worthy than the citizens of any other country. It happened because those men and women who founded this land made a solemn covenant that they would be the people of God and that this would be a Christian nation.

God in turn has watched over our land—*shed His grace on us*, as the song says. He has prospered our endeavors. He has given victory to our forces in battle. He has kept us safe from storm and pestilence, and our material wealth has grown exponentially.

Yet in recent years our thanks to Him for His gracious bounty has been as follows:

- The highest court in our land has ruled God out of our schools and forbidden the teaching of His Word. It has prohibited even a simple prayer for God's blessing on a high school graduation or a similar prayer on a state road map.

- This same court opened the floodgates for our citizens to murder twenty-eight million innocent babies, and then lower courts have caused certain of God's people who protested to be hauled off to jail, where brutal police have tortured some of them, strip-searched some of them, and in several incidents sexually molested them.

- Now our government has not only given positions of power to those whose lifestyle is called an "abomination" by God, but we are beginning to teach little children all over the land to engage in sexual practices that have been described by the apostle Paul as evidence that "God has given a people up."

- Our people, our entertainers, our authors, our journalists, our politicians make blasphemy of God's name a staple of their vocabulary.

- The elites of this nation for thirty years have been carrying on an all-out assault on the people of God throughout this land, to harass them, humiliate them, and strip them of their rights. (My staff gathered more than two thousand incidents of anti-Christian bigotry in just two weeks. Selected, verified examples of various cases are included in the Appendix.)

The Destiny of the Cursed

The people of Israel stationed on Mount Ebal had a totally different message from those on Mount Gerazim. There was a warning of potential curses. Here is what God's warning was to Israel:

"If you do not obey the voice of the Lord your God, to observe carefully all His commandments and His statutes, [then] all these curses will come upon you":

- Cursed you will be in the city and in the country.

- Cursed shall be the fruit of your body, the produce of your land, and the increase of your livestock.

- The Lord will send on you cursing, confusion, and rebuke in all you set your hand to until you are destroyed.

- The Lord will make the plague cling to you until He has consumed you from the land.

- The Lord will strike you with consumption, with fever, with inflammation, with severe burning fever. The Lord will strike with tumors, with the scab, with the itch, from which you cannot be healed.

- The Lord will cause you to be defeated before your enemies, and you shall become troublesome to all the kingdoms of the earth.

- Your sons and your daughters will be given to another people, and your eyes shall look and fail with longing for them all day long; and there is nothing you can do about it.

- The alien who is among you shall rise higher and higher above you, and you shall come down lower and lower. He shall lend to you, but you shall not lend to him.

Now consider how many of these curses have now settled on our land:

- In Vietnam, for the first time in America's history, our armed forces were defeated in a major war, a war whose beginning coincided with the Supreme Court decision to ban God from our schools.

- The United States by virtue of its uncontrolled inflation, huge budget deficit, and debasement of its currency, has become "troublesome to all the kingdoms of the earth." In fact, if there is a major worldwide economic collapse, it is clear that the policies of the United States that began shortly after 1962 will have caused it.

- In the thirty years since the Supreme Court insulted God, we have had a president assassinated. Then a series of tragedies. One president was forced not to seek reelection and his

principal rival was assassinated. One president was driven
from office in disgrace. One president was humiliated by an
old cleric in a Third-World power. Another president was
involved in a Middle East quagmire and the scandal that
arose out of it. Our current president is wallowing in
confusion, ill-considered initiatives, unpopular selections of
subordinates, and ongoing scandal. Now our government has
uncontrolled debt and gridlock—"Cursing, confusion, and
rebuke in all that you set your hand to."

- At least two foreign powers have amassed huge trade
  surpluses with us and have then been loaning our money back
  to us. They and their products have been rising higher and
  higher while we have been falling lower and lower. At the
  present our economy is dependent on foreign sources for at
  least 50 percent of our petroleum, which places us at the
  mercy of the OPEC oil producers. The oil crisis that drained
  hundreds of billions of our wealth took place the same year
  our Supreme Court legalized the murder of unborn babies.

- Since 1962 our children have been given over to "another
  people." They have been victimized by marijuana, heroin,
  hallucinogens, crack cocaine, glue, PCP, alcohol, unbridled
  sex, a pop music culture that has destroyed their minds, the
  occult and Hindu holy men, and an epidemic of disease.
  Many belong to a subculture that is totally at odds with
  anything hitherto known in this society.

Just as the Bible says, "Your eyes shall look and fail with longing
for them," but there is nothing you can do about it. How many parents
look on as their children are wasted by drugs, rebellion, illicit sex, and
the heavy metal music of the counterculture and realize there is absolutely nothing they can do to stop what has been happening to those
they love? They have truly been given over to "another people."

- Our healthcare costs are so enormous they are consuming
  more of our national wealth than any other single segment

other than government itself. The venereal disease in our midst has stricken at least forty million people with boils, scabs, itches, and fevers for which, in the case of genital herpes there is no cure.

In the case of AIDS there is no cure for a disease that produces burning fever, tumors, and death. Alcoholism claims at least ten million victims, and various types of substance abuse claim as many more.

The Bible says, "The Lord will make the plague cling to you." A recent news report tells of a mysterious rodent-borne plague that has arisen in New Mexico that easily could spread to our major cities. Even tuberculosis (the biblical consumption) is reappearing in our cities after we thought it had been eradicated.

- The biblical warning says "cursed shall be the fruit of your body." How more cursed can the fruit of our bodies be than for twenty-eight million of them to die horribly in their mothers' wombs in the short space of just two decades? The mothers of this land have turned cruel to destroy their unborn or to abandon their little children to unloving institutional day care.

Just as every blessing that God promised to the nation that serves Him and obeys His commandments has come upon the United States of America—every single one—even so every curse that is promised to a nation that forsakes Him and flagrantly violates His commandments is in the process of coming upon the United States of America. Every one except the ultimate destruction of the nation has taken place.

While these curses are being sent upon us, it seems as if God has also lifted His hand of protection that has protected us from natural disaster. The superlatives of disaster mount one upon another. Hurricane Andrew hit the Homestead area of Florida with killer winds that included the phenomenon of 210 mile-an-hour tornadoes within a massive hurricane. The devastation from that storm cost $25 billion, the most costly in America's history. Hurricane Andrew, coupled with

Hurricane Hugo, which devastated Charleston, South Carolina, at a cost of $3 billion, and the San Francisco earthquake, which did $10 billion in damage, make up the three most costly disasters in U.S. history. They were the worst until the rains came in July and August 1993 and produced the worst flood in the history of America, with initial estimates of financial losses at $12 billion, and the possibility that losses might be much higher.

In June 1992 more tornadoes struck the United States than during any month in its history. Yet every natural disaster in the history of the land would seem as nothing beside the "big one"—the earthquake that seismologists tell us is sure to strike Los Angeles sometime in the future. If that isn't enough, a quake along the New Madrid fault in the Midwest, which would devastate the heartland of America from St. Louis to Chicago, is forecast by some experts as a definite possibility.

The Chosen People

The nation of Israel was considered a peculiar treasure to God. The Israelites were the chosen race, the heirs of the patriarch Abraham, who had received a special covenant promise from the Lord. Time and time again when the people turned away from God, He sent prophets to warn them—as Jeremiah put it, "Rising up early and speaking." He endured their sins, forgave their transgressions, and called out over and over again to bring them back.

Yet even though the promised Messiah was destined to come forth from the tribe of Judah, a time came when the sins of the chosen people were too great to ignore any more. When that day came, God permitted Assyria to invade Israel in 721 B.C. and carry the survivors into captivity and ultimate extinction as a race. Then, despite spiritual revivals under Kings Hezekiah and Josiah in the kingdom of Judah, God permitted the king of Babylon in 586 B.C. to sack the country, slaughter the inhabitants, and lead a remnant away from the land. This remnant was enough to provide the world with a Messiah, but only after the generation taken into captivity had died and a new generation had been born in Babylon to take their place.

Why There Is Hope

Again the lesson is clear: If God did not spare His chosen people, what possible reason can the United States give to escape God's wrath unless we change our way? As things stand now, this nation's gracious Friend and Protector has become the nation's Judge and its Avenger of evil.

As an evangelical Christian I believe that this is more than a biblical metaphor, and I am convinced that it is a faithful analysis of what is taking place in this land today. In fact, I will even go so far as to say that the only thing holding back even worse wrath on the nation is the sizable body of faithful believers who are praying each day for revival in the land. In great denominations like the Southern Baptists and the Assemblies of God, and in tens of thousands of individual congregations of all types, there is a genuine spiritual revival underway. The movement back to biblical Christianity is accelerating in many quarters. As Americans, these Christians are refusing to accept the nation's slide into moral oblivion, and the culture wars are intensifying between them and the ruling liberal elite.

Perhaps an even more pressing reason why I personally believe that God is withholding ultimate judgment on America is the existence in our land of powerful ministries that are reaping a spiritual harvest of unprecedented magnitude in every continent on the globe. In God's eyes, this final worldwide, spiritual harvest, which has been financed and sustained by American Christians, is vastly more significant than punishing an entire nation for what its liberals have done in their rebellion against Him.

Nevertheless, this nation is now operating on borrowed time. On the one hand, the tide of conservative thought is clearly flowing in this land as it is all over the world. On the other we have a president and his wife and many key officials in government who are clearly committed to a radical, unbiblical agenda.

So in my opinion this nation is going to be gripped by an intense struggle as those who are alarmed by the threat to our nation posed by the radical nihilistic agenda do battle with its proponents. I believe that in this struggle, conservatives must understand that the Radical Left controls all of the citadels of power—the presidency, the Congress, many courts, public education, the universities, the press, the motion picture and television industry, the major foundations, and the National Council of Churches. The strategy needed for Christian conservatives will resemble in part that of Douglas MacArthur in his campaign against the Japanese in the Pacific.

Christians must take all the territory that is available with minimal struggle, then surround and isolate each stronghold and prepare to blast the enemy out of its positions. In the process they must bypass less strategic targets and concentrate on those that are most significant.

Christians will immediately recall the words of the apostle Paul: "We do not wrestle against flesh and blood, but against principalities, against powers, the rulers of the darkness of this age, spiritual hosts of wickedness in the heavenly places." But he adds, "the weapons of our warfare are not carnal but mighty through God to the pulling down of strongholds."

This means that without the power of prayer all else will be to no avail. Nevertheless, each of us must recognize that the situation is desperate. If the present condition of radical liberalism is permitted to remain triumphant for the next seven years, and if the moral decline of the nation accelerates for the rest of this decade at an ever-accelerating rate, this nation will have passed the point of no return. If that happens, the righteous and the unrighteous may be forced to share the pain together, as this once proud, richly blessed Christian nation topples into anarchy, lawlessness, and economic and political collapse.

There Is Still Time

For now, even though the danger is very real, America has not yet passed the point of no return. This nation can in 1994 and 1996 elect a responsible, conservative Congress and in 1996 elect a conservative president committed to upholding moral values. The people can mobilize enough votes to bring in school vouchers and break the back of the powerful NEA and the leviathan grasp of monopoly education. All over the land, coalitions of common-sense conservatives can elect school boards of concerned parents who hold strong moral convictions. They can build on the cases already won in the courts to expand the rights of believers to express their faith in the public schools and other parts of the public square. Conservatives can also continue to resist the liberal media, build alternate means of communication, and encourage trends already in place toward wholesome family entertainment.

All of us can speak out and expose the agendas of the radical feminists, homosexuals, Planned Parenthood, the ACLU, People for the American Way, and their radical allies. We can certainly become informed, vote our conscience instead of our pocketbook, and seek to persuade others to do likewise. We can call, write, and speak out. But we cannot be silent in the face of grave danger. We must not be afraid, for truth is our most powerful weapon. Our own fear and apathy are the most dangerous weapons against us.

But let us not stop short until there is a complete restoration of the time-honored traditions of this nation, the complete fall of liberalism, and God's blessings once again upon the land. We should never leave the liberals in place to gorge themselves at the banquet table just because they have been willing to buy us off with a few scraps of concessions. Nor should we be content with elected leaders of either party who with their lips profess allegiance to our goal but by their actions give the lie to their words.

Gloria Steinem said that the goal of the feminists was not just to destroy capitalism but the entire patriarchy. Today the goal of common-sense conservatives is not only to tear down liberalism, but the entire socialist, welfare state. With men and women of goodwill united together —including economic, political, and religious conservatives of every stripe—we will succeed.

So take heart. Common sense is rising in the land, and the tide is turning. But you must recognize that the choice between the two destinies before us is in your hands, and the decision you make now is absolutely critical. Our nation and our entire future are at risk. Either we decide to serve God and obey His commandments and then join together in a bond of common commitment to reassert our historic values and beliefs, or we can witness the imminent collapse of our culture.

If we rise together with conviction and with the weight of history behind us, then, with God's help, the turning tide before us will swell into a mighty, unstoppable wave of justice, virtue, and compassion for every man, woman, and child. Let that be our destiny.

Appendix

The War Against Christianity

• The U.S. Supreme Court upheld a ruling forbidding a fifth-grade teacher in Denver from displaying his own Bible on his desk at school, even though books dealing with other religious subjects (mythological legends) sit on nearby bookshelves.

• Despite the practice that the Supreme Court begins its sessions with the words "God save this honorable court," a federal court ordered a state judge in North Carolina to stop his practice of beginning each morning with a brief, nonsectarian prayer. The U.S. Supreme Court upheld this ruling as well.

• A Christian group was denied access to a public library in Clark County, Nevada, although it had been used by other civic groups, because their scheduled event included a prayer.

• In Washington, D.C., the Department of the Interior adopted regulations that prohibit free speech activities, including evangelism, on sections of Constitution Avenue.

• In Michigan, a five-year-old girl in kindergarten tried to thank Jesus quietly before her Friday snack. Her teacher told her to stop because prayer is not allowed in school. The girl went home in tears.

• At Moorehead State University in Minnesota, officials told co-ed students they could not include a fish in a mural on a dormitory wall because it is a religious symbol. This despite the fact that the gates of that university have etched on them in stone, "The truth shall set you free" (John 8:32).

All of these stories are true. Nothing has been changed to protect the guilty. The good news is that thanks to the American Center for Law and Justice some of these situations have been reversed. The bad news is that they happened at all, but this is the tiniest sample of what's taking place in the United States.

How could such atrocities have been committed in a nation founded by men and women of God, pilgrims seeking freedom from government oppression to practice their religious beliefs freely?

Despite our nation's strong Christian heritage, in our own century Christians failed to watch vigilantly as the precious religious freedoms on which this nation was built have been gradually stripped away. Even though the founders of the United States promoted Christianity and the Bible as the chief foundation for all of society, including government, over the last few years we have seen literally thousands upon thousands of horror stories from all across America.

One reason we have lost so many of our religious freedoms is that the liberal educational establishment has worked hard to eliminate our knowledge of the Judeo-Christian heritage of America. The facts nonetheless reveal the true convictions of our founders. Without question, they believed that although no one Christian denomination should dominate the nation, the principles of the Bible and Christianity should underlie our government and American education as well.

President George Washington's Farewell Address includes this observation: "Of all the dispositions and habits which lead to political prosperity, religion and morality are indispensable supports. In vain would that man claim the tribute of patriotism, who should labor to subvert these great pillars of human happiness. . . . The mere politician . . . ought to respect and cherish them. . . . Reason and experience both forbid us to expect that national morality can prevail in exclusion of religious principle." Washington also said, "It is impossible to govern rightly without God and the Bible."

John Quincy Adams, sixth president of the United States, noted, "The highest glory of the American Revolution was this: it connected, in one indissoluble bond, the principles of civil government with the principles of Christianity."

On the subject of education, a founding father whose name is synonymous with education in early America, Noah Webster, said: "In my view, the Christian religion is the most important one of the first things in which all children, under a free government, ought to be instructed. . . . No truth is more evident to my mind than that the Christian religion must be the basis of any government intended to secure the rights and privileges of a free people."

Such views have filled multitudes of books, yet the liberal establishment pretends instead that the founders intended that Christian principles be utterly divorced from virtually anything related in even the smallest way to the government, including public education.

Horror Stories

For well over a decade on "The 700 Club," we have documented the consistent abuses of religious freedoms that Americans, including children in our schools, have suffered at the hands of those who have pushed a militant secular ideology. Beyond that, literally thousands more complaints have poured into our CBN offices and into those of the American Center for Law and Justice.

This is just a sampling of the incidents that have taken place over the past few years. Some have since been resolved, but this list serves as an example of the mind-set of the liberals in this nation who are determined to eradicate virtually any trace of Christianity from our government.

• An appeals court in Colorado ruled in June 1993 that a stone monument depicting the Ten Commandments, located on state property in Denver, violated the separation of church and state. The four-foot high monument, not far from the state capitol building, consists of two tablets bearing Jewish and Christian symbols. The court ruled it unconstitutional because it carried "an essential religious message." But the only connection to the state government comes from the fact that the Colorado attorney general's office periodically cleans it. The monument was first commissioned by a civic organization.

• In Vancouver, Washington, a teacher tore up a picture drawn by a third-grade boy as part of an assignment. The picture included a caption that played off an athletic shoe advertising campaign. The caption said, "If Bo don't know Jesus, Bo don't know Didley."

• A woman in Oregon was told that the state's laws forbade her from using the word *Pray* on her license plates. She filed a lawsuit against the state.

• In Kelseyville, California, officials granted permits for musical groups, including rock, country, and classical, to perform in a city park (with city-paid electricity). When a church applied for a permit for a well-known Christian musician, the city flatly denied it, citing separation of church and state and fear of a lawsuit. The city eventually allowed the musician to perform, but only under certain restrictions, including no preaching or distribution of Christian literature.

• A district judge ordered a picture of Jesus Christ removed from Bloomingdale High School in Grand Rapids, Michigan. He ruled that the two-foot-by-three-foot print, which had been hanging outside the principal's office for thirty years, violated the separation of church and state.

• The American Civil Liberties Union tried to stop a jail in Tarrant County, Texas, from running a unit for Christians called the "God Pod." The problem: The inmates had access to Bible teaching, religious television stations, and videos. The ACLU said that was unconstitutional.

• The ACLU accused the school board in St. Tamany Parish, Louisiana, of "bias against the voodoo religion" after it voted to ban a book called *Voodoo and Hoodoo*. The book explained voodoo rituals and spells, including some for murder and others in explicit sexual detail. The ACLU claimed the students have a First Amendment right to see the book. (But as their actions in a wide variety of other cases have shown, the ACLU clearly believes students don't have the same rights to see Christian literature.)

• In Chicago, a group known as the Chicago Nativity Scene Committee placed a Christmas scene in the city's Daley Plaza in 1986. They were told to tear it down. The committee's chairman said, "It would be easier to put a Nativity scene in Red Square than here in Chicago." To prove his point, he displayed an identical scene for two weeks in Moscow in 1993.

• In Adrian, Michigan, no part of a church-based school can display anything religious while a state-funded special education teacher is working there. The pastor reported that the state wanted the picture of Christ on the wall and the crosses covered up in the St. John's Lutheran Church School. The state said that the law requires this for any school receiving public funding, and a state-funded special education teacher constitutes public funding. The special education teacher himself is a Christian and doesn't mind the picture or crosses, but the state nonetheless demanded that these items be covered. Apparently no vestiges of Christian belief can be permitted in any area blessed with Michigan's state tax dollars.

• In Bremerton, Washington, when children in a kindergarten class were invited to sing their favorite songs, one little girl began to sing "Jesus Loves Me." The teacher stopped her, saying songs like that aren't allowed in school.

• In Selkirk, New York, in 1992, a teacher told a third-grade girl that she should bring material for free reading time. When the student brought her children's Bible, the teacher asked her, "What are you reading?" The girl responded, "My Bible." The teacher told her, "Put it away and never bring it back again." The girl has since had dreams and nightmares about this incident.

• In Hayward, California, a pastor was told that he could not pray at a birthday for his wife at a rented hall in the city park.

• In Texas, a first-grade class watched "Teenage Mutant Ninja Turtles" during television time. One youngster didn't like it, and his mother suggested he take his Noah's Ark video to show the class. The teacher, however, told the boy to put it away because it was against the law.

• In Beloit, Wisconsin, a woman tied sixty-six thousand feet of yellow ribbons around the city to remind people to pray for our servicemen during Operation Desert Storm. After Desert Storm, she put up ribbons with the word *Life* on them in support of the pro-life movement. They also meant life with Christ. The city council agreed to allow her to put up ribbons with the word *Pray* in blue with three red hearts on either side. But after she put them up, the city manager ordered her to remove them.

• The Florida Civil Liberties Union took up a case for a chapter of the American Atheists. The lawsuit's goal: to remove a statue of Christ from a federal park. The fact that the land was three miles offshore under twenty feet of water did not deter the FCLU in its quest for total secularism on the part of the government.

• In Nazareth, Texas, the ACLU filed a complaint with the local post office during Christmas 1992. Their offense: their postmark showed a nativity scene. The supervising postmaster in nearby Lubbock ordered the Nazareth post office to stop using the special postmark, even though the Nazareth postmaster said that she had obtained permission from Washington to use it.

• In Oceanside, California, a mother attended her second-grade daughter's Thanksgiving program in 1992. The children, dressed as Pilgrims and Indians, were going to eat a meal. The mother asked if they could have a prayer, and the teacher responded, "No! Everyone knows we can't pray at school." The mother said the Thanksgiving prayer was the whole reason for the holiday, but the teacher ultimately had her way.

• In Wisconsin, the ACLU argued that "Sex Respect," a teenage sex-education program that promoted abstinence and traditional values, should not be used in public schools because it "discriminated" on the basis of religion and other values.

• In Shreveport, Louisiana, in 1993, a small group of parents sued the Caddo Parish school board over "Sex Respect" and another program called "Facing Reality." They claimed teaching abstinence promotes religion, and that the statement "human reproduction has a higher meaning than animal reproduction" supports a religious view.

• In Duval County, Florida, Planned Parenthood sued the school board in an attempt to remove another sex-education curriculum called "Teen Aid." Planned Parenthood, along with some local parents, claimed that the program "promulgates the teachings of a particular set of religious beliefs" because it did not discuss birth control or promote abortion.

• From Sacramento, California, a sixth-grade student was assigned a presentation on the subject of her choice for extra credit. The girl's hobby was stringing beads together, often in the form of a cross. When she stood up to present a cross in class, the teacher told her she couldn't. As a result, she lost her extra credit and was forced to sit down.

• All across America, school officials have stopped traditional and historic prayers at the beginnings of sporting events such as football and basketball games, even when the public clearly supports such practices. The examples are too numerous to detail.

• Similarly, school districts around the nation no longer honor the Christmas holidays; instead, they celebrate "Winter Festival" or something similar.

• In Stockton, California, a third-grade chorus in a public school was preparing for its Winter Festival. Included in its list of songs was the classic hymn "Joy to the World." But instead of singing the words "Lord," "Savior," and "King," the children were told they must hum or remain silent at those points. The principal cited separation of church and state and a desire not to offend anyone. One child's mother told the principal, "I'm offended!"

• In DeKalb County, Georgia, members of a Bible club called Youth on Fire were told they could not pass out Christian newspapers at their high school in 1992. They were told they could not hand them out on the public sidewalk in front of the school. This case is still in the court system.

• At nearby Henderson High two years earlier, students were suspended for "possession of Christian material."

Compare the incidents cited above with the widespread growth of New Age and similar occult materials on school grounds and in the classrooms themselves as part of the courses. One such story recently came to us from Texas. There, a third grader came home crying but wouldn't tell her parents why. Finally, the girl became so unhappy her mother pulled her out of the school. Then she told her mother what had happened. The teacher had a crystal ball and taught fortune telling. The children were given material on psychic readings and told not to take the material home. The mother contacted the school board, which agreed such things shouldn't be part of the school curriculum. But the board did nothing to the teacher, even though other parents had complained as well.

In addition, we have received various reports of students who were told they could not read the Bible on their own free time in school. One parent told us that even other students told her son that he would get in trouble for simply having a Bible in school.

• One trend in recent years has been the creation of so-called bubble zones, gospel-free zones, speech-free zones, and so forth. Essentially, any speech or expression on certain topics (such as abortion or religion itself) within a certain range (for example, a hundred feet) of a facility, such as an abortion clinic, is illegal. One such "bubble law" was signed by the governor of Colorado in April 1993. That statute made it illegal to get within eight feet of someone to give them printed information or counsel them. So even talking to someone using politically incorrect pro-life or religious speech or literature, is illegal under such laws or court rulings.

• A superior court judge in Georgia, Joseph Newton, was threatened by an ACLU lawsuit in late 1992. His crime: permitting local pastors to open his court with prayer.

These are but the tip of the iceberg. Yet despite the gloomy outlook this snapshot gives of the erosion of religious freedom in our land, many of those cases have been reversed and other important victories have been won.

Turning the Tide Back for Religious Freedom

Approving a prayer [at a public school graduation] is like buying a lawsuit.

> Doug Bates, a lawyer representing the
> Utah education department

The very soundest legal position—and the safest course this year —is to have nothing [religious] at the ceremony.

> Gwendolyn Gregory, a lawyer for the
> National School Boards Association

Those quotes come from the June 13, 1991, issue of *USA Today*. At the time this perception was arguably true—but what a difference time and smart court victories have made.

What happened in between? Even though the persecution of those who believed, lived, and upheld Christian doctrine continued throughout the land in the public schools, the government, and elsewhere, important court victories by the American Center for Law and Justice (ACLJ) have begun to turn the tide.

On April 1, 1993, the ACLJ began a national campaign to protect a student's right to have prayer at graduation ceremonies. The center based its mail campaign on a decision by the Fifth District Court of Appeals, *Jones v. Clear Creek Independent School District*. In that case the court ruled that prayer at such ceremonies was protected as long as it was initiated and led by the students themselves. The case had gone to the Supreme Court, and the ACLU, Americans United for Separation of Church and State, and People for the American Way believed that the Supreme Court would reverse the district court and outlaw student-led prayer. Instead, on June 7, 1993, the Court supported the ACLJ's position on the issue and let the district court ruling stand that upheld graduation ceremony student prayers.

The center mailed special bulletins about student-led graduation prayer to fifteen thousand school districts—virtually every district in the nation. Follow-up letters were sent to every school principal in the country. In addition, four hundred thousand bulletins were sent to individuals throughout the U.S. The result: 6,791 people from all fifty states contacted the center's offices.

The Indiana Civil Liberties Union sent out a counterletter of its own, saying bluntly that the ACLJ's position was legally wrong. The ICLU threatened:

1. We will sue both the school corporation and any individuals who approved or authorized graduation prayers.

2. We will win—the Supreme Court has already decided the issue.

3. You will pay your own and our attorney's fees, an amount that could run as high as $250,000.

Despite that and similar threats, calls came into the ACLJ from students, school board members, school principals, and school board attorneys. After those contacts, the ACLJ had a 100 percent success rate in the actual legal cases that followed.

We Are Winning

• In New Auburn, Wisconsin, the 1993 class salutatorian at New Auburn High School, Steve Jerabek, was told he would have to edit his speech because it included a prayer. If the prayer wasn't taken out, he was told, he couldn't give the salutatorian address at the his own high school graduation ceremonies. But with the help of an ACLJ trial counsel, Stuart Roth, Steven was able to give his speech—prayer included.

• At Columbia Falls High School in Montana, the school principal decided the student choir could not perform two songs at their graduation ceremonies ("Don't Stop Praying for Me" and "Thy Will Be Done") because they had a religious message. The center's office quickly contacted the school district leaders and informed them that if the choir could not sing, a lawsuit would be filed. The district changed its policy, and the choir sang its songs.

• In Hawaii, Naho Inoue, a committed Christian, intended to speak about God in her address as the class valedictorian of her school. But both the principal and the student adviser told her she couldn't. Within hours of receiving a letter from the center demanding that the school reconsider, the principal wrote back and said that Naho could give her speech as planned, complete with her references to God.

• In Rockingham County, Virginia, the school board told Jason Nauman he couldn't pray during his graduation speech or he would be breaking the law. But Jason took matters into his own hands and consulted with attorneys from the ACLJ, then he told his school board they were getting bad advice from their lawyers. He went ahead with his prayer in his commencement speech.

• The ACLU filed suit in two cases in Idaho and Florida to prevent graduation prayers, including those initiated and led by students. The ACLJ won and the ACLU lost in both cases.

As you can see, taking the offensive against the leftists in the war over Christianity in the public arena has already begun to pay major dividends for our country and its future.

Another important triumph also came in the Supreme Court in a unanimous decision on July 7, 1993. The case was *Lamb's Chapel v. Center Moriches Union Freech School District.* The school district had forbidden a church, Lamb's Chapel, from using the school's auditorium to show a film series from James Dobson's Focus on the Family ministry. The school district had allowed the facilities to be used for a wide range of social, recreational, and civic activities, but it had adopted a rule specifically prohibiting their use for religious purposes (such a practice is not uncommon across the country, as some of the previous examples demonstrated). The American Center for Law and Justice appealed to the Supreme Court.

The High Court ruled that the school district was practicing religious discrimination. Justice Byron White wrote, "The government violates the First Amendment when it denies access to a speaker solely to suppress the point of view he espouses on an otherwise includable subject."

The Court also ruled that the "First Amendment forbids the government to regulate speech in ways that favor some viewpoints or ideas at the expense of others." Significantly, the Court also held that allowing a religious organization to use the public school facilities for an openly religious purpose was not a violation of the First Amendment's establishment clause, which liberals claim sets forth the separation of church and state.

This victory by the ACLJ quickly bore fruit. Just eight days later, a U.S. district court in the Midwest ruled on a case where high school students had been denied the use of a high school for a religious baccalaureate service. But this time the district court ruled that the students could have their religious service at the high school. The ruling was based on the *Lamb's Chapel* decision. The district court ruled that "the [school] board violated the First Amendment by denying the baccalaureate group access to facilities contrary to its previous policy of open and equal access to the facilities by discriminating against a particular point of view."

The victories have extended into other areas as well.

Evangelism Issues

• In one case mentioned at the beginning of this appendix dealing with the Interior Department's decision to prohibit free speech activities on sections of Constitution Avenue in Washington, D.C., the ACLJ won a victory in the U.S. Court of Appeals for the District of Columbia. The court ruled completely in favor of the Center that evangelism could not be forbidden on the street. This case has set a significant precedent and has been cited in many other cases across the country; it's been called a major victory for public evangelism in this nation.

• The First Circuit Court of Appeals ruled unanimously in the ACLJ's favor that evangelism must be permitted in the terminals of the Massachusetts Bay Transportation Authority. The MBTA had attempted to shut down evangelism in those locations to the point of arresting people who were passing out Christian literature.

• The Georgia Supreme Court unanimously ruled evangelistic activities could take place in the public access areas of Stone Mountain Park. Previously, officials had tried to stop evangelism there. One reason this case is so important is that Atlanta is the site of the 1996 Olympic Games, and Stone Mountain is one of the most popular tourist sights in the area.

The ACLJ has won victories for freedom of speech for pro-lifers as well. One important case involved the "speech-free zones" mentioned earlier. In this particular instance, a judge's injunction prohibited peaceful prayer, preaching, and literature distribution within a hundred feet of an abortion clinic. The Texas Supreme Court ruled unanimously in the ACLJ's favor on June 30, 1993.

In addition, the center is challenging the "zone" law passed in Colorado that was mentioned earlier, as well as similar laws in other states.

Horror Stories with Happy Endings

Just as the first half of this appendix listed examples of the hostile climate toward religion in so much of our nation today, we can also point to those stories that show that the tide is turning back toward the faith of our nation's heritage. One key factor to remember is that in recent years the victories have started to balance out the defeats. Now, while the forces of atheism and secularism still rage against religious values and liberties, the other side is beginning to rise up steadily to turn back those who would keep the knowledge of God out of American life.

Look at this list of recent victories from across America:

• A second-grader in Bakersfield, California, wrote about Jesus for an assignment to discuss her hero. But the teacher wouldn't let her read her report in front of the class as other children did. The girl's father confronted the teacher, who said that the assignment was supposed to deal with living people. The father replied that Jesus is a living person. The teacher attempted to bring up separation of church and state, but the father knew how to answer that argument. He told a CBN staff member that he had been informed of his Christian rights by watching ACLJ Chief Counsel Jay Sekulow on "The 700 Club."

• As mentioned at the beginning of this appendix, a Christian group had wanted to use the library facility in Clark County, Nevada, just as other civic groups did. But a library regulation prohibited prayer and religious activities on the premises. In that case, the ACLJ threatened a lawsuit, warning the library district that the Christian group had the same right to free speech as the other civic groups. The district changed its policy, and now religious groups can meet there as well.

• In Russell, Kansas, the senior class sponsor told the seniors that they would have to vote unanimously to keep their school prayer at graduation. They did. But the ACLU threatened a lawsuit, which would have stopped the traditional graduation prayer for the first time in the school's history. One student's mother wrote the ACLJ for information and passed it on to the students. The students took the issue to the school board. After a long-drawn-out debate, the board president moved that no prayer be allowed. But no one would second the motion. The students had their invocation at graduation.

• In 1991, in Norman, Oklahoma, the parents of a fifth-grader filed a lawsuit against the city's public schools after their daughter could not read her Bible or pray on school grounds. The parents reached an agreement with the school system out of court allowing their daughter to do those things as long as she wasn't disruptive and didn't interfere with the First Amendment rights of others.

• In Vegas Verdes, Nevada, in 1992, Kara Russell, an eleven-year-old elementary student, wanted to sing a solo at the school's winter concert (not Christmas concert). At first, the teacher told Kara she could sing anything she wished. When Kara said that she wanted to sing "The First Noel," her teacher told her she couldn't because of church-state issues. The teacher, who was sympathetic to Kara, said the principal had told the teachers at the beginning of the year that there would be no religious songs or celebrations at Christmas. Kara's mother contacted the ACLJ, and, after an exchange of several letters, the school district agreed to let Kara sing "The First Noel."

• In Arlington, Texas, Louanne Fulbright wanted to write a book about Jesus for her class project. Her teacher said no. Louanne's parents complained to the principal, who in turn said Louanne could write the book but it couldn't be displayed with the other children's work. Louanne would have to write a second book if she wanted it to be displayed. Her parents contacted the ACLJ. After the center became involved, the school immediately backed down.

• At Robert McQueen High School in Reno, Nevada, in 1992, Jena Pagni was both senior class president and master of ceremonies for graduation ceremonies. She was asked to help plan those ceremonies, and she asked for student-led prayer. The school said no. She then asked if she could thank God for bringing her and the students to this important day in their lives. The school said no again. Jena was told that when she stepped on the platform, she became an official representative of the school and therefore her prayer would mean the government was establishing a religion. But after the ACLJ intervened and explained that students were permitted to pray as part of free speech, officials changed their minds and Jena prayed.

• In Ottawa, Illinois, citizens ultimately won a long-running battle over whether or not they could put paintings of Christ in the public park at Christmastime. They had done this faithfully for more than twenty years, but one resident objected and the ACLU filed suit. The ACLU won the case, and in 1988 the paintings came down. But the people of Ottawa persisted, arguing on appeal that the paintings were an expression of free speech. They finally triumphed, and the pictures of the One who is supposed to be honored by Christmas could be displayed once more in the town's park.

• Also in Illinois, the city of Zion finally won a long-running battle over its city seal. The words "In God We Trust" were ruled permissible on the seal by a federal judge. The original seal had pictured a cross and included the motto "God Reigns." But the American Atheists had sued and forced Zion to change its seal, which had dated back to 1902. After a long court battle, Zion won. The judge ruled that the words "In God We Trust" were "an essentially empty gesture drained of any traditional religious meaning" (but perhaps some citizens of Zion and other communities felt differently).

• Another gospel-free zone was overruled in November 1992, this time in Wisconsin. A witch in that state had gone to court against an evangelical preacher to try to prevent any attempts at preaching in her area. ACLJ attorneys argued that would establish a gospel-free zone that would rob the preacher of his freedom of religious expression. The important point was that someone who opposed Christianity tried to establish a zone, not around an abortion clinic, but simply around her property. The precedent set by these zones around abortion clinics, if ever upheld, could conceivably be extended to a wide variety of locations deemed politically correct by a local judge or other authority.

• In Braintree, Massachusetts, in 1993, a pastor was denied permission to conduct a free concert in the city's public park. The reason: When his band had done it the year before, they had preached and passed out gospel literature. But after the ACLJ sent a letter demanding the pastor's band be allowed to perform, the attorney for the park commission advised the board to permit the concert. Ultimately, it did.

• The Bible an obscene book? That's what a Minnesota man claimed in late 1992. The self-proclaimed atheist filed a petition with the Brooklyn Center Independent School District claiming that the Bible had to be removed from the school libraries because it was lewd, indecent, and violent. In a unanimous decision, the school board rejected the petition.

• Does drug free equal Christian free? High school officials told student Alan Sheaffer that he couldn't distribute Christian literature in a drug-free zone because the ban also included a prohibition on such material.

After negotiations between the school board and the ACLJ, Alan was free to pass out his materials.

• In Concord, California, a Christian group was denied the use of a display case in a public library because of its religious content. The display was called "What Christmas Means to Me" and included short essays by children that mentioned Jesus, a Christmas tree, and a small Nativity scene. When the head librarian saw the display, she called the group's leader and demanded that it be taken down. The same case had been used by a local pagan group two months earlier to display spells and various implements used in the practice of Wiccan witchcraft. The ACLJ immediately intervened, and the Christian display remained in place. (However, since then, the library has revised its policy to prevent any religious displays, so this case may well resurface.)

• In Gulf Shores, Alabama, the evening meetings of a ministry group known as Strike Force were cut short after two nights when school officials locked the ministry out of the school auditorium. The same group earlier in the year had given a nonreligious version of its anti-drug and abstinence program, but this time students were invited to night meetings, which were scheduled for four nights and included an evangelistic message. According to the pastor involved in the meetings, the principal asked him to drop the gospel message and altar call. The pastor refused, and officials locked Strike Force out of the gymnasium. One pastor had recently traveled to Russia, where the gospel was welcomed by the people, and he told a CBN News reporter, "It's that eerie feeling that you get that you're not in your own country." After the ACLJ filed suit in federal court, the school system settled before the case came to trial, and Strike Force returned to Gulf Shores for four more meetings.

• In Pennsylvania, fifth-grade student Jason Bishop was told by his teacher that his Bible was "an illegal book." After the ACLJ worked things out, both the school system and teacher publicly apologized to Jason.

• A new trend has developed in the last few years called "See You at the Flagpole." This is a student-initiated and student-led movement that supports prayer in the public schools. This year, on September 15, an estimated 1.5 million students are expected to take part. The ACLJ will send bulletins to every high school principal in the country, along with personal correspondence to every state school superintendent. A national education campaign, including ads and a video presentation to be aired on the major television networks, is also being planned.

The Shape of Things to Come

We can only pray that victories such as these represent the tide turning in favor once again of religious freedom in our nation. Yet this is only the beginning. The liberals have worked diligently for decades through the legal system, the universities, the media, and every other avenue at their disposal to indoctrinate the nation with their tortured view of the Constitution and the role of religion and the Bible in our society. Their ideas are certainly not those of the framers of our foundational documents, and their efforts toward creating a completely secular society have only left us on the road to ruin. The best hope for our nation is found in the principles that originally conceived, built, and strengthened it—the very principles the liberals wish to keep from our society and especially from our young people.

Even as this book goes to press, the ACLJ faces a rapidly increasing number of religious freedom battles. Some of these cases could have a profound impact on our nation's liberties, just as previous victories already have. Others, while not as important nationally, will still reclaim lost ground and will help each individual or group looking to exercise the freedom our founders intended us to have. These are just a few of the significant cases still in the legal system:

• A husband-and-wife team in Vermont who own a printing business are pro-life Catholics facing a lawsuit because they refused to print pro-abortion material. The suit charges discrimination. The ACLJ has argued that the freedom of the press allows printers to refuse a job they find morally objectionable. This case could have important constitutional implications.

• Can a student hand out Christian literature, or can the school deny him that right based on the content of that material? This is the case in DeKalb County, Georgia, referred to earlier, and it could prove to be very important.

The price of liberty is eternal vigilance. May God grant that once we reclaim the true freedom of religion and speech in our nation, we never again let it slip through our fingers.

Notes

Chapter 1 • The Wave of the Future

1. Irving Kristol, "The Coming 'Conservative Century,'" *Wall Street Journal*, 1 February 1993.

2. Sylvia Nasar, "Confidence in Clinton Is Slipping Among Many Business Leaders," *New York Times*, 24 May 1993, 1, 9.

3. Ibid.

4. Special report, "Nobelists Rate Clintonomics," *Wall Street Journal*, 23 March 1993, A14.

5. Marlin Maddoux, *A Christian Agenda: Game Plan for a New Era* (Dallas: National Christian Media, 1993).

Chapter 2 • The World Turns

1. Karel van Wolferen, *The Enigma of Japanese Power: People and Politics in a Stateless Nation* (New York: Alfred A. Knopf, 1989), 273.

2. Robert C. Christopher, *The Japanese Mind: The Goliath Explained* (New York: Simon & Schuster, 1983), 71.

3. Yuri Kageyama, "'In-Family Divorces' Common in Japan," *Los Angeles Times*, 16 May 1993, 6A.

4. Steve Berg, "Japan and the U.S.—Startling Contrasts: Differences in Cultural Values Shape Economic Competition," *Minneapolis Star Tribune*, 11 January 1993.

5. Quoted in Andrew Tanzer, "Consumer Frenzy in China: This Time It's for Real," *Forbes*, 2 August 1993, 58f.

Chapter 3 • Clinton Against the Tide

1. Maureen Dowd, "Washington Is Star-Struck As Hollywood Gets Serious," *New York Times*, 5 May 1993.

2. Ibid.

3. Michael Novak, "The Lines Are Drawn," *Forbes*, 26 April 1993, 162f.

4. Fred Barnes, "Right Back: The GOP Lives," *New Republic*, 5 July 1993, 19f.

5. Ralph Reed, personal interview, 24 May 1993.

6. Irving Kristol, "What Ever Happened to Common Sense?" *Reader's Digest*, February 1990, condensed from *Wall Street Journal*, 17 January 1984.

7. I discuss this important article in greater detail in chapter 7.

8. Norman Lear, "Worship of Bottom Line Has Left Us with a Void," *Washington Post*, 30 May 1993.

9. Charles Krauthammer, "Liberals Led Assault on Our Spiritual Basis," *Washington Post*, 4 June 1993.

Chapter 4 • The Cookie Monster

1. Martin Gross, *The Government Racket: Washington Waste from A to Z* (New York: Bantam, 1992); see also, Paul Beckner, *Wasting America's Money II* (Washington, D.C.: Citizens for a Sound Economy, 1992).

Chapter 5 • A Crisis of Law

1. Mark Pulliam, "The Need for Tort Reform," cited in *Wall Street Journal*, 1 June 1993.

2. From his speech at Elmira, New York, 3 May 1907.

3. Walter K. Olson, *The Litigation Explosion: What Happened When America Unleashed the Lawsuit* (New York: E. P. Dutton, 1991), 339.

4. Note Proverbs 14:12: "There is a way which seems right to a man, but its end is the way of death."

5. *Moseley v. General Motors*, 90V-6276 (Georgia, Fulton County State Court, 4 January 1993).

6. Charles Murray and Louis A. Cox, Jr., *Beyond Probation: Juvenile Corrections and the Chronic Delinquent* (Beverly Hills, Calif.: Sage Publications, 1979).

7. John Silber, *Straight Shooting: What's Wrong with America and How to Fix It* (New York: Harper & Row, 1989), 213.

8. Ibid., 231.

9. Russell Kirk, *The Roots of American Order* (Washington, D.C.: Regnery Gateway, 1991), 462—63.

10. Ibid., 272.

11. Ibid., 13.

12. Harvey C. Mansfield, Jr., *America's Constitutional Soul* (Baltimore: Johns Hopkins University Press, 1991), 24.

13. Rob Gregory, "Benedictions, Invocations and the God Who Still Cares," *Dallas/Fort Worth Heritage*, July 1993, 3.

Chapter 6 • The Fifth Column

1. S. Robert Lichter and Stanley Rothman, "Media and Business Elites," *Public Opinion*, October/November 1981, 42–45, 59–60.

2. *Notable Quotables*, Media Research Center, Alexandria, Va., 2 September 1991.

3. Quoted by David Shaw in "Trust in Media Is on Decline," *Los Angeles Times*, 31 March 1993, 1.

4. Harrison Rainie et al., "Warning Shot at TV," *U.S. News & World Report*, 12 July 1993, 48f.

5. Norm Alster, "A Few Good Films," *Forbes*, 26 April 1993, 58–62.

6. Ibid., 60.

7. Harold Lavine, *The Fifth Column in America* (New York: Doubleday, Doran, and Co., 1940).

8. Barry Sussman, *What Americans Really Think: And Why Our Politicians Pay No Attention* (New York: Pantheon, 1988). Though Sussman is personally sympathetic to the perspective of the Left, his candid documentation of media manipulation of the 1983 Reagan-Mondale debates is startling evidence of the power and influence of the mainstream, liberal media.

9. Larry Sabato, *Feeding Frenzy: How Attack Journalism Has Transformed American Politics* (New York: Macmillan Free Press, 1991).

10. William F. Buckley, "Agenda for the Nineties," *National Review*, 19 February 1990, 37.

11. Ibid.

12. Peter Collier and David Horowitz, *Destructive Generation: Second Thoughts about the '60s* (New York: Summit Books, 1989), 15.

13. Ibid., 335.

14. Ibid.

15. Sharon Cohen, "From Abortion to Zionism: Scholars Look at Fundamentalism," Associated Press, 17 May 1993.

16. Larry Barrett, "The Religious Right and the Pagan Press," *Columbia Journalism Review*, July-August 1993.

17. Michael Medved, *Hollywood vs. America: Popular Culture and the War on Traditional Values* (New York: HarperCollins/Zondervan, 1992).

18. Carl F. H. Henry, "Secularization," in *In Search of a National Morality*, ed. William Bentley Ball (Grand Rapids, Mich.: Baker Book House, 1992), 24. (Includes author's citation from Frederick Case, "Minds at Risk," *Washington Post*, 29 July 1991, C5.)

19. Ibid., 23f.

20. Dinesh D'Souza, *Illiberal Education: The Politics of Race and Sex on Campus* (New York: Vintage Books, 1992) remains the classic statement on this problem.

21. Charles Colson, "Can We Be Good Without God?" *Imprimis*, April 1993, was originally presented at the Seventy-third Shavano Institute for National Leadership. *Imprimis* is the newsletter of Hillsdale College, in Hillsdale, Mich.

Chapter 7 • He Made Them Male and Female

1. Alcia Swasy, "Stay-at-Home Moms Are Fashionable Again in Many Communities," *Wall Street Journal*, 23 July 1993.

2. *Monitor*, an annual report of Yankelovitch Partners, Westport, Conn., 1992.

3. *The Boomer Report*, 15 October 1992.

4. Barbara Dafoe Whitehead, "Dan Quayle Was Right," *Atlantic*, April 1993, 47–84.

5. Daniel Patrick Moynihan, "Defining Deviancy Down," *American Scholar*, Winter 1993, 17.

6. Whitehead, "Dan Quayle Was Right," 64.

7. Judith Wallerstein and Sandra Blakeslee, *Second Chances: Men, Women, and Children a Decade After Divorce* (New York: Ticknor & Fields, 1989).

8. This statement has been repeated often and was printed in the *Congressional Record* in February 1987.

9. Myron Magnet, "The American Family, 1992," *Fortune*, 10 August 1992, 43.

10. Whitehead, "Dan Quayle Was Right," 71.

11. Mortimer B. Zuckerman, "The Crisis of the Kids," *U.S. News & World Report,* 12 April 1993.

12. William Galston, *Mandate for Change* (Washington, D.C.: Progressive Policy Institute, 1992).

13. See Douglas W. Allen, "Marriage and Divorce: Comment," *American Economic Review,* June 1992, 679–85. This article reviews the correlation between no-fault divorce laws and the rising rate of divorce nationwide.

14. These and other scenes even more graphic were recorded by CBN News camera crews in Washington, D.C., during the gay and lesbian demonstrations of May 1993.

Chapter 9 • What Every Child Should Know

1. Peter Brimelow and Leslie Spencer, "The National Extortion Association?" *Forbes,* 7 June 1993, 79.

2. Samuel Blumenfeld, *Is Public Education Necessary?* (Old Greenwich, Conn.: Devin-Adair, 1981), 95f.

3. David Barton, *America: To Pray or Not to Pray?* (Aledo, Tex.: Wallbuilders Press, 1991).

Chapter 10 • A Portrait of America

1. Ironically, this line, in its original form, comes from George Bernard Shaw's 1921 play, *Back to Methuselah,* where it is spoken by the Serpent to Eve.

2. E. Michael Jones, *Degenerate Moderns,* 11.

3. William Kilpatrick, *Why Johnny Can't Tell Right from Wrong* (New York: Simon & Schuster, 1992), 208.

4. Ibid., 210.

5. Thomas Hine, *Facing Tomorrow: What the Future Has Been, What the Future Can Be* (New York: Alfred Knopf, 1991), 15.

6. Paul Weyrich quoted in *No Longer Exiles: The Religious New Right in American Politics,* ed. Michael Cromartie (Washington, D.C.: Ethics & Public Policy Center, 1993), 25f.

7. E. J. Dionne, Jr., *Why Americans Hate Politics* (New York: Touchstone, 1991), 354f.

8. Ann Trebbe Oldenburg, "Incorrect Is Making a Comeback," *USA Today*, 21 July 1993, D1.

9. Cited in *First Things: A Monthly Journal of Religion and Public Life*, June/July 1992, 71.

10. These and portions of subsequent data appear in John W. Wright, ed., *The Universal Almanac 1993* (Kansas City: Andrews & McMeel, 1992).

11. Cited in Wright, *The Universal Almanac 1993*, from *American Demographics*, July 1992.

12. Charmaine C. Yoest, ed., *Free to Be Family: Helping Mothers and Fathers Meet the Needs of the Next Generation of American Children* (Washington, D.C.: Family Research Council, 1992), 19.

13. Amitai Etzioni, *The Spirit of Community: Rights, Responsibilities and the Communitarian Agenda* (New York: Crown Publishers, 1993), cited in *Utne Reader*, May/June 1993, 53.

14. Ibid., cited in *Utne Reader*, 54.

15. Gerald L. Schroeder, *Genesis and the Big Bang: The Discovery of Harmony between Modern Science and the Bible* (New York: Bantam Books, 1990).

Chapter 11 • The Cornerstone of Democracy

1. Alexis de Tocqueville, *Democracy in America*, trans. George Lawrence (New York: Harper & Row, 1988), 47.

2. James Madison, "Memorial and Remonstrance, 1785," in A *Documentary History of Religion in America*, ed. Edwin S. Gaustad, vol. 1 (Grand Rapids, Mich.: Eerdmans, 1982), 262f.

3. James Madison, *Notes of Debates in the Federal Convention of 1787* (New York: Norton, 1987), 209f.

4. Noah Webster, *The History of the United States* (New Haven: Durrie & Peck, 1833), 309.

5. Robert Royal, "1968, Twenty-Five Years Later: Some Burkean Reflections," *American Character*, Spring 1993.

6. George Gallup, Jr., and Robert Bezilla, "The Role of the Bible in American Society" (Princeton, N.J.: Princeton Religion Research Group, 1990), 1–5.

7. A 3 percent rise in this report from the mid- to late-1980s is a good sign, but premature perhaps as a sign of the turning tide.

8. Os Guinness, *The American Hour: A Time of Reckoning and the Once and Future Role of Faith* (New York: Macmillan Free Press, 1992), 363.

9. Chuck Lindell, "Religion to Return, Says Atheist O'Hair," *Austin American-Statesman*, 18 July 1993, B1–2.

10. David B. Larson, M.D., "Physician, Heal Thyself!" *Guideposts*, March 1993, 41.

11. Mark Hartwig, Ph.D., "For Good Health, Go to Church," *Focus on the Family Citizen Magazine*, 21 July 1993, 10ff.

Selected Bibliography

Anderson, Martin. *Impostors in the Temple*. New York: Simon & Schuster, 1992.

Aquinas, Thomas. *Treatise on Law*. Washington, D.C.: Regnery Gateway, 1991.

Ball, William Bentley. *In Search of a National Morality: A Manifesto for Evangelicals and Catholics*. Grand Rapids, Mich.: Baker Books with Ignatius Press, 1992.

Barlett, Donald L., and James B. Steele. *America: What Went Wrong?* Kansas City: Andrews & McMeel, 1992.

Barton, David. *America: To Pray or Not to Pray*. Aledo, Tex. Wallbuilder Press, 1991.

———. *The Myth of Separation*. Aledo, Tex. Wallbuilder Press, 1989.

Bloom, Allan. *Giants and Dwarfs: Essays 1960–1990*. New York: Simon & Schuster, 1990.

Burnham, James. *Suicide of the West: An Essay on the Meaning and Destiny of Liberalism*. Washington, D.C.: Regnery Gateway, 1985.

Collier, Peter, and David Horowitz. *Destructive Generation: Second Thoughts about the '60s*. New York: Summit Books, 1989.

Colson, Charles. *The Body: Being Light in Darkness*. Dallas: Word, 1992.

Diggins, John Patrick. *The Rise and Fall of the American Left*. New York: W. W. Norton, 1992.

Dionne, E. J., Jr. *Why Americans Hate Politics*. New York: Simon & Schuster, 1991.

D'Souza, Dinesh. *Illiberal Education: The Politics of Race and Sex on Campus*. New York: Vintage Books, 1992.

Etzione, Amitai. *The Spirit of Community: Rights, Responsibilities and the Communitarian Agenda*. New York: Crown Publishers, 1993.

Fitzgerald, Frances. *America Revised: History Schoolbooks in the Twentieth Century*. New York: Vintage Books, 1980.

Fraser, Steve, and Gary Gerstle. *The Rise and Fall of the New Deal Order: 1930–1980*. Princeton, N.J.: Princeton University Press, 1989.

Gallup, George, Jr., and Robert Bezilla. *The Role of the Bible in American Society*. Princeton, N.J.: Princeton Religion Research Group. 1990.

Gaustad, Edwin S., ed. *History of Religion in America*. Vol. 1. Grand Rapids, Mich.: Eerdmans, 1982.

Gray, John. *Post Liberalism: Studies in Political Thought*. New York: Routledge, 1993. [Companion volume to *Liberalisms: Essays in Political Philosophy*. Routledge, 1989.]

Gross, Martin. *The Government Racket: Washington Waste from A to Z*. New York: Bantam, 1992.

Guinness, Os. *The American Hour: A Time of Reckoning and the Once and Future Role of Faith*. New York: Free Press, 1993.

Halberstam, David. *The Next Century*. New York: Wm. Morrow, 1991.

Hart, Benjamin. *Faith and Freedom*. Dallas: Lewis and Stanley, 1988.

Hartz, Louis. *The Liberal Tradition in America*. New York: Harcourt Brace Jovanovich, 1983.

Hayek, F. A. *The Fatal Conceit: The Errors of Socialism*. Chicago: University of Chicago Press, 1988.

Hine, Thomas. *Facing Tomorrow: What the Future Has Been, What the Future Can Be*. New York: Knopf, 1991.

Hoffman, Mark S. et al., eds. *The World Almanac and Book of Facts, 1993*. New York: Pharos Books, 1993.

Kilpatrick, William Kirk. *Why Johnny Can't Tell Right from Wrong*. New York: Simon & Schuster, 1992.

Kirk, Russell. *The Roots of American Order*. 3d ed. Washington, D.C.: Regnery Gateway, 1991.

Levinson, Sanford. *Constitutional Faith*. Princeton, N.J.: Princeton University Press, 1988.

Lichter, S. Robert et al. *Watching America*. New York: Prentice Hall, 1991.

Lutzer, Erwin W. *Exploding the Myths That Could Destroy America*. Chicago: Moody Press, 1986.

Jones, E. Michael. *Degenerate Moderns: Modernity as Rationalized Sexual Behavior*. San Francisco: Ignatius Press, 1993.

Madison, James. *Notes of Debates in the Federal Convention of 1787*. New York: W. W. Norton, 1987.

Mansfield, Harvey C., Jr. *America's Constitutional Soul*. Baltimore: Johns Hopkins University Press, 1991.

Medved, Michael. *Hollywood vs. America: Popular Culture and the War on Traditional Values*. New York: Harper/Zondervan, 1992.

Mora, Gonzalo Fernandez de la. *Egalitarian Envy: The Political Foundations of Social Justice*. New York: Paragon House, 1987.

Murray, William J. *My Life Without God*. Nashville: Thomas Nelson, 1982.

Olson, Walter K. *The Litigation Explosion: What Happened When America Unleashed the Lawsuit*. New York: E. P. Dutton, 1991.

O'Rourke, P. J. *Give War a Chance*. New York: Vintage Books, 1993.

Pines, Burton Yale. *Back to Basics: The Traditionalist Movement That Is Sweeping Grass-Roots America*. New York: Wm. Morrow, 1982.

Reisman, Judith A., et al., eds. *Kinsey, Sex and Fraud: The Indoctrination of a People*. Lafayette, La.: Lochinvar-Huntington, 1990.

Robertson, Pat. *The New Millennium*. Dallas: Word, 1990.

———. *The New World Order*. Dallas: Word, 1991.

Sabato, Larry. *Feeding Frenzy: How Attack Journalism Has Transformed American Politics*. New York: Free Press, 1991.

Scammon, Richard M., and Ben J. Wattenberg. *The Real Majority*. 2d ed. New York: Primus, 1992.

Schroeder, Gerald L. *Genesis and the Big Bang: The Discovery of Harmony Between Modern Science and the Bible*. New York: Bantam Books, 1990.

Silber, John. *Straight Shooting: What's Wrong with America and How to Fix It*. New York: Harper & Row, 1974.

Sussman, Barry. *What Americans Really Think: And Why Our Politicians Pay No Attention*. New York: Pantheon, 1988.

Sykes, Charles J. *A Nation of Victims: The Decay of the American Character*. New York: St. Martin's, 1992.

Tocqueville, Alexis de. *Democracy in America*. New York: Doubleday, 1969.

Tyrrell, R. Emmett, Jr. *The Conservative Crack-Up*. New York: Simon & Schuster, 1992.

Watt, James G. *The Courage of a Conservative*. New York: Simon & Schuster, 1985.

Wattenberg, Ben J. *The First Universal Nation*. New York: Macmillan/Free Press, 1991.

Wills, Garry. *Under God: Religion and American Politics*. New York: Simon & Schuster, 1990.

Wolferen, Karel van. *The Enigma of Japanese Power: People and Politics in a Stateless Nation.* New York: Alfred A. Knopf, 1989.

Wright, John W., et al., eds. *The Universal Almanac, 1993.* Kansas City: Andrews & McMeel, 1993.

Yoest, Charmaine C., et al., eds. *Free to Be Family: Helping Mothers and Fathers Meet the Needs of the Next Generation of American Children.* Washington, D.C.: Family Research Council, 1992.

Index